Kant's Compatibilism

HUD HUDSON

Kant's Compatibilism

Cornell University Press · Ithaca and London

First published 1994 by Cornell University Press

Library of Congress Cataloging-in-Publication Data

Hudson, Hud.
     Kant's compatibilism / Hud Hudson.
          p.   cm.
     Includes bibliographical references and index.
     ISBN 0-8014-2923-4 (alk. paper)
     1. Kant, Immanuel, 1724–1804.   2. Free will and determinism.
I. Title.
B2799.F8H83   1994
123'.5'092—dc20   93-41809

Printed in the United States of America

For Warren Harbison and Alan Brinton

Contents

Preface

This is a book about the philosophy of Immanuel Kant and about the metaphysics of causal determinism and human freedom. The primary thesis of this work is that Kant holds a profoundly insightful, compatibilistic view of human free will and causal determinism, a view that is not only consistent with the whole of his mature, critical writings but also philosophically respectable and philosophically satisfying. In short, Kant holds a position on this classical problem worthy of adoption.

Whereas I have attempted to combine my investigations into Kant's thought with my investigations into current discussions regarding free will, determinism, compatibilism, and the philosophy of mind, in order to present a unified and comprehensive treatment of the relevant issues, I have also attempted to divide the results of those investigations into five largely self-contained chapters. I chose this strategy so that readers with different degrees of proficiency in eighteenth-century philosophy, Kant studies, and analytic metaphysics will readily be able to identify the material they are most likely to find of interest, and so that they will be able to avoid explanatory material on which they already have extensive background knowledge.

The opening chapter serves both to introduce the issues and to preview the rest of the work. Then, after examining and finding unsatisfactory the traditional interpretations of Kant's position, I develop and defend my reading of Kant's compatibilism in Chapter 2. In Chapter 3, I offer a critical evaluation of that reading from a contemporary perspective, an evaluation that seeks to produce both current critiques of the Kantian position and Kantian critiques of current positions. Since I ascribe to Kant a thesis of causal determinism (which contains controversial commitments from the standpoint of Kant interpretation), and since I draw on a particular characterization of Kant's theory of free will in my reconstruction and defense of his compatibilism, I devote Chapters 4 and 5 to an extended discussion of Kant's views regarding causal determinism and human free will. Because these final chapters are addressed primarily to Kant scholars, who may want to see a sustained defense of the positions I ascribe to Kant, they presuppose a fair amount of familiarity with the original texts and the secondary literature.

In writing this manuscript, I have become indebted to several persons and to some institutions. I acknowledge the Woodrow Wilson National Fellowship Foundation for the award of a Charlotte W. Newcombe Fellowship in the 1990/91 academic year, during which the first drafts of this manuscript were written. I also thank the editors of *Kant-Studien* for their kind permission to use, in revised form, portions of my article "*Wille, Willkür*, and the Imputability of Immoral Actions," an article which is an ancestor of the present chapter on Kant's theory of free will, and for their permission to reprint portions of my review of Henry E. Allison, *Kant's Theory of Freedom*. Both pieces appeared in *Kant-Studien* 82, no. 2 (1991).

Many individuals have influenced my thoughts about Kant and about the metaphysics of freedom and determinism over the past several years, and others have provided valuable assistance at one stage or another of this project. I thank an anonymous referee for Cornell University Press, who stimulated me to undertake substantial revisions of the original manuscript. I also extend my appreciation to Ralf Meerbote and Richard Feldman for their criticism, direction, and expert advice during the early stages of this work; to Lewis White Beck for hours and hours of delightful and unfailingly instructive conversation on Kant's philosophy; to my *commilitones*, William Schneider, Kelly Jolley, and Robert Epperson; and finally to my teachers, friends, and family, Warren Harbison, Alan Brinton, Andrew Schoedinger, Deborah Modrak, Randy Olson, Paul Johnson, Mary DiPietro, Linda Jacobs, and especially Tara Hughes, for their inspiration, guidance, support, and friendship.

HUD HUDSON

Bellingham, Washington

Chapter 1

Prolegomena to Kant's Compatibilism

Compatibilism is the philosophical thesis which maintains that the doctrine that human agents have free will does not entail the falsity of the doctrine of determinism, or, if one prefers, that granting determinism is not tantamount to denying the claim that human agents have free will. Compatibilism is not the dual thesis that human beings have free will and that determinism obtains, although it is clearly a requirement for that state of affairs; rather, compatibilism is merely a statement of the logical relation of consistency holding between two philosophical positions, and not a pronouncement on the truth or falsity of those positions.

Despite its modest claim, compatibilism has frequently been the target of severe criticism. One way to appreciate the motivation for this criticism is to consider three propositions which together form an inconsistent triad:

(F) Human agents have free will.
(D) Determinism obtains.

(I) Human agents have free will just in case determinism does not obtain.

One cannot consistently adopt (F) and (D) and (I), and so the obvious problem is deciding which proposition to reject. The proponent of compatibilism rejects (I) and thus is free to adopt (F) and (D) consistently. One may, however, think that we have much better evidence in support of (I) than we have in favor of compatibilism; indeed, there is no shortage of purported proofs and demonstrations of the truth of (I), some of which certainly appear extremely plausible. Consequently, one may also think that we are faced with a particularly difficult choice: philosophers who are inclined to accept (I) may also either accept (F) and thereby reject (D), or they may accept (D) and thereby reject (F). The former group have traditionally been known as libertarians, and the latter group have traditionally been known as hard determinists. Moreover, whereas libertarians and hard determinists cannot wholly reconcile their differences, at the very least they can join in opposing the compatibilist.

Whether one should side with the compatibilist, the libertarian, or the hard determinist depends crucially on a further investigation into (F) and (D). Compatibilism comes in different varieties, and the reason for this is that accounts of human free will and accounts of determinism also come in different varieties.

Proposition (F) announces that human agents have free will. Now suppose you happen to believe that a necessary condition on any respectable theory of free will is that it require the ability to do otherwise. In other words, suppose you adopt the principle that an agent freely does x only if the agent could have done otherwise than x.[1] Then, if you also happen to think that the ability to do otherwise is incompatible with determinism, you have a reason for thinking that free will is incompatible with determinism.[2] But if you should happen to believe that a

[1] In a widely discussed article, Harry Frankfurt has cast doubt on a related principle that maintains that the freedom to do otherwise is a necessary condition on action for which an agent is morally responsible. See his "Alternate Possibilities and Moral Responsibility," *Journal of Philosophy* 66 (1969): 829–839. But for a defense of a similar principle, see Peter van Inwagen's response to Frankfurt-style counterexamples, in his "Ability and Responsibility," *Philosophical Review* 87 (1978): 201–224.

[2] Reasons for thinking that the ability to do otherwise is incompatible with deter-

theory of free will can retain its respectability without that principle, then you may not have a reason for thinking that free will is incompatible with determinism, whether or not you are correct in your belief that the ability to do otherwise is incompatible with determinism.

Alternatively, suppose you happen to believe that a necessary condition on any acceptable theory of free will is that it provide for a notion of moral responsibility. In other words, suppose you adopt the principle that an agent freely does x only if the agent is morally responsible for doing x. Then, if you also happen to think that moral responsibility is incompatible with determinism, you once again have a reason for thinking that free will is incompatible with determinism. But if you should happen to believe that there are counterexamples to that principle, then you once again may be without a reason for thinking that free will is incompatible with determinism, whether or not you are correct in your belief that moral responsibility is incompatible with determinism.[3]

The lesson in each case is the same: different analyses of free will and its related concepts (e.g., the ability to do otherwise and moral responsibility), may lead to different conclusions regarding the plausibility of (I). Of course, it may turn out that free will is sufficient after all for the ability to do otherwise and for moral responsibility, but, if so, this does not in turn guarantee (I), unless the arguments for the incompatibility of determinism and the ability to do otherwise or for the incompatibility of determinism and moral responsibility are sound.[4]

Proposition (D) announces that determinism obtains. It does not,

---

minism abound in the literature, and they have ancestors in the ancient writings of various Stoic philosophers. One of the most sophisticated attempts to argue for this view is offered by Peter van Inwagen; see his *An Essay on Free Will* (Oxford: Clarendon Press, 1983).

[3]Peter van Inwagen has also offered an argument designed to show the incompatibility of moral responsibility and causal determinism which has the interesting feature of not moving through any particular conception of free will. To the extent that one takes free will to be sufficient for moral responsibility, however, this argument may yet provide a reason for denying the compatibility of free will and causal determinism. See his "The Incompatibility of Responsibility and Determinism," in *Moral Responsibility*, ed. John Martin Fischer (Ithaca: Cornell University Press, 1986), pp. 241–249.

[4]I suspect the soundness of prominent representatives of both types of argument, and I return to these considerations in Chapter 3, where I take these matters up in some detail.

however, specify just which type of determinism is at issue. There are several species of determinism, including logical determinism (sometimes termed fatalism), ethical determinism (allegedly held by Socrates), theological determinism (sometimes termed the problem of God's foreknowledge), psychological determinism, physical determinism, and causal determinism. Just as competing analyses of free will can affect the plausibility of (I), so too distinct versions of determinism can make all the difference regarding the acceptability of (I).

Identifying strategies for arguing in favor of the compatibilism of free will with one type of determinism may lead to insights into similar defenses of the compatibilism of free will with another type of determinism, but the truth of compatibilism in one area is not a reliable guide to the truth of compatibilism in another. For instance, one may have a formidable defense of the compatibilism of free will and *causal* determinism, a defense that turns on some fact about the contingency of causal laws and the past, and yet have no comparable defense of compatibilism with respect to free will and *theological* determinism, since the relevant analogue to the causal laws in the latter case, namely, God's beliefs, may not be contingent at all.[5]

Therefore, to clarify the controversy between a particular brand of compatibilist and incompatibilist which is the subject of this book, and to facilitate my investigation into Kant's defense of this particular brand of compatibilism, I presuppose for the sake of argument the following two conditions on a theory of free will: (i) free will requires the ability to do otherwise, and (ii) free will is sufficient for moral responsibility.[6]

[5]For an excellent introduction to some of the differences between what I am calling causal determinism and theological determinism, and their respective types of compatibilism and incompatibilism, see John Martin Fischer's "Introduction: God and Freedom," in his anthology *God, Foreknowledge, and Freedom* (Stanford: Stanford University Press, 1989), pp. 1–56.

[6]As we see in Chapter 2, there are reasons to believe that Kant would have denied (i) in his precritical period. By his critical period, however, he clearly maintains that human agents enjoy this particular ability. Consequently, Kant will not be able to sidestep certain incompatibilist arguments by denying that the ability to do otherwise is a necessary condition on free action. Also, Kant commentators have often been puzzled about how Kant can account for the truth of (ii), given his restrictive views regarding the autonomy of the will. I return to these topics in Chapters 3 and 5, respectively.

Furthermore, in this book I restrict my discussion of determinism to the thesis of causal determinism; hence, let us amend (D) so that it now reads "Causal determinism obtains."

Given this clarification of (F) and (D), we are now in a position to listen to arguments in favor of libertarianism, hard determinism, and compatibilism. On the one hand, the hard determinists maintain that we have better evidence to accept the truth of (D) than of (F), and they then face the challenge of eliminating (or reinterpreting) many of our concepts and reactive attitudes which seem to rely on the truth of (F), such as moral responsibility, imputability, praiseworthiness, blame-worthiness, moral permissibility, moral obligation, gratitude, respect, and punishment.[7] On the other hand, the libertarians maintain that we have better evidence to accept the truth of (F) than of (D), and they then face the challenge of making intelligible either a thesis of agent causa-tion (interpreted as substance causation), or a thesis of singular causa-tion (causation without causal laws), or a thesis regarding a certain con-tingency of the causal relation, or some other metaphysical claim that would falsify (D).[8] Finally, the compatibilists deny that we have to make a choice between (F) and (D), and consequently they are not subject to either difficulty just sketched. Instead, the compatibilists must face the challenge of providing compelling reasons for rejecting (I); if they are successful in meeting that challenge, then the point of agreement be-tween the hard determinists and the libertarians is undermined and arguments concerning their subsequent disagreement are rendered un-necessary.

On my view, Kant is one compatibilist who provides compelling rea-sons for rejecting (I). As is well known, Kant continually modified and improved his views on causation and free will throughout his precritical and critical periods, and although the particulars of his compatibilistic resolution were altered accordingly, his basic sympathy for a compati-bilistic stance remained unchanged throughout his professional life. In 1755, in the form of a brief dialogue, Kant defended a compatibilist position in his very first strictly philosophical publication, the *Nova*

---

[7]For a careful investigation into "what our not having free will would mean," see van Inwagen, *An Essay on Free Will*, pp. 153–189.

[8]In Chapter 4, I return to the various means by which someone might argue for the falsity of causal determinism, and I construct a Kantian argument for that thesis.

dilucidatio. And although he later abandoned the rationalistic metaphysics of the early treatise in which that defense appeared, in 1781 he
again offered a compatibilist solution to the problem of freedom and
determinism in his resolution to the Third Antinomy in the *Critique of
Pure Reason*. For the remaining two decades of his life, Kant was in-
trigued with the relation of the solution of that problem to his ethical
and religious works as well as to its epistemological significance. Consequently, his fascination with compatibilism has left an unmistakable
mark on all his major critical writings, most notably the *Foundations of the
Metaphysics of Morals*, the *Critique of Practical Reason*, the *Critique of Judgment*, the *Metaphysics of Morals*, and *Religion within the Limits of Reason
Alone*.

Interpretations of his solution have been varied. The Kant literature in
this area is sharply divided between those who, in the final analysis,
take Kant to be an incompatibilist after all, those who admit but want to
apologize for his compatibilism and who maintain that a superior view
can be constructed from the Kantian corpus, those who think he is
either inconsistent or hopelessly confused, and those who believe that a
straightforward compatibilism is exactly the position that Kant should
be recognized and praised for having adopted. In this book I defend the
final approach, and I attempt to explain both why I believe that alternative, standard readings of Kant's compatibilism fall under one of the
other approaches just characterized and why I believe that those approaches are ultimately unsatisfactory, both from the standpoint of Kant
interpretation and from the standpoint of philosophical merit. To this
end, I embark on four separate tasks in this work:

1. I construct and defend a reading of Kant's compatibilistic resolution
to the apparent inconsistencies arising when one affirms both that causal determinism obtains and that human beings have free will. I begin
this task by examining Kant's precritical writings on compatibilism and
by reviewing the particulars of the Third Antinomy from the *Critique of
Pure Reason*, in which Kant explicitly addresses the issue of compatibilism. I then turn to a critical analysis of the standard readings of Kant's
compatibilistic resolution, found in the commentaries of prominent
Kant scholars such as Allen Wood, Jonathan Bennett, Lewis White Beck,
Robert Butts, Ralf Meerbote, and Henry Allison. On the strength of
these investigations, I then submit and develop my own interpretation

of Kant's compatibilism. In the course of developing this reading, I ascribe to Kant a token-token identity thesis regarding natural events and transcendentally free, human actions, but I also ascribe to Kant a type-type irreducibility thesis regarding the distinct sorts of descriptions with which we characterize natural events and transcendentally free, human actions. Finally, I explain how the resulting compatibilistic theory can best accommodate the traditional, problematic passages from Kant's texts which have been partially responsible for the numerous and diverse readings of Kant's compatibilism.

2. I critically evaluate the resulting Kantian position, drawing on various themes and arguments that have emerged in contemporary debates regarding free will, determinism, compatibilism and selected topics in the philosophy of mind. In particular, I investigate the similarities between Kant's nonreductive token physicalism (a corollary thesis to his compatibilistic resolution between free will and causal determinism) and Donald Davidson's anomalous monism, and I defend the Kantian compatibilist from contemporary arguments in favor of incompatibilism, arguments that turn on attempts to demonstrate the incompatibility of causal determinism and the ability to do otherwise (construed as a necessary condition of free agency).

3. I offer a reconstruction and defense of a Kantian argument for causal determinism, together with an extended discussion of the recent literature regarding Kant's attempt to provide a proof of a key premise in that argument, namely, the Law of Universal Causation. I here maintain that Kant is committed not only to the universality of the causal connection (the widely recognized target of the proof he offers in the Second Analogy) but also that he is similarly committed to the necessity and to the generality of the causal connection, three suppositions of a thoroughgoing causal determinism.

4. I offer an account of Kant's theory of free will in which I identify, analyze, and exhibit the interconnections between two senses of 'will', the legislative function of practical reason and the executive function of the power of choice, and four senses of 'freedom of the will': spontaneity, independence, autonomy, and heteronomy. I here maintain that proper attention to specific features of Kant's theories of human will and of free agency reveals that Kant is not subject to certain routinely accepted objections raised against his ethical theory, or to the complaint

that his indeterminist conception of freedom prevents him from consistently adopting the type of compatibilism I ascribe to him in Chapter 2.

The result of these investigations, I argue, is that Kant endorses a sophisticated compatibilistic resolution that neither sacrifices the epistemology of the *Critique of Pure Reason* nor leaves him with only an impoverished theory of human free will. Moreover, I argue that Kant's position has exercised considerable influence on contemporary thought with clearly recognizable descendants in the current literature, and I argue that the Kantian compatibilist position has not been rendered obsolete, as is sometimes suggested, by current defenses of incompatibilism. Finally, I conclude that we can place Kant's views in a modern context and that we can align him with certain contemporary philosophers who share not only his compatibilism but also, to a surprising degree, the particulars of his version of compatibilism.

Chapter 2

Kant's Theory of Compatibilism

According to Kant, at any moment of time, the entire world at that time and the laws of nature together determine a unique future; that is, causal determinism obtains.[1] Also according to Kant, the human will, independent of pathological necessitation, is capable of both autonomous and heteronomous spontaneity of action; that is, the human will is free.[2]

Kant gives his official reconciliation of causal determinism and human free will in his Third Antinomy of Pure Reason. The Antinomy of Pure Reason can be found in the second division of the Transcendental Logic in the *Critique of Pure Reason*, known as the Transcendental Dialectic. Now, for Kant the term 'Dialectic' means a logic of illusion, and under this heading he investigates, with the purpose of exposing the illusion,

[1] A sustained analysis and defense of this claim is the focus of Chapter 4 of this book.

[2] A sustained analysis and defense of this claim is the focus of Chapter 5 of this book.

three kinds of dialectical inference. Common to each of these inferences, in Kantian terms, is reason's attempt to rise from a conditioned synthesis (the proper realm of experience) to a knowledge of the unconditioned (which lies beyond the scope of the understanding). In more familiar terms, Kant provides a critique of rational psychology, rational cosmology, and transcendental theology by showing that in each case reason makes an illegitimate demand to extend our knowledge to objects that lie beyond the bounds of possible experience, and that only by granting these unjustifiable extensions can we arrive at the corresponding transcendental doctrine of the soul, transcendental science of the world, or transcendental knowledge of God [A333–335/B390–392].[3]

The Dialectic contains the third series of arguments by which Kant hopes to establish his doctrines of transcendental idealism and empirical realism, and the centerpiece of his discussion is the Third Antinomy and its resolution. Kant never seemed to be satisfied with his exposition of the Third Antinomy and its resolution, though. In almost every major work after the *Critique*, he endlessly repeated his solution, rephrased it, then summarized it, rehearsed it in numerous footnotes, and tugged and pulled at all its corners until he succeeded in shrouding it in more obscurity than ever. In his obsession not to be misunderstood on this topic, he commented so often on his achievement that he gave critics and sympathizers alike several apparently conflicting quotations from his later works to hurl at one another in their attempts to attack or defend his position.[4]

In this chapter, I give a reading of the Third Antinomy and its resolution which draws on the results of my investigations into Kant's views on causal determinism and the freedom of the will. In the first section I begin with an investigation into Kant's precritical work, the *Nova dilucidatio*, in which he explicitly defends a compatibilistic line, in order to

---

[3]References to the *Critique of Pure Reason* appearing in the text are to the standard pagination of the first and second editions, indicated as A and B, respectively. English translations are from Norman Kemp Smith's translation (New York: St. Martin's Press, 1929).

[4]*Critique of Practical Reason*, trans. Lewis White Beck (New York: Macmillan, 1956), p. 6; *Kants Gesammelte Schriften* (Berlin: Königlich Preussische Akademie der Wissenschaften, 1902), 5:6 (Prussian Academy Edition hereafter cited Ak. Ed.). Kant here confesses that the objections brought against his resolution of the Third Antinomy are one of the two "most weighty criticisms of the *Critique* which came to [his] attention."

establish some facts about Kant's early thinking on this topic. In the second section I sketch the problem at issue in Kant's Third Antinomy and I reconstruct and comment on the proofs for the thesis and antithesis which constitute that antinomy. In the third and fourth sections I address three traditional (but conflicting) readings of the Third Antinomy and I argue that they are unsuccessful, though instructive, for a proper reading. Finally, in the fifth section I offer a new reading of Kant's compatibilistic resolution in the Third Antinomy to the problem of free will and causal determinism, and in the course of my discussion I comment at some length on the passages that seem most at odds with my primary thesis.

The Precritical Kant on Compatibilism

Despite Kant's rejection of the extravagant theory of preestablished harmony which served as the supporting structure for Gottfried Wilhelm Leibniz's metaphysics of freedom and determinism, the precritical Kant adopted a position somewhat similar to Leibniz's (and to that of Leibniz's intellectual descendant, Christian Wolff) on the debate over compatibilism. For these philosophers, the controversy regarding compatibilism was one regarding the relation of free will to logical and to theological determinism, that is, to different aspects of the problem of God's foreknowledge. Much of what they have to offer by way of defending their position, however, can be carried over directly to the case concerning causal determinism as well.

Leibniz holds the doctrine that there are truths of reason and truths of fact. The former, as one might expect, are logically necessary, certain, and provable a priori. The latter, as one might not expect, though logically contingent are also certain and provable a priori. The provability of the former rests on the logical Law of Contradiction, and the provability of the latter rests on the Principle of Sufficient Reason.[5] Now, human actions, one and all, are described through truths of fact, and these truths, though certain, are not logically necessary. Thus, for Leibniz, although it is a priori certain that Judas will betray Christ

[5]Gottfried Wilhelm Leibniz, *Discourse on Metaphysics* (1686), sec. 13; *Monadology* (1715), secs. 32–33.

(owing to the fact that this free act is contained in the complete concept of Judas), since this a priori certainty attaches merely to a truth of fact, it is not logically necessary that Judas will betray Christ. Hence, Judas's freedom is thus far not affected.[6] In other words, even though it is logically necessary that if it is a priori certain that Judas will betray Christ, then Judas will betray Christ, and even though it is a priori certain that Judas will betray Christ, it does not follow from these facts that Judas *must* betray Christ. The inference form in question is widely recognized as fallacious in modal logic. Given the premises (i) necessarily, if P obtains, then Q obtains, and (ii) P obtains, one can derive only that Q obtains, and not that necessarily Q obtains. Hence, in our present example, what follows is that Judas will betray Christ, and not that Judas must betray Christ.[7] But merely granting the actuality of Judas's action, as opposed to its necessity, does nothing for the argument in favor of incompatibilism, which purports to demonstrate that it is impossible for Judas to have acted otherwise.

According to Leibniz, when God makes actual the finest set of compossible monads, or simple substances, included in that set are individuals whose complete concepts contain some freely chosen, evil actions. The justification for including them in the set of actual beings, rather than replacing them with other possible individuals whose complete concepts do not contain freely chosen, evil actions, is that the former individuals belong to that unique set of compossible individuals which constitutes the most perfect or greatest state of affairs possible and, hence, that replacing them with other individuals who would freely make different choices would have been repugnant to God's nature inasmuch as the final product of His creation would be lacking in perfection.

There is a danger of making a similar error here in modal reasoning as in the argument discussed immediately above. According to Leibniz,

---

[6]Leibniz, *Discourse on Metaphysics*, sec. 30; *Theodicy* (1710), secs. 20, 158, 282.

[7]Clearly, Leibniz needs to make reference to God in order to account for his notion of the a priori provability of logically contingent truths of fact which require an infinite analysis, and so in this context references to God are fair game. Nevertheless, at this early stage I am purposefully avoiding a discussion of the argument that maintains that God's foreknowledge of Judas's betrayal provides the incompatibilist with a way to avoid the modal fallacy just mentioned.

that Socrates will drink hemlock is a contingent, but certain, fact that is contained in the complete concept of Socrates. Nevertheless, one might think that, even though it is not logically necessary that Socrates drink hemlock, it is nevertheless hypothetically necessary; that is, given that this possible Socrates is a member of the actual world, which depends on certain of his actions for its perfection or value, he cannot fail to drink the hemlock. One might think that if he could fail then this would not be the best of all possible worlds, and Leibniz's God would be lacking in perfection insofar as His creation suffered from defect. Once again, however, this is a mistaken inference. What follows is that Socrates does not fail to drink the hemlock, not that he cannot fail. The former is all that Leibniz requires in order to preserve the integrity of the actual world and the status of God's perfection, but the latter would be required in order to begin to construct an argument in favor of incompatibilism.

Leibniz hastily takes his point a step farther, though, when he writes, "absolutely speaking, our will as contrasted with necessity, is in a state of indifference, being able to act otherwise, or wholly to suspend its action, either alternative being and remaining possible . . . . it is, however, true, and has been assured from all eternity that certain souls will not employ their power upon certain occasions."[8] Leibniz, then, not only advocates compatibilism but also insists that our freedom is a freedom to do otherwise than we in fact do. Wolff almost surely followed Leibniz in this particular, just as he followed Leibniz in most matters dealing with the soul. Unfortunately for Wolff, however, the misrepresentation of his views on this issue to Friedrich Wilhelm I led to his dismissal from the University of Halle in 1723 and to a threat on his life. Wolff was accused of suggesting that deserters from the military should not be punished since they could not do otherwise than desert, and this view was alleged to follow from his determinism. But Wolff maintained that this follows no more from his determinism than from Leibniz's, and in fact both men would have assented to the proposition that if an agent acts freely, then the agent can do otherwise than the agent in fact does. Naturally, then, neither believed that he needed to relinquish the no-

---

[8]Leibniz, *Discourse on Metaphysics*, trans. George Montgomery (La Salle, Ill.: Open Court, 1902), sec. 30, p. 49.

tions of responsibility, the imputability of actions, praiseworthiness or blameworthiness, or punishment. For instance, according to Leibniz, it is quite appropriate, and even demanded by the principle of fitness, that one's punishment should be suited to the evil actions that one freely performs.[9]

It is only fair to point out, however, that strictly speaking the argument Leibniz has given thus far is merely a defensive one. Leibniz has shown that the only relevant information one may deduce from, say, the a priori certainty regarding Socrates' behavior is that Socrates will drink hemlock. He rightly points out to the incompatibilist that this does not show that it is impossible for Socrates to do otherwise, and thus on Leibniz's view it does not jeopardize Socrates' freedom. The incompatibilist might return the favor, though, and point out that this does not show that it *is* possible for Socrates to do otherwise either. In short, that Socrates will drink hemlock certainly implies that it is possible that Socrates will drink hemlock, but it does not imply that Socrates cannot fail to drink hemlock or that Socrates can fail to drink hemlock. Leibniz, it seems, has simply taken for granted the view that Socrates can do otherwise, and whereas he has defended himself from one incompatibilist attack, he has failed to demonstrate that an agent is free in a sense which he seems to regard as crucial. One positive argument attributed to Leibniz (and Wolff) for the claim that an agent can do otherwise is the following: among those actions an agent does not in fact do, any action that is not self-contradictory, that is, which is not logically impossible, is something the agent is free to do in place of what the agent actually does.[10] Although this would certainly solve Leibniz's problems, it is hardly a credible principle to adopt regarding sufficient conditions for free agency.

Before one attempts to search for a better argument to establish an agent's ability to do otherwise on behalf of Leibniz and Wolff, one might first consider whether defending this ability is necessary for a successful defense of compatibilism. The precritical Kant's disagreement with Leibniz and Wolff begins with just this point. Kant exhibits his precritical position on this issue not in a response to Leibniz or Wolff directly

[9]Leibniz, *Theodicy*, sec. 74.

[10]Lewis White Beck, *Early German Philosophy* (Cambridge: Harvard University Press, 1969), pp. 239 (and n. 136), 274.

but rather in a partial defense of their joint position from objections raised against it by Christian August Crusius.[11]

Kant begins by reporting Crusius's objection to Leibniz and Wolff and by then joining him in making exactly the sort of error in modal inference noted above. He argues along with Crusius that "if whatever happens cannot happen unless it have a reason determining it antecedently, it follows that *whatever does not happen could not happen*, because clearly there is no reason for its happening, and without a reason it is quite impossible that it should happen."[12] Thus, he argues merely from the lack of the actuality of a sufficient reason for some action (which would therefore result in the actual nonoccurrence of that action) to the impossibility of the action's occurring. Similarly, he is willing to argue from the actuality of a sufficient reason for some action (which will therefore result in the actual occurrence of that action) to the impossibility of the action's not occurring. In other words, he (unsuccessfully) attempts to argue from actuality to necessity. Kant is entitled only to the more modest claim that the action will occur, or to the modal claim that necessarily, given its sufficient reason, the action will occur, but not to the claim that necessarily the action will occur. Even though one might wish that Kant did not here take the distinction between absolute and hypothetical necessity to be of no value in assessing the modal status of actions that are in fact performed,[13] there is nevertheless an interesting aspect of this mistake to investigate: Kant here concedes the impossibility of an agent's ability to do otherwise (albeit in this instance on improper grounds), yet he is still quite willing to attempt to defend the compatibility of the freedom of the will with a determinism that he believes renders necessary every action performed by an agent.

As Kant maintains when he begins to address the nature of free

[11]Christian August Crusius, *Entwurf der nothwendigen Vernunft-Wahrheiten* (1745).

[12]*Nova dilucidatio* [*A New Exposition of the First Principles of Metaphysical Knowledge*], trans. John A. Reuscher, in *Kant's Latin Writings*, ed. Lewis White Beck (New York: Peter Lang, 1986), pp. 57–109; the relevant discussion is found in the text following proposition 9, pp. 75–90; Ak. Ed. 2:398–406.

[13]Kant draws attention to Leibniz's attempt (*Theodicy*, sec. 132) and Wolff's attempt (*Vernünftige Gedanken von Gott, der Welt, und der Seele der Menschen, auch allen Dingen überhaupt* [1729], 4th ed., sec. 565) to utilize this distinction but rather hastily joins with Crusius's rejection of it (*Entwurf*, sec. 126). See *Nova dilucidatio*, p. 79; Ak. Ed. 2:400.

actions that are also necessitated, "what we want to know is the *source* of [a] thing's necessity." And he reminds us that "God's action is not less free because it is determined [here read as "necessitated"] by reasons which, as certainly inclining His will, include motives of His own infinite intelligence, and which do not originate in some blind power of nature."[14] Similarly, Kant claims that "the characteristic mark of freedom" is the internal determination of the actions one performs, actions that "are elicited only through motives of the intellect applied to the will." He contrasts this internal determination (i.e., providing oneself with reasons that determine the will) with external determination, appropriate for animals, in which "everything happens in necessary conformity with external solicitations and impulses without any spontaneous inclination of the will."[15] For the moment, let us note that (at least in his precritical writings) Kant does not think that necessity interferes with freedom, even if it does interfere with the ability to do otherwise. Rather, he here argues that freedom is a matter of the *source* of an action's necessity, and he suggests that the type of necessity appropriate for imputations of freedom of action is the necessity with which reasons determine action when "motives of the intellect are applied to the will."

In the dialogue between Caius, "the defender of the freedom of indifference," and Titius, "the supporter of reasons of determination," which follows these introductory remarks, Kant makes it clear that by "spontaneous inclination of the will" he does not mean that it is possible that the will should not have so inclined; rather, he explains that the correct interpretation of spontaneity "is action proceeding from an *internal principle*."[16] Significantly, Kant does not wholly retract this characterization of this crucial term in his discussion of spontaneity in the *Critique of Pure Reason*, and this is one reason to be initially suspicious of interpretations of his later use of the term 'spontaneity' which would make it equivalent to the power to disrupt the uniformity of nature or to violate

[14]*Nova dilucidatio*, p. 82; Ak. Ed. 2:402.
[15]*Nova dilucidatio*, p. 80; Ak. Ed. 2:400. (In Chapter 5 we see a similar distinction drawn in Kant's critical writings between types of elective will, or the power of choice, through which the sort of will that can be determined through practical reason is separated and elevated above the sort that is pathologically necessitated. Also in Chapter 5, I investigate further the notion of freedom Kant makes reference to when he maintains that this internal determination is a *spontaneous* inclination of the will.)
[16]*Nova dilucidatio*, p. 82; Ak. Ed. 2:402.

the necessity of nature. Spontaneity simply indicates what Kant claims we are here concerned with, namely, the source of the necessity of a freely performed action. Consequently, when an agent spontaneously inclines his will, then the will is determined internally, that is, through reasons the agent has represented to himself.

Much of the rest of the dialogue is devoted to defending the notions of the imputability of actions and the appropriateness of punishment and to addressing the problem of evil and God's relation to human action. As is not surprising, Kant maintains that an agent is to be held responsible for an action when the action follows on a determination of the agent's will from conscious motives that the agent has represented to himself, or, in other words, when the agent has acted spontaneously, that is, freely.[17]

The Kant of the critical period does not introduce his defense of compatibilism with an error in modal reasoning as he does here. The error, as I have noted, is in concluding that necessarily Q from the premises (i) necessarily, if P, then Q, and (ii) P. In the critical writings, Kant (correctly) argues from the same two premises only to the actual occurrence of Q. As we see in Chapter 4, however, Kant eventually locates the relevant necessity of the causal connection (what he would term, in this case, the empirical or real necessity of Q) in the impossibility of both the occurrence of P and the nonoccurrence of Q, not simply in the impossibility of the nonoccurrence of Q.[18]

So, in the course of responding to Crusius on behalf of Leibniz and Wolff, Kant partially disagrees with the very philosophers he is defending, but the disagreement leads to interesting consequences. Moreover,

[17]*Nova dilucidatio*, esp. pp. 85–87; Ak. Ed. 2:403–405. Kant adopts a Leibnizian approach on these other matters: evil in the world turns out to be a necessary condition of God's creating the most perfect universe. And Kant borrows Leibniz's distinction between permitting and assenting to evil in order to absolve God of any guilt for the evil actions that God foresees will be freely willed by some of the members of this best world. *Nova dilucidatio*, p. 87; Ak. Ed. 2:404–405.

[18]In his Third Postulate of Empirical Thought, Kant announces that he will use the term 'necessary' to describe any event which "in its connection with the actual is determined in accordance with universal conditions of experience" [A218/B266]. Although this may look like a repetition of the same modal error at first glance, it becomes clear that Kant intends to defend only the necessity of the conditional and not the necessity of the consequent of the conditional [see A228/B280].

as we see in later chapters, his mature compatibilistic stance contains many of the same elements found in his precritical position, and his later views are supported by many of the same considerations that he here employs against Crusius, or, if one prefers, which Titius employs against Caius in the dialogue.

Kant's Third Antinomy

Let us begin with a brief review of what is at stake in the Third Antinomy. An antinomy arises when two conflicting propositions can each be demonstrated with an equally compelling proof, so that neither the thesis nor the antithesis has a superior claim. According to Kant, such an antinomy surfaces when the demands of reason and the limits of the understanding are in conflict. More specifically, with respect to a series (say, a causal series), whereas reason demands a completeness in the series (i.e., an unconditioned condition of the series), the understanding is only capable of acquiring knowledge of the conditioned members of the series and cannot venture out beyond these members to acquire any knowledge of the completeness of the series itself. In the Third Antinomy [A444–451/B472–479], we find ourselves with one proposition, the antithesis, which is defended by an appeal to a rule of the understanding through which some such series may be generated indefinitely, and we find ourselves with a contradictory proposition, the thesis, which is defended by an appeal to reason through which we seek a unity or unconditioned condition for that series.

Thesis: Causality in accordance with laws of nature is not the only causality from which the appearances of the world can one and all be derived. To explain these appearances it is necessary to assume that there is also another causality, that of freedom.

Antithesis: There is no freedom; everything in the world takes place solely in accordance with laws of nature.

Thesis Proof
Note that the thesis makes a claim to "necessity" (which Kant demotes to "logical possibility" in his resolution); also note that the proof offered by Kant resembles a Aristotelian/Thomistic proof of a first

cause, but without any theological overtones. The proof takes a reductio form:

(1) There is no other causality than that in accordance with laws of nature. (reductio assumption)
(2) There is at least one experienceable event. (unstated assumption)
(3) Every such event requires a previous event from which it follows according to a rule. (Second Analogy)
(4) So, our event in (2) requires an ancestor, which requires an ancestor, etc., thereby guaranteeing no completeness in this series but only relative or subordinate beginnings for its members. (2), (3)
(5) But the law of nature requires sufficiency of the cause determining such an event. (Second Analogy)
(6) Due to the incompleteness of this series, and due to the absence of any other types of causality, no such sufficiency is available. (1), (4)
(7) Hence, there are no experienceable events. (5), (6)
(8) Hence, (1) is false. (2), (7)

Kant concludes more generally with "we must, then, assume a causality through which something takes place, the cause of which is not itself determined in accordance with necessary laws, by another cause antecedent to it, that is to say an *absolute spontaneity* of the cause, whereby a series of appearances, which proceeds in accordance with laws of nature, begins *of itself*." This, he declares, is transcendental freedom, or what he sometimes terms the causality of reason.

This general conclusion follows, however, only if Kant is correct in assuming that there are just these two types of causality at issue. Only under such an assumption is showing that (1) is false sufficient warrant to conclude the proof with this stronger claim. Nevertheless, as has been repeatedly shown, not all is well with Kant's proof. For example, a careful reader will note that (5) claims that every experienceable *event* must have a sufficient cause and that (6) claims that there is no sufficiency in the *series of events*. But then one may object that any event in that series has a sufficient cause after all; it is the series itself that does not have a sufficient cause. Another problem stems from the fact that Kant represents the proponents of both the thesis and the antithesis as in agreement about the universality of natural causality. Now, since the argument form is indirect, at the conclusion of the reductio we must deny something. But why not deny the truth of (3) or (5) rather than of (1)? In other words, one might attempt to argue, this is more persuasive as an argument against the principle of the Second Analogy than it is as a proof of the thesis. I return to the impact of these representative problems for Kant's thesis proof below. First, though, let us note some problems that naturally arise at this juncture. Any reading of the antinomy that claims that both propositions may be true when properly interpreted (which, to anticipate a bit, is Kant's professed reading) must provide answers to the following questions: what does it mean to say that the 'cause' of some event is not itself causally determined? what does Kant mean by 'absolute beginnings' in a series of appearances? and why does he believe, as he writes in his observation on the thesis [A448/B476], that we can know *that* transcendental freedom is possible but not *how* it is possible, that is, that we cannot comprehend or understand its possibility? These are frequently the very questions the traditional answers to which are cited in favor of Kant's *incompatibilism*, and consequently we need to return to them and to their answers in the following sections.

Antithesis Proof

Again, the proof takes a reductio form.

(1) There exists the causality of transcendental freedom. (reductio assumption)
(2) So, some series has its absolute beginning in this causality of freedom, and thus this cause will not be determined in accordance with fixed laws (of nature). (1)
(3) There is a unity of experience (i.e., there is a thoroughgoing interconnection between all members of a causal series such that any member follows from some other and a law. (Second Analogy)
(4) The members of some series (which have their absolute beginning in the causality of freedom) are causally independent of events prior to that beginning. (2)
(5) The unity of experience is forfeited; there are no thoroughgoing interconnections in experience. (4)
(6) Hence, (1) is false. (3), (5)

Kant concludes more generally with, "the illusion of freedom . . . [and] unconditioned causality . . . is blind, and abrogates those rules through which alone a completely coherent experience is possible" [A447/B475].

Once again, though, we should note that Kant has assumed that there are only two types of causality at issue. And whereas he may well be right in doing so, unless we make this assumption explicit, a denial of (1) is not sufficient warrant for the claim that causality in accordance with the laws of nature is the only type of causality. Once again, as Kant's opponents have been happy to point out, not all is well with Kant's proof. For instance, since the contradiction seems to be between transcendental freedom and necessary conditions for experience, perhaps we once again must make explicit the assumption that there exist some experienceable events. Moreover, we have the same problem we had with the thesis proof: the argument form is indirect, and at the conclusion of the reductio we must deny something. But why not deny the truth of (3) rather than of (1)? In other words, one might attempt to argue that this too is more persuasive as an argument against the principle of the Second Analogy than it is as a proof of the antithesis.

For better or worse, these are the proofs (somewhat charitably reconstructed) that Kant is wholeheartedly willing to vouch for in his presentation of the Third Antinomy. In fact, Kant was so impressed with his own efforts on this score that he challenged all readers to find the slightest flaw in the arguments, and he brashly pretended to rest the whole of his case for transcendental idealism on the success of *any* of his eight proofs found in the text of the antinomies.[19] Historically, critics have not tended to share Kant's enthusiasm for his achievement and have delightedly taken up his offer to find fault with the arguments. A host of objections have been advanced against the two proofs in their present form, the common conclusion of which is that Kant has not succeeded in presenting a genuine antinomy, since one or both of the proofs is drastically inadequate. Nevertheless, there are also sympathetic defenses in the literature which improve the arguments by stressing the fact that all Kant needs to show is that they can be defended on

---

[19]See the Appendix of the *Prolegomena to Any Future Metaphysics,* where Kant is railing against a reviewer of the *Critique of Pure Reason;* Ak. Ed. 4:377–380.

principles that would have to be accepted by a transcendental realist, and by interpreting his proof structure rather liberally.[20]

Setting aside these objections and the replies offered in response, though, we can take Kant's problem seriously whether or not it is couched in the form of an antinomy.[21] Kant is concerned to show that the interests of practical reason, which are committed to the popular dogmatist thesis that there is a causality of reason (or transcendental freedom), can be satisfied along with the interests of speculative reason, which are committed to the empiricist antithesis that the only causality is that of nature. He hopes to do this by showing that the compatibility of these two theses depends on a distinction between things in themselves and appearances, and his problem and its solution both remain philosophically significant whether or not Kant is correct in his additional (and somewhat implausible) belief that he has furnished an independent proof of both thesis and antithesis as well.

The distinction between things in themselves and appearances (leaving aside for the moment the controversial question of whether it deserves an ontological or an epistemological interpretation) allows Kant to resolve the antinomy by maintaining the possibility of the truth of both thesis and antithesis; both may be true, provided that they are interpreted under the different senses provided by the distinction [A531–532/B559–560]. It is this strategy, then, that underlies Kant's defense of the compatibilism of causal determinism and freedom of the will, and we may now turn to an investigation of this crucial distinction and the compatibilist thesis it justifies.

Wood on Kant's Compatibilism

Kant motivates his discussion of compatibilism with a conditional statement of incompatibilism from the first *Critique*: if one does not

[20]Henry E. Allison has provided a fresh look at the Third Antinomy in which he sympathetically defends it from traditional (and widely accepted) objections, see his *Kant's Theory of Freedom* (Cambridge: Cambridge University Press, 1990), pp. 11–28.

[21]After all, that the Fourth Paralogism is not a genuine paralogism does not alter the force of Kant's critique of problematic idealism in his discussion of rational psychology.

distinguish between things in themselves and appearances, then one "could not, therefore, without palpable contradiction, say of one and the same being, for instance the human soul, that its will is free and yet is subject to natural necessity; that is, is not free. For I have taken the soul in both propositions in *one and the same sense*" [Bxxvii]. And again in the second *Critique*, "if one takes the attributes of the existence of things in time for attributes of things in themselves, which is the usual way of thinking, the necessity in the causal relation can in no way be united with freedom. They are contradictory to each other."[22] Kant vouches for the truth of the conditionals but is not committed to the consequent since he denies the antecedent, that is, Kant does distinguish between things in themselves and appearances and locates freedom in the former and causal determinism in the latter.

Allen Wood puts his view of the distinction as follows: "Kant's compatibilism . . . is based on the aggressively metaphysical distinction between phenomena and noumena; far from unifying our view of ourselves, it says that freedom and determinism are compatible only because the self as free moral agent belongs to a different world from that of the self as natural object."[23] Under this two-worlds hypothesis, Wood assigns the causality of reason to the intelligible world and the causality of nature to the sensible world. Let us call this metaphysical or ontological interpretation a two-selves or two-worlds reading of Kant's distinction. We might also note that it is a plain, textual fact that, in many of those passages where Kant draws his distinction, he seems to speak with just the sort of metaphysical language that suggests an ontological reading.[24] The question, then, is whether this two-worlds hy-

---

[22]*Critique of Practical Reason*, p. 98; Ak. Ed. 5:94.

[23]Allen Wood, "Kant's Compatibilism," in *Self and Nature in Kant's Philosophy*, ed. Wood (Ithaca: Cornell University Press, 1984), pp. 73–101.

[24]For example, one of the most frequently cited passages for a two-worlds reading is in the *Foundations of the Metaphysics of Morals*, Ak. Ed. 4:451. But the number of passages in favor of a two-worlds reading (e.g., those found in the chapter "Phenomena and Noumena" from the first *Critique*) can be sharply reduced if we read their metaphysical language as simply holding out a possibility (attractive to Kant) that there might well be *some* types of noumena that are not also phenomena (e.g., God). A universal ontological separation of phenomena and noumena does not, however, follow from this possibility.

pothesis is ultimately the best way to interpret Kant's distinction, both
with a view to consistency against the rest of the Kantian corpus and
with a view to the philosophical merit of the resulting position.

Kant's primary question throughout the resolution of the Third Antinomy is "whether freedom [as a causality of reason] is completely excluded by this inviolable rule [viz. the principle of the Second Analogy],
or whether an effect, notwithstanding its being thus determined in
accordance with nature, may not at the same time be grounded in
freedom" [A536/B564]. In other words, Kant wants to show the mere
logical compatibility of the two senses of causality. Wood, however,
goes on to attribute a much stronger view to Kant. Wood proposes that,
whereas empirical causes are real and not merely apparent causes, nevertheless they are not complete or self-sufficient causes. His idea is that,
without a free act of the will, certain events would not come into being,
their natural causes being insufficient in themselves to produce their
effects. He expresses this idea by suggesting that "empirical causality
regarding human actions is an effect of intelligible causality," and that
the causal efficacy behind the production of our actions is to be found
only in the intelligible world.[25] This view is stronger than Kant's professed aim inasmuch as it makes transcendental freedom *necessary* for
the production of certain events; it is not just that it is *possible* to think its
coexistence along with natural necessity. After presenting a final aspect
of Wood's interpretation, I return to this difficulty.

In locating the human agent and causal efficacy in the ontologically
distinct, intelligible world, Wood also attributes to Kant the hypothesis
that human beings are timeless beings and that they engage in timeless
agency. Wood believes that the doctrine of timeless agency also permits
Kant to defend an additional thesis that Wood (correctly) believes Kant
to maintain: that an agent can do otherwise than the agent in fact
does.[26] According to Kant's hypothesis (on Wood's view), human beings engage in a timeless choice of character through which the empirical character is wholly fixed, and through which the empirical character
is exhibited in the course of nature. A being could have done otherwise
with respect to some specific empirical action, then, by having made a

[25]Wood, "Kant's Compatibilism," pp. 86–89.
[26]Again, despite his precritical views on this matter, by the writing of the first
Critique Kant believes that human agents enjoy this particular ability.

different timeless choice concerning the character he has.[27] If an image would be of assistance, it would be that of the myth of Er from Book 10 of Plato's *Republic* in which souls choose the pattern of their lives from among alternatives offered by the Fates (or, in Kant's language from the *Religion within the Limits of Reason Alone*, where one chooses the fundamental maxim of one's character). One's timeless choice, then, restricts the number of possible worlds that might become actual, since it guarantees that one will do certain things and avoid others. Finally, one's timeless choice is to be appropriately connected to one's empirical actions by being "considered simultaneous with each act as it occurs in the temporal order."[28] This, then, serves as the basis for Wood's reading of the passages in which Kant declares that our free actions are not themselves determined in the time order of appearances and thus are not causally conditioned.

Here is one reading of Kant's compatibilism. Wood is not alone in his interpretation. Although he professes not to see much (if any) philosophical merit in the resulting position, Jonathan Bennett has lent his support to Wood's reading of Kant by saying that with the exception of one (minor) point "the interpretation is flawless."[29] As I have reconstructed it, the interpretation is characterized by three theses: (i) Kant's distinction between things in themselves and appearances is an ontological, two-worlds one; (ii) the intelligible cause is the source of causal efficacy, and the empirical cause, which is the effect of the intelligible cause, is not self-sufficient for its effect in the world of appearance; and (iii) human beings participate in timeless agency. It is worth noting that on Wood's view Kant is not committed to the truth of (i)–(iii) but rather only to the coherence of the hypothesis characterized by these theses. In other words, Wood suggests that, if Kant can demonstrate the coherence of this hypothesis and can show that no one could ever be in a position to refute that coherent hypothesis, then he has all he needs to

---

[27]Wood's view on these matters bears a close resemblance to the position Schopenhauer adopts when praising Kant's distinction between the empirical and the intelligible character. See Arthur Schopenhauer, *The World as Will and Representation*, trans. E. F. J. Payne (New York: Dover, 1969), sec. 55, 1:289–290.

[28]Wood, "Kant's Compatibilism," pp. 90–101.

[29]Jonathan Bennett, "Commentary: Kant's Theory of Freedom," in *Self and Nature in Kant's Philosophy*, pp. 102–112.

protect his doctrines regarding freedom from incompatibilist opponents, even if it should turn out that our actions are determined by natural causes. Nevertheless, if these were Kant's views, he would be in trouble, for they not only conflict with his other views but are internally inconsistent as well.

With respect to thesis (iii), we are offered a truly incredible doctrine: although intelligible acts of choice are timeless, in order to connect the choice of the agent with the empirical event it is supposed to condition (say, my rising from my chair now—rather than the Lisbon earthquake), we are forced to regard the choice as simultaneous with the relevant empirical event. This is simply an outright contradiction. Suppose that some activity x is timeless. Then there is no time at which x occurs.[30] But if x is simultaneous with something y, x and y occur at the same time. Thus, there is no y such that x and y are simultaneous. In short, to purchase compatibilism at the price of ignoring the incoherence of timeless choices that are also simultaneous with empirical events seems an awfully high price to pay.

Moreover, this strategy would wreak havoc on much of Kant's moral philosophy. For example, choosing actions to perform and choosing a character are clearly temporal processes, and nowhere does Kant give an analysis of a nontemporal sense of 'choice' which allows us to conclude that he thought otherwise. On the contrary, he emphasizes repeatedly how one's choices are always pathologically affected but not necessitated. On Wood's view, these passages cannot be adequately accommodated. 'Being pathologically affected' is another temporal relation and, worse yet, one that certainly cannot occur if the senses belong to a being in one world but the choice is made by an agent in another. Hence, Wood's account cannot make sense of Kant's discussions of moral failure or moral evil; barring any affection by the senses on the act of choice, one cannot give a coherent account of how the agent might be sensuously inclined to adopt them into a maxim and thus transgress the moral law. Furthermore, as Wood himself points out, this reading creates difficulties for the possibility of moral improvement, for the notion

---

[30]Given the context, I take it that 'timeless' here means "without temporal location or duration," as opposed to "existence at all times."

of human striving, and for several other themes intimately related to Kantian ethics.

In conclusion, let us simply note that there is no external, textual support for the thesis of timeless agency, and let us also note that what Kant does commit himself to—namely, the claim that the content of a description of transcendental freedom does not involve its object in conditions of possible experience or time determination—does not serve as evidence for timeless agency either. In other words, one should not draw inferences from the atemporality of the content of a description to the atemporality of the object that falls under that description.

Thesis (ii), as already pointed out, commits Kant to a necessity claim whereas he believes himself to have established only a thinkability or possibility claim, and this, as it turns out, is untenable for the following reasons. If an empirical cause were not itself sufficient for its effect, the argument of the Second Analogy would be forfeited and Kant's causal determinism would be in ruins. As we see in Chapter 4, according to Kant an empirical cause is not only sufficient for its effect in the sense of producing it but necessitates its effect under an empirical law of nature. But if an empirical cause is sufficient for its effect after all, then either Wood is mistaken or Kant is inconsistent when he resolves his Third Antinomy. Since Wood's construal of Kant's hypothesis commits Kant to a weaker view of the efficacy of empirical causes than Kant has argued for, and since it is the weaker view responsible for the problems just noted, I suggest that it is Wood who is here mistaken.

Furthermore, it is unclear in what sense we are to understand the term 'effect' in the proposal, "intelligible causality has as its effect empirical causality." As I intend to show below, Kant does have a way of relating an intelligible cause to an empirical effect which does not violate his condition that the only proper relata of causal connections in nature are empirically given, natural events, but I do not see how that relation can be defended when the relata are taken to be not events but rather types of causality themselves. Finally, if Wood simply means by the insufficiency of empirical causes that there must be something "behind" the appearances (that there must be something appearing), and if he intends to locate transcendental freedom merely in this fact, then it would turn out that on Kant's view everything is the product of such freedom. Everything would be free, because every appearance is conditioned by noumena in this minimal fashion. It is not simply in virtue of having a noumenal counterpart that an action is free but rather in having the right sort of thinkable determining ground for the action, which as it turns out is subject to a description that shares important features with other noumenal descriptions.

Last, with respect to thesis (i), is Kant's distinction an ontological one? There is a great (largely German) tradition of interpretation in favor of this thesis.[31] Since it is reasonable to suppose that thesis (i) leads naturally (as evidenced by Wood's article) to theses (ii) and (iii), we might argue that (i) is to be rejected because (ii) and (iii) are. But this move (perhaps illegitimately) begs the question of Kant's consistency. So, let us investigate this thesis on its own as well.

We may begin by contrasting it with its rival, a two-aspects or two-descriptions, methodological or epistemological reading of the distinction. On the two-worlds interpretation, we have ontologically distinct kinds of objects, and we have two levels of reality in which they reside. The two-descriptions interpretation differs from Wood's precisely in the respect that there are not two selves and two worlds to put them into but one self and one world, a self and a world which admit of different types of descriptions. These descriptions, one concerned with intelligible aspects and the other with sensible aspects of their mutual object, can be regarded as two self-contained worlds only metaphorically; they are isolated realms only in that, although their descriptions refer to the same object, no inference is permitted from an instance of one type of description to an instance of the other type. Thus, there is some sense in which even a two-descriptions reading may be considered a two-worlds reading, but this sense is restricted by the fact that such "worlds" are then regarded as containing the very same token inhabitants, considered under irreducibly different description types.

Is such a reading plausible, or is Kant stuck with a hopeless, ontologically motivated, two-worlds view? One defense of a methodological or epistemological reading is suggested by Gerold Prauss in his remarks on the German constructions Kant uses for drawing his distinc-

---

[31]But recent Anglo-American commentators endorse it as well: Bennett, again, in *Kant's Analytic* (Cambridge: Cambridge University Press, 1966), and Robert Paul Wolff in *Kant's Theory of Mental Activity* (Cambridge: Harvard University Press, 1963).

tion. Prauss argues that such terms as 'in itself', 'for itself', and 'itself' are used adverbially, modifying a manner of consideration or reflection, rather than substantivally, such that the distinction should be drawn between the thing considered in itself and the thing considered as appearance.[32] The obvious but crucial point is that one and the same thing is at issue; specifically, it is one and the same object/event multiply described.

Another compelling defense of an epistemological reading has been offered by Henry Allison in a discussion of the problem of the thing in itself in his commentary on the first *Critique*. Allison interprets the distinction between an appearance and a thing in itself simply as a function of the two ways we can consider one and the same object in transcendental reflection: first, in relation to conditions of human cognition, and then, apart from any relation to conditions of human cognition. In his clear treatment of this issue, Allison considers (and rejects) a causal reading and a semantic reading of the distinction, but he then modifies the semantic interpretation, bringing it into line with the position articulated by Prauss.[33]

Furthermore, the epistemological reading is reinforced in most of the passages in which Kant draws the distinction by his explicit insistence on the sameness or identity of the referent involved in each case. Neither is his commitment to this version of the distinction a correction of some earlier and failed attempt to make a two-worlds reading work.[34] Rather, it is fully evident in the Preface[35] and in the Analytic[36] of the

---

[32]Gerold Prauss defends the two-descriptions view in *Erscheinung bei Kant* (Berlin: Walter de Gruyter, 1971), and again in *Kant und das Problem der Dinge an Sich* (Bonn: Bouvier Verlag H. Grundmann, 1974). Prauss's suggestion replaces a common construal of the distinction as one between a consideration of a thing in itself and a consideration of an appearance.

[33]Henry E. Allison, *Kant's Transcendental Idealism* (New Haven: Yale University Press, 1983); esp. chaps. 1, 2, 11. For Allison's modification, see pp. 237–242.

[34]Beck argues, for example, that it is only after recognizing the failure of a two-worlds theory that Kant revises his position into a two-descriptions theory. But in the opening of the next section I argue against Beck's evidence for this position. See his "Five Concepts of Freedom in Kant," in *Stephan Körner: Philosophical Analysis and Reconstruction*, ed. J. T. J. Srzednicki (Hingham: Kluwer, 1987), pp. 41, 43, and esp. 44–45.

[35]E.g., Bxixn–Bxxii, and esp. Bxxviii–Bxxix.

[36]E.g., at B55, B69, B186, B258, A249–A253, B306, B333.

first *Critique*; it is repeated in the *Foundations*, where Kant rightly points out that the concept of duty or obligation makes sense only under a two-descriptions view and not under a two-worlds view;[37] and it is confirmed in the second *Critique*, where Kant continually insists on the sameness of the subject in two different relations.[38] But, most important, it is the very reading Kant himself gives to the distinction while invoking it in the resolution of the Third Antinomy: he asks, "Is it truly a disjunctive proposition to say that every effect in the world must arise *either* from nature *or* from freedom; or must we rather not say that, in one and the same event, in different relations, both can be found?" [A536/B564]. In answering this question with the latter alternative, Kant commits himself to a two-descriptions theory, and thus we can turn to an investigation of his compatibilism which begins with that interpretation, and we can turn away from the ontological, two-worlds approach with its doctrine of timeless, human agency.

Beck and Butts on Kant's Compatibilism

Lewis White Beck and Robert E. Butts are two commentators who endorse a version of the nonontological reading of Kant's distinction. Beck, however, endorses the view for reasons quite different from those just presented. According to Beck, Kant is driven from a two-worlds view to a two-descriptions view because of a problem that supposedly arises when he attempts to hold both that freedom does not infringe on the mechanism of nature but that nevertheless it is adequate to the needs of ethics.[39] Beck rightly points out that Kant maintains that all an agent's actions, as events, are fully determined, and that if we knew all the empirical facts and natural laws we could predict the agent's actions with perfect certainty [see A549–550/B577–578; and also second *Critique*, Ak. Ed. 5:99]. That Kant simultaneously maintains that such an agent is free seems to Beck to be no more intelligible than the "hoary

[37]E.g., Ak. Ed. 4:453, and again at 4:450, 451, 456, 457. In other words, it is one and the same being who has a dual nature, partially rational and partially sensuous, and thus it is one and the same being who is subject to the prescriptions of the moral law.
[38]E.g., Ak. Ed. 5:6n, and again at 5:42, 43, 65, 87, 95, 114.
[39]Beck, *A Commentary on Kant's "Critique of Practical Reason"* (Chicago: University of Chicago Press, 1960), pp. 190–191.

mystery" of the compatibility of human freedom and God's foreknowledge. Beck condenses his criticism by posing a dilemma for Kant, a
dilemma that straightforwardly advances an incompatibilist sentiment:
"If the possession of noumenal freedom makes a difference to the uniformity of nature, then there is no uniformity; if it does not, to call it
'freedom' is a vain pretension."[40]

This dilemma, in Beck's opinion, forces a two-descriptions approach
to resolving the antinomy.[41] Beck states, though, that "Kant does not
seem to have felt the paradox in his own views." But perhaps there is no
genuine paradox to be felt. This is not the turning point for Kant from a
two-worlds to a two-descriptions view; he held the latter view only.
And the reason we cannot blame him for failing to appreciate the force
of an objection like Beck's is that the dilemma is not successful, since, as
it stands, the proposition corresponding either to its first or to its second
horn is false.

As is clear from the structure of his dilemma, Beck believes that the
possession of noumenal freedom is inconsistent with the uniformity of
nature (i.e., with the claim that those phenomenal events that are free
actions are subject to causal determination through the laws of nature).
His idea seems to be that genuine freedom requires the ability to choose
from among alternative courses of action, but that the uniformity of
nature (i.e., the strict ordering of nature in accordance with natural
laws) would unacceptably restrict the range of alternatives in every case,
leaving only whatever action the agent is causally determined to perform. Possession of genuine freedom, Beck implies, would (sooner or
later) lead to the actual performance of some action that was not in
accordance with the history of the phenomenal world and the natural
laws governing it. In other words, if we possess genuine freedom, the
thesis of the uniformity of nature is false.

In this spirit, the proposition corresponding to the second horn of the
dilemma states that, "if the possession of noumenal freedom does not

---

[40]Beck, *Commentary*, pp. 191–192; he repeats a similar worry in "Five Concepts of
Freedom in Kant," pp. 42–43.

[41]Beck's view is often characterized somewhat loosely, as it is here, as a two-
descriptions view. As we soon see, however, it is a nonstandard two-descriptions
view inasmuch as it simply endorses an incompatibilist line and straightforwardly
denies that any single object is the proper recipient of a description of both types.

make a difference to the uniformity of nature, to call it 'freedom' is a vain pretension." Let us make Beck's objection as strong as possible: suppose for the moment (contrary to fact) that, if one is able to make a difference to the uniformity of nature, one is able to perform an action that directly violates some law of nature. Even on this exceedingly strong reading of an agent's ability to make a difference to the uniformity of nature, the proposition corresponding to the second horn of the dilemma is false. It is false quite simply because it conflates possessing an ability with exercising the ability. Even this very strong reading—in which one's exercising this peculiar ability would make a difference to the uniformity of nature by acting in such a way as to violate a natural law—does not imply that the uniformity of nature *will* be disrupted by a being possessing such a fantastic ability—unless possessing an ability commits one to exercising it. Since there is no such commitment, it is not a vain pretension to term such an ability "freedom." Hence, as originally formulated, the dilemma is not successful.

Perhaps someone will think that I am missing the point of the real dilemma. Suppose we replace the words "makes a difference" with "can make a difference" in the hopes of reestablishing the dilemma. But then the proposition corresponding to the first horn is false, since it now says that, if the possession of noumenal freedom can make a difference to the uniformity of nature, then there is no uniformity. This proposition is false, since it once again patently conflates the possession of an ability with the exercise of that ability.

Finally, someone might attempt to convey the point of Beck's critique by simply advancing the claim that motivated the dilemma in the first place: "genuine freedom requires the ability to do otherwise, and if an agent's actions are causally determined, then she lacks the ability to do otherwise; accordingly, to maintain that such an agent is free is nothing more than a vain pretension." Now, we may grant that an agent can do otherwise than she in fact does (or is causally determined to do); moreover, we may grant that her so acting would make a difference to the uniformity of nature. In response to the objection, however, I would not permit the exceedingly strong reading of the ability to make a difference to the uniformity of nature (which we considered just now in order to make a point about the dilemma as it stood).[42] Instead, we may argue

---

[42]That is, for the sake of the argument we can grant that an agent has the ability to make a difference to the uniformity of nature, but we no longer grant that an exercise

that the agent could make a difference to the *manner* in which nature is uniform, or that she could make a difference to *which* nature is uniform. Let me explain. Two schools of compatibilism have surfaced in recent debate, and they have been classified according to a particular strategy they adopt when responding to certain incompatibilist arguments. Theorists known as "divergence-miracle" or "altered-law" compatibilists attempt to tell a plausible story in which, if freedom were to make a difference to the uniformity of nature, it would do so by making a difference to the manner in which nature is uniform, by making a difference in the set of actual empirical laws. Theorists known as "altered-past" compatibilists attempt to tell a similar plausible story in which, if freedom were to make a difference to the uniformity of nature, it would do so by making a difference to which nature is uniform, by making a difference in the events of the past. Furthermore, to defend their respective positions, neither sort of compatibilist is constrained to endorse the obviously false claim that an agent can perform some action that has as a causal consequence a change in the laws of nature or in the events of the past. The point is simply that there are ways to make a difference to the uniformity of nature that are not tantamount to violating the uniformity of nature. I comment on these counterintuitive proposals at some length in the next chapter when I defend Kant's position from contemporary incompatibilist arguments. For the moment, let us simply note that the dilemma and its critique are only as strong as the arguments for incompatibilism on which they so clearly rest, and since, as I intend to show, the best versions of those arguments have been refuted, Beck's original dilemma and both its revisions fail.

It is significant that the dilemma fails, because Beck believes that once even the first version is granted there is "only one way out of the dilemma," and this belief leads Beck to assign the two theses to Kant which constitute his, Beck's, interpretation of Kant's resolution to the Third Antinomy. The first thesis is that Kant held the two-descriptions rather than the two-worlds theory. The second thesis is that both freedom and natural necessity are to be read as regulative Ideas, rather than freedom's being subordinate to the constitutive principle of natural ne-

---

of this ability would directly violate a natural law. The point of granting this latter claim in the earlier case was only to show that the original dilemma failed no matter what interpretation we gave to that ability to make a difference, and not to suggest that this was a plausible interpretation of that particular ability.

cessity.[43] Beck's first thesis is in accidental agreement with my discussion against Wood's two-worlds interpretation, but the pseudo-dilemma that led him to this thesis also leads him to the second, which I will first reconstruct and then attempt to give further reasons for abandoning.

Beck's second thesis requires a fundamental restructuring of our ordinary views of the epistemology of the *Critique of Pure Reason*. "Specifically, it requires that the sharp distinction between constitutive category and regulative Idea be given up, that even the categories be regarded as devices for the regulation of experience and not as structures necessarily given in a fixed constitution of our experience of nature."[44] Beck notes that the only evidence indicating that this is Kant's view is section 70 of the *Critique of Judgment*, in which Kant presents an antinomy Beck believes Kant solves in the way he ought to have solved the Third Antinomy. Beck's interpretation of that later resolution of the Antinomy of Teleological Judgment serves as a model for the Third Antinomy as follows: Kant could have interpreted the thesis and antithesis in the Third Antinomy as regulative principles that correspond to maxims governing our investigations in two fields. Our two maxims would then be

(a) Always (in science) search for mechanical causes and allow no non-natural causes to enter into the explanation of natural phenomena.
(b) Always (in ethics) act as if the maxim of the will were a sufficient determining ground of the conduct to be executed or judged.[45]

Note the advantages of such a reading: neither maxim makes an ontological claim committing Kant to a two-worlds view. Both retain their a priori structure and can make a defensible claim to cover all relevant experience. Finally, neither maxim makes a declarative statement, and thus the principles do not conflict with one another, since they lack truth values (i.e., this is one way to solve the antinomy). Beck considers the remaining type of conflict, which is characterized by the command to pursue two incompatible courses of action, but argues that even this sort of conflict never arises with respect to maxims (a) and (b).[46]

[43]Beck, *Commentary*, p. 192.
[44]Beck, *Commentary*, p. 193.
[45]Beck, *Commentary*, p. 193; "Five Concepts of Freedom in Kant," p. 45.
[46]Stemming from his own incompatibilist stance, Beck ultimately argues that, not

Robert E. Butts also opts for such a reading of the Third Antinomy, but he makes a stronger claim than Beck regarding it. Beck's position is that Kant was a two-worlds theorist in the first *Critique*, did not appreciate the paradoxes regarding his solution to the Third Antinomy when invoking that desperate ontological move, finally came to a realization in the third *Critique* of the improvements available through a two-descriptions view, and changed his mind about the constitutive character of his categories in order to accommodate his new discovery. Hence, Beck's real reading of the Third Antinomy is that Kant fails as a two-worlds theorist; his charitable reading is that Kant can be saved in the manner of the third *Critique*.[47] Butts claims that the regulative reading of the thesis and antithesis is already present in the first *Critique* and that Beck's way of resolving the Third Antinomy by noting that such rules are nonpropositional and thereby cannot conflict is Kant's early view as well. Butts explicitly supports Beck's motivational dilemma but adds to Beck's solution that "the one way out" which he believes leads to the regulative reading of the categories is already present in Kant's Dialectic from the first *Critique*.[48]

Here, then, are two slightly different readings of Kant's compatibilism. Insofar as they are responses to the dilemma Beck presents, they are both prompted by a straightforward incompatibilism, as suggested by Beck in the form of a secularized version of the relation between God's foreknowledge and human free will. For reasons already given, though, that version of incompatibilism and Beck's dilemma are unsuccessful, and there is more than only one way out. But this simply shows that Beck and Butts are incorrect in thinking that Kant must adopt this reading of his compatibilism in order to remain consistent. That is important, but it does not by itself show that Kant did not take just this approach; it does not by itself show that he is not permitted to have

---

only is it the case that we cannot ascribe freedom and causal necessity to the same event, it is also the case that we never find ourselves in a position that would require us to do so, for the sake of either science or ethics. But see my discussion at the end of this section for considerations against both of these views.

[47]See his "Five Concepts of Freedom in Kant," pp. 44–45.

[48]Robert E. Butts, *Kant and the Double Government Methodology* (Dordrecht: D. Reidel, 1984), pp. 248–273. Butts endorses Beck's dilemma on p. 260 and pp. 271–272. The primary piece of evidence he cites for his reading is from the text of the Fourth Antinomy at A561–562/B589–590.

resolved his problem in this fashion. So, with reference to the latter claim, is this a proper reading of Kant's compatibilism?

Beginning with the stronger reading first, Butts's claim that this is already Kant's view in the first *Critique*, we can oppose his single citation from the antinomies with an overwhelming number of passages. Throughout the Preface, Introduction, Aesthetic, and Analytic of the first *Critique*, Kant argues that we bring a structure to our experience such that we legislate, through the nature of our understanding, a priori, constitutive principles of our experience, which he later contrasts with the regulative Ideas of reason. Perhaps, given the location of Butts's evidence, though, we are to understand that certain conclusions reached in the Dialectic are to be read back into those earlier sections containing the positive epistemology of the first *Critique*. Even strictly confining ourselves to the Dialectic, though, we can find passages that cannot plausibly be interpreted as being consistent with a regulative reading of the category of causality. For example, from the resolution to the Third Antinomy, Kant writes, "that all events in the sensible world stand in thoroughgoing connection in accordance with unchangeable laws of nature is an established principle of the Transcendental Analytic, and allows of no exception" [A536/B565]; and again, "the thoroughgoing connection of all appearances, in a context of nature, is an inexorable law" [A537/B565]; and again, "this law is a law of the understanding, from which no departure can be permitted, and from which no appearance may be excepted" [A542/B570].

Butts faces another difficult problem. On his view, the thesis and antithesis when not reinterpreted as regulative are in inescapable conflict; when reinterpreted as regulative, they do not conflict because they do not, as maxims, have truth values. But if they do not have truth values, then Butts attributes to Kant a resolution of his Third Antinomy which contradicts what Kant says about how he will resolve the problem in the text of the Third Antinomy: Kant claims that, given a certain distinction, both thesis and antithesis may be true [A531–532/B559–560]; Butts's reconstruction of the resolution allows neither to be true.[49]

---

[49]Ralf Meerbote raises this objection to Butts in a review of his book and adds that, since Butts believes the thesis and antithesis form a genuine contradiction unless read as regulative principles, he cannot resort to their declarative form for a reading in which both may be true either. See "Butts' *Kant and the Double Government Methodology*," *Nous* 13 (1989): 266–270.

Butts slightly anticipates this objection when he declares that "they both can be 'true', that is, reasons can be given for adopting one in this context, the other in another context."[50] Butts's hesitancy reveals itself in his use of scare quotes, however, and it seems fairly unlikely that this is the sense of 'truth' Kant appeals to in this regard. To make it a plausible reading, Butts needs to provide us with some further reason for believing it to be Kant's usage. For instance, is there a similar, diluted sense in which both thesis and antithesis in the mathematical antinomies are false? If not, what justification is there for maintaining that Kant switched his way of dealing with the antinomies in this important manner?

Let us now examine Beck's reading. Beck does not have to answer the questions of internal inconsistency in the Dialectic which Butts faces, since Beck believes Kant to be a confused two-worlds theorist in the first *Critique*. But, as I have argued, it is not clear that Kant ever endorsed the two-worlds theory in his first *Critique*. It is understandable how a sympathetic and incompatibilist critic, such as Beck, who believes that there is only one way out of the dilemma, might attribute an unsuccessful ontological distinction to Kant (since he can see no other way to accommodate Kant's obvious compatibilistic desires in the first *Critique*), and then, armed with a story of philosophical development and Kant's more mature texts, attempt to correct the philosopher's earlier views with the help of his later ones. But, despite the fact that there is more than one way out of the dilemma, it remains to be seen if the proposal really solves the antinomy after all, and, if so, at what cost.

Recall that the proposal requires us to regard moral and natural laws as coordinate, rather than the former subordinate to the latter in experience. Then we raise the question of freedom or natural necessity with respect to some action or event either within the context of an investigation into ethics or within the context of an investigation into nature, but not both. Beck accuses Kant of presenting, at best, a paradox when he asserts at the same time of the same action that it is both necessitated and free, and he argues that "one does not ever need to do so, either for the sake of science or morals"; the maxims tell us "what we must do in order to be a spectator or an actor, but one cannot be both at the same time and with respect to the same item of conduct."[51]

[50]Butts, *Kant and the Double Government Methodology*, p. 262.
[51]Beck, "Five Concepts of Freedom in Kant," p. 47; *Commentary*, p. 193.

According to the first claim, we are never required to do so; according to the second, we cannot even manage it if we try. But why should this be so? As I write these lines, there is one event, among others, which I describe as the effect of some natural cause with the phrase "my hand rising," and which I describe as the outcome of my free agency with the phrase "my raising my hand." There is only one event under two descriptions here. On Beck's account, however, it would seem that I am incapable of simultaneously ascribing causal necessitation and freedom to this event; I must first ascribe one and then change the context and ascribe the other. On the contrary, though, as in the standard rising/raising example, we succeed in making these dual judgments all the time. The real question (and the one that occupies our attention in the next chapter) is just the familiar incompatibilist worry about whether any object is ever a proper recipient of both types of description.

Beck continues to presuppose an incompatibilist approach to these matters when he explains that, if he knew what empirical cause produced some action, he "would no longer say (with Kant) that this action was a free one and the defendant was responsible for it."[52] I take it that this is because he believes that causation interferes with our freedom in some important way (most likely, with our ability to do otherwise than we in fact do). But unless a defense can be offered for this presupposition, something beyond Beck's dilemma (which simply assumes it) and beyond the analogy with the problem of God's foreknowledge (which actually differs from it considerably), we need not be led to this form of incompatibilism, and neither do we need to invoke this approach, so opposed to Kant's project in the first *Critique*, to rescue Kant from any untenable position.[53]

Finally, a brief comment about the price of such a revision to Kant's epistemology is in order. The consequences are staggering. On this regulative interpretation, we are to understand that only those actions

---

[52]Beck, "Five Concepts of Freedom in Kant," p. 47.

[53]In other words, we need an argument for incompatibilism which *motivates* the dilemma Beck has offered. Moreover, for numerous reasons we should not (as Beck sometimes implies) rest the case for incompatibilism of causal determinism and free will on considerations regarding the incompatibility of God's foreknowledge and human free will. An introduction to the relevant differences between the two problems can be found in John Martin Fischer's "Introduction: God and Freedom," pp. 1–56.

that are uncaused are free and also that there are such actions, that is, that some events do not in fact have a sufficient natural cause.[54] In short, to grant this revision is to reject the main task of the first *Critique*. There is no longer any justification for metaphysical, synthetic a priori judgments, since without the full strength of the categories as constitutive principles these judgments lose their claim to strict necessity and universality. Also, Kant's causal determinism would be in shambles, since it depends on the universality and necessity of this causal principle. Last, as we see in Chapter 4, Kant would be landed in exactly the kind of skepticism he repudiates, since his account of the empirical knowledge of events, which also depends on the full strength of the principle of the Second Analogy, would be forfeited. For an unnecessary revision, that price is too high.

Kant's Compatibilism Reconsidered

Let me sketch the lessons we have drawn from the discussions in the preceding sections. Kant admits only a conditional incompatibilism but denies the antecedent of the conditional, and hence he is permitted to defend a version of compatibilism. Denying the antecedent in this case amounts to drawing a distinction between things in themselves and appearances. In the former Kant finds grounds for the possibility of freedom; at the same time, he is able to maintain a strict and thoroughgoing causal determinism for the latter.

This view did not turn out, as it might have appeared at first blush, to be the superficial compatibilism Wood finds in Kant. That version followed on reading the distinction between things in themselves and appearances as an ontological, two-worlds distinction. It is difficult to see, though, how the resulting compatibilism is any more philosophically significant than is showing the compatibility of ascribing 'being merely two-dimensional' and 'being three-dimensional' to a body by saying that the first ascription belongs to the reflection of the body in a glass whereas the second belongs to the object casting the reflection. It seems to be a shallow compatibilism that professes to eliminate incom-

[54]Beck, *Commentary*, p. 193; "Five Concepts of Freedom in Kant," p. 48.

patibilism by maintaining that the competing ascriptions hold of entirely distinct objects.

Then we were led with Prauss and Allison to construe the distinction along the lines of a two-descriptions reading in which one and the same thing is considered in itself (under one description) and is considered as appearance (under another description). In so doing, we also relinquished Wood's attempt to deny the sufficiency of empirical causes for their effects in the hopes of connecting those causes with some other, intelligible cause that would supply the required efficacy of the causal relation, and we relinquished Wood's attempt to locate those intelligible causes in the mysterious field of human, timeless agency.

Committing Kant to a two-descriptions view of this sort, though, did not turn out to be subject to the dilemma raised by Beck, and hence it is not necessarily joined with Beck's and Butts's way out of the dilemma. Interpreting Kant's claim that one and the same event is causally determined insofar as it is considered as an appearance and free insofar as it is considered as having an intelligible determining ground does not require treating causality/freedom as an either/or proposition, nor does it require that the distinction between constitutive category and regulative Idea be abandoned; thus, it does not endanger the scope or force of the principle of the Second Analogy.

Merely cautioning against taking certain paths to interpreting Kant's compatibilism does not, however, show us which path to take instead, or even if there is a path which leads to a coherent reconstruction of his view. On the face of it, there are serious obstacles to our reaching such a reconstruction. The following four problems attest to this. Taking a two-descriptions reading as fixed, we need to discover whether Kant contradicts himself by stating (i) that events that are free human actions are causally determined and yet arise from a will with the freedom of independence from pathological necessitation; (ii) that these events are members of a series in which every member follows from some other member and a strict law and yet have their absolute beginning in a determining ground (or causality of reason) which is such that it does not follow from some other member in that series and a strict law; (iii) that they are one and all in time and subject to conditions of time determination and yet are related to a merely intelligible ground that is not subject to the conditions of time determination at all; and (iv) that they are fully explicable and predictable as events in nature and yet rise from unknowable and incomprehensible grounds. For convenience let us refer to these as the problems of independence, of absolute beginnings, of atemporality, and of incomprehensibility, respectively.

Since Kant rests his compatibilism on the distinction I have interpreted as a two-descriptions view, it is fitting to begin here in our search for a resolution to these problems. The most striking feature of the two-descriptions view (at least from the standpoint of traditional Kant studies) is that Kant claims not merely association but numerical identity of free human actions and empirical events in nature under the scope of the principle of the Second Analogy. Such token-token identity of actions and events has frequently been rejected as Kant's view by Kant commentators who either see only incompatibilism as an option after a token-token identity is granted or who believe that one of the four problems just mentioned is sufficient to refute the notion that Kant advocated the token-token identity thesis. Nevertheless, in addition to the arguments so far offered against the two-worlds reading and in favor of the two-descriptions reading, consider the following sample passages drawn from all the major writings of the critical period:

In the *Foundations* Kant writes that "actions [proceeding from the causality of reason] must be regarded as determined by other appearances, namely desires and inclinations belonging to the world of sense." In the *Prolegomena* he writes, "Nature and freedom therefore can without contradiction be attributed to the very same thing, but in different relations." In the *Critique of Practical Reason* he writes, "All instances of possible actions are only empirical and can belong only to experience and nature," and again, "a law of freedom is to be applied to actions which are events occurring in the world of sense, and thus, to this extent, belonging to nature." In the *Critique of Judgment* he writes, "For the will, as the power of desire, is one of the many natural causes in the world, namely the one that acts in accordance with concepts."[55] But, most important, in the *Critique of Pure Reason* Kant puts the question

[55]*Foundations of the Metaphysics of Morals*, 2d ed., trans. Lewis White Beck (New York: Macmillan, 1989), p. 71; Ak. Ed. 4:453. *Prolegomena to Any Future Metaphysics*, trans. Lewis White Beck (Indianapolis: Bobbs-Merrill, 1950), p. 92; Ak. Ed. 4:344. *Critique of Practical Reason*, p. 70; Ak. Ed. 5:68. *Critique of Judgment*, trans. Werner S. Pluhar (Indianapolis: Hackett, 1987), p. 10; Ak. Ed. 5:172.

beyond dispute when he writes, "Every action [viewed] as appearance, in so far as it gives rise to an event, is itself an event or happening, and presupposes another state wherein its cause is to be found" [A543/B571] and "the same cause does, indeed, in another relation, belong to the series of appearances" [A552–553/B580–581]. These passages are merely representative and can be joined to numerous additional texts from the chief writings in which Kant comments on his own resolution to the Third Antinomy. They all share, in one way or another, Kant's explicit identification of a free action and an event in nature. In other words, they all share an endorsement of the token-token identity thesis.

This fact does not solve our original problem, though; it only redirects our attention. Does Kant escape the fatal problems awaiting a two-worlds theorist only to be lost in the absurdity of one of the predicaments that arise on presupposing the two-descriptions theory?

Before I answer, a preliminary investigation is worthwhile. As I argue in Chapter 5, Kant's theory of human agency can be adequately represented with Donald Davidson's pro-attitude belief model of human agency. Under this model, an agent selects from among alternative means-end relations, furnished by pure or empirical practical reason, the selection being dependent on a belief in the propositional representation of the means to some end which has been conceptualized by the agent and for which the agent has some (rational or sensuous) desire. This, then, provides us with one sense of the phrase 'being determined to act': an agent's actions are determined by his belief in the proposition expressing a relation of means to some end which is an object of desire for that agent. This sense of 'determination', however, does not appear to be of the nature of a competitor to the sense of 'determination' applicable to natural events under the scope of the Second Analogy.

In the case of what we might call pro-attitude, propositional determination (what Kant would term "the determination corresponding to an intelligible cause"), if an agent S in performing action x is determined by something y, then y is S's practical reason for performing x, and y consists in the conjunction of a desire for some end and a belief in a proposition expressing means to that end. Whereas such determination is necessary but not sufficient for its corresponding action (for reasons I discuss below), that is, whereas some agent's having a practical reason for performing some action is not invariably followed by a performance of that action, the sense of 'determination' at work in the Second Analogy differs in precisely this regard. In the case of what we may call empirical, causal determination (the only case Kant allows as a productive or efficacious usage of the term), if an event x is determined by something y, then (as we discover in Chapter 4), y is an event, which together with a causal law, necessitates the occurrence of x.

A commentator on Kant must admit that, in addition to saying that events determine other events, he also says that actions determine events and that acts of will are themselves determined by the causality of reason. But we need not convict Kant of a confusion if we recognize that sometimes he uses his term in one way and sometimes in the other. Accounting for some action's being determined by the causality of reason would involve us in the task of providing reasons for that action utilizing some story concerning propositional representations, beliefs, and desires, but it does not introduce a new productive force into nature. Rather, since Kant holds the identity theory of actions and events, any free action that is subject to this determination of the causality of reason is token-token identical with some event that is determined (in the strong sense of empirical causal necessitation) by some antecedent event and a natural law. Hence, in thinking about the determination of a causality of reason, we do not introduce any supernatural productive forces into nature, nor (owing to the identity theory) do we lose an account of the efficacy of the causal connection.

On this reading, intelligible causes do not determine natural events at all, but this claim must be understood only as a denial of a sense of 'determination' which is both distinct from determination of causes under the principle of the Second Analogy and sufficient for an account of causal efficacy. (Kant nowhere provides an account of a productive sense of 'determination' which is not empirical causal determination.) Nevertheless, whereas a free action is productive (i.e., brings consequences into being) only by being token-token identical to an event that is the effect of some natural cause, it also can be regarded as being determined by the causality of reason in our sense of pro-attitude, propositional determination.

That the efficacy of intelligible causes is due to their being identical to natural events is Kant's own conclusion as well in an important footnote in the *Critique of Judgment*: "Even the *causality* of freedom (of pure and practical reason) is the *causality* of a natural cause (the subject regarded as a human being and hence as an appearance) subject to [the laws of] nature." And again in the text of the third *Critique*, "It is true that when we use the word *cause* with regard to the supersensible, we mean only the *basis* that determines natural things to exercise their causality to produce an effect in conformity with the natural laws proper to that causality."[56]

Now, according to Kant, reason is such a supersensible faculty in agents, and (in its practical employment) it is the intelligible cause that determines the agent's will [A546–547/B574–575]. Moreover, Kant maintains, that we regard our reason as having causality is clear from the imperatives that are constructed when we employ pure or empirical practical reason in the hopes of attaining some desired end [A547/B575]. This causality is distinct in type from that at issue in the Second Analogy, since these imperatives are always formulated with an 'ought' (a term that has no place in empirical descriptions or natural law). Thus we have the form of the propositional representations required in Kant's analysis of human agency;[57] that is, when one is determined by the causality of reason, Kant maintains that one believes in something equivalent to a statement of the form "if I desire end x, I ought to do action y," and that one in fact desires x. An agent who then performs y might well adduce his desire and belief in this proposition as his (practical) *reason* for doing y. All this is consistent, though, with regarding y as token-token identical with an event that is the effect of a natural *cause*, that is, which has been determined in the strong sense Kant regards as productive of events in the world.

I here purposefully set aside various difficulties associated with identifying the set of proper restrictions on practical reasons that function as the causes of free actions, restrictions suggested by familiar cases involving deviant causal chains or externally manipulated desires and beliefs. There are troublesome scenarios in which we are inclined to say that,

[56]*Critique of Judgment*, p. 36, 36n.; Ak. Ed. 5:195–196.

[57]As he does elsewhere, Kant expresses his view that the intelligible determining grounds of a will which are given through the causality of reason are always bound up with an 'ought' in *Prolegomena to Any Future Metaphysics* [Ak. Ed. 4:345]. This is intimately connected with Kant's view that the activity of the human will is always mediated by a maxim, or that human agency essentially involves imperatives.

even though the action was performed as a result of what appears to be the right sort of belief-desire pair, the agent was not free in the performance of the action owing to some nonstandard causal origin of the belief-desire pair itself (e.g., hypnosis, neurophysiological manipulation, demon interference). Nevertheless, I intend to concentrate simply on the noncontroversial cases to determine whether, as Kant maintains, some causally determined events can also be free actions. Even he must grant that freedom is not compatible with all types of causal determination.

An agent's ability to determine himself in this manner through the causality of reason by representing means-end relations (i.e., to act on reasons or in accordance with a conception of laws) is regarded by Kant as the mark of a rational being, or of an intelligence, or of a being with personality. Moreover, he tells us that "so far as we consider a being (man) entirely according to this objectively determinable reason, he cannot be considered as a being of sense; this property is a property of a thing in itself."[58] Here, as elsewhere, we do not take a different referent in making the switch from "a being of sense" to "a thing in itself" but rather take the same object but considered apart from the conditions of our knowledge of it, that is, considered apart from conditions of spatial or temporal determinations of it through which we could connect it to other appearances in nature and thereby come to make empirical knowledge claims concerning the object in question.

So, Kant is here telling us that, insofar as we regard man as an intelligible cause through reason, insofar as we entertain the notion of a transcendentally free agent, we apply descriptions that are of such a nature that they cannot be used in generating any empirical knowledge concerning their object. It is absolutely vital to understand that this is not to say that no descriptions exist which, if applied to the same object, would be of a sort to yield empirical knowledge of that object; of course, such empirical, natural descriptions are available. It is merely to say that empirical knowledge is not forthcoming while restricting oneself to the intelligible descriptions concerning an ordering not of the way things are but of the way they ought to be, that is, an ordering thought in the employment of free human agency.

[58]*Critique of Practical Reason*, pp. 130, 89; Ak. Ed. 5:87, 125. *Prolegomena to Any Future Metaphysics*, pp. 92–93; Ak. Ed. 4:345.

We may now begin to discover Kant's further use of the two-description theory through an inquiry into the nature and limitations of the types of descriptions in question. To this extent, Beck and Butts are right to look to the third *Critique* for clues in interpreting the Third Antinomy from the first *Critique*. For it is in that work that Kant carefully crafts the distinction between the intelligible descriptions appropriate to a thing considered in itself and the natural descriptions appropriate to a thing considered as a being of sense. Without reducing the category of causality from a constitutive principle to a regulative Idea, we can benefit from Kant's treatment of regulative principles in the third *Critique*. As Ralf Meerbote argues, "The concepts of a purpose and a reason for an action are ideas [Ideas of reason, in Kant's technical sense], and descriptions of agents acting on reasons are descriptions in a language of regulative principles."[59] His point is that the purposive activity of human beings—the activity requiring the use of reason and thus, as Kant tells us, the activity described as belonging to a thing considered in itself rather than to a thing considered as a being of sense—admits of noncausal, teleological description. Meerbote identifies these as "nondetermining descriptions," meaning thereby descriptions that are not determining in the sense of empirical causal determination. We may adopt this terminology, provided that we remember that some subclass of nondetermining descriptions in Meerbote's sense may yet be such that they are determining in our sense of pro-attitude, propositional determination.[60]

By saying that action descriptions are nondetermining descriptions, one maintains at the very least that such descriptions afford neither causal inferential connections between the action and the events that precede and follow it nor determination of their objects in space or time. Consequently, to say that a person employs transcendental freedom

[59]Ralf Meerbote, "Kant on the Nondeterminate Character of Human Actions," in *Kant on Causality, Freedom, and Objectivity*, ed. William Harper and Ralf Meerbote (Minneapolis: University of Minnesota Press, 1984), p. 139.

[60]It is worthwhile to note that, whereas on this reading all intelligible causes and all instances of pro-attitude, propositional determination are expressed in terms of nondetermining descriptions, not all nondetermining descriptions express pro-attitude, propositional determinations. If they did, we would once again have to contend with the non-Kantian view that everything in the empirical world is the product of transcendental freedom.

(exercises a causality of reason with its attendant pro-attitude, propositional determination) is to apply a nondetermining description to that person. Such nondetermining descriptions (which in these contexts are used to express the purposes and reasons for action) are not reducible to any determining descriptions, owing in part to the presence of the irreducibly intelligible term 'ought' that occurs in them essentially and in part to their failing to supply information necessary to ground claims to empirical knowledge concerning their objects.

Making exactly this point seems to be Kant's intention when he applies his distinction between things in themselves and appearances (to man as agent) in his resolution of the Third Antinomy [A545–547/B573–575]. After reaffirming the full strength and scope of the principle of the Second Analogy, he draws the distinction between types of characters along the lines of how descriptions express the information in virtue of which an object is experienceable or knowable for us. His result, the empirical contrasted with the intelligible character of an agent, is just the result of contrasting determining with nondetermining descriptions of one and the same object.[61]

Specifically, then, the Kantian compatibilist can claim to have located the empirical cause of an action with a determining description regarding a certain belief-desire pair functioning as a reason for action (i.e., in a certain neurophysiological event that tokens the reason) but can also claim to have satisfied the Kantian demand for an intelligible character of the action in virtue of the applicability of a nondetermining description to that token, a description expressing a practical reasons connection. The empirical character of the action, then, can serve an explanatory role in empirical-causal contexts, and the intelligible character can serve a regulative function in the conception of ourselves as rational agents by providing nonempirical grounds for imputational and justificatory contexts. Consequently, the action of such an agent is free (admits of noncausal, nondetermining descriptions that concern a pro-attitude, propositional determination of the agent's will by practical

[61]Henry Allison argues for an interesting reading of the distinction between the empirical and the intelligible character which has rational agency (rather than the agent itself) as the subject of this dual character, see *Kant's Theory of Freedom*, pp. 29–53. I believe, though, that this approach ultimately leads Allison to misconstrue the nature of Kant's compatibilism, as we see below.

reason) and is causally determined (is token-token identical to an event in nature which is necessitated as the effect of an antecedent event and a causal law).

I here include the clause that makes reference to pro-attitude, propositional determination in order to isolate those nondetermining descriptions that are relevant for ascriptions of freedom. Once again, anything admits of a nondetermining description and, even though it is necessary in ascriptions of freedom to show that nondetermining descriptions may be applied to natural events, such application is not sufficient to regard those events as free actions. Rather some, but not all, types of nondetermining descriptions are appropriate for a discussion of free agency. What makes them appropriate is that they are the special sort of nondetermining descriptions that express the pro-attitude, propositional determination of an agent's will. Insofar as this is their status, they are merely intelligible and thus, according to Kant, incomprehensible; "incomprehensibility" in this context is not to be taken in any pejorative sense, however, since it simply serves as a way of stressing the fact that, from the Kantian point of view, no empirical knowledge or understanding of an object is available through intelligible or nondetermining descriptions.

Contrary to popular opinion, then, Kant's mature brand of compatibilism bears striking resemblance to the version of compatibilism he defended against Crusius in the *Nova dilucidatio*. Admittedly, when writing that piece he had not developed his mature theories of the autonomous and heteronomous spontaneity of action in which the will is determined by pure or empirical practical reason, together with an independence from pathological necessitation. Nevertheless, his notion of 'spontaneity' as action proceeding from an internal principle (its determination being through reasons the agent has represented propositionally to herself) is very similar to the account I have just attributed to Kant in the first *Critique*. That account is one in which freedom does not consist in some special productive power of spontaneous action different from the role of an empirical cause but rather in the fact that an agent can regard her actions as determined through her desires and beliefs in the imperatives formulated through her rational activity in accordance with a conception of natural laws.

With the present account of Kant's compatibilism in hand, let us return to the four problems I mentioned at the outset of this section. My task is now to determine whether the problems of independence, of absolute beginnings, of atemporality, and of incomprehensibility still present us with any obstacles to reconstructing a satisfactory interpretation of Kant's compatibilism.

Independence

How can Kant say that actions are causally determined and yet belong to an agent with the freedom of independence from pathological necessitation? To some extent we can provide the beginning of an answer to this problem if we note that the absence of pathological necessitation is not absence of all types of determination, inasmuch as pathological necessitation limits itself to sense and imagination. According to Kant, something pathologically necessitated "cannot be determined save through sensuous impulses" [A802/B830]. A rational agent, in contrast, is not such a being precisely because he can be determined "through motives which are represented only by reason" [A802/B830]. Determination, so considered, is our pro-attitude, propositional determination, and Kant's claim that this is independent of causal determination can now be read as follows: an imperative can determine the will in the sense of providing the propositional component of a practical reason for an agent's action, and such pro-attitude, propositional determination is not expressed with causal, determining descriptions. Significantly, this commitment does not count against the resulting free action's being token-token identical to a natural event. Consequently, in granting the freedom of independence Kant is still able to preserve the scope and force of the principle of the Second Analogy while providing an account of the efficacy of actions in producing their consequences.

This independence Kant insists on has extremely important consequences. Since he thereby denies type-type reducibility, unless he also adopted a token-token identity theory he would be committed to a much stronger thesis about the type of determination involved in the causality of reason. In other words, he would have to make reasons efficacious, not by being identical to some event that is a natural cause, but by construing as lawlike the relation between an agent's having a practical reason for performing some action x and his subsequent perfor-

mance of *x*. This would effectively make nonsense of Kant's discussions
of deliberating about competing means-end relations and of his account
of the possibility of moral failure and moral evil, which depend on a
plurality of such practical reasons in an agent only one of which is acted
upon. Similarly, Meerbote has argued that treating reasons as efficacious leads to lawlikeness, which leads to integration or reducibility of
mental descriptions to physical descriptions (the nondetermining to the
determining), which in turn leads to a rejection of the freedom of independence as I have just described it.[62] As we have seen, though, Kant
accepts a token-token identity thesis and denies a type-type reducibility
thesis, thereby preserving the freedom of independence without violating the causal determinism to which he is committed.[63]

Absolute Beginnings and Atemporality

How can Kant say that any action is a member of a series in which
every member is subject to conditions of time determination, and in
which every member follows from some other member and a strict law,
and yet has its absolute beginning in a causality of reason that is not
subject to conditions of time determination, and which beginning does
not follow from any other member and a strict law?[64]

Kant states that "the absolutely first beginning of which we are here
speaking is not a beginning in time, but in causality" [A450/B478]. His
theory of causality commits him to as much, since *any* happening is
temporal and thus has only a relative beginning in the causal series.

[62]Meerbote, "Kant on the Nondeterminate Character of Human Actions," pp. 151–
153.

[63]It is this compound thesis, complete with the sense of independence just described, that has led Ralf Meerbote to call Kant's theory a version of anomalous
monism, by way of comparing it to the view advocated by Donald Davidson; see his
"Kant on the Nondeterminate Character of Human Actions." I have much more to
say about Kant's Davidsonian tendencies (or, rather, about Davidson's Kantian tendencies) in Chapter 3.

[64]Given Kant's view concerning the intimate relation between causality and time
determination, it is fitting that these two problems stand together. In Chapter 4,
following the lead of Gordon G. Brittan, Jr., I argue that Kant actually holds a causal
theory of time which anticipates views held by Hans Reichenbach and Adolf Grünbaum. See Brittan's *Kant's Theory of Science* (Princeton: Princeton University Press,
1978), esp. chaps. 7, 8.

With this clue, though, we can introduce our distinction once again to read these passages. As Kant writes in the *Prolegomena*, "every beginning of the action of a being from objective causes regarded as determining grounds is always a *first beginning*, though the same action is in the series of appearances only a *subordinate beginning*" in accordance with the principle of causality.[65] His reason for regarding the event as having a first beginning under its action description is that the relation expressed between an action and its intelligible determining ground is not a temporal and a fortiori not a causal relation: "The action in so far as it can be ascribed to a mode of thought as its cause does not *follow* therefrom in accordance with empirical laws," since "pure reason, as a purely intelligible faculty, is not subject to the form of time, or consequently to the conditions of succession in time" [A551/B579]. In other words, the intelligible cause is not orderable in time or locatable in an empirical causal chain insofar as it falls under nondetermining, intelligible descriptions. Therefore, insofar as we regard it under such a description, the pro-attitude, propositional determination of the causality of reason does not follow from any natural law, and in this independence from nature it can itself be regarded as a first beginning. Alternatively, as Kant explains in his *Religion within the Limits of Reason Alone*, a first beginning "is the derivation of an effect from its first cause, that is, from that cause which is not in turn the effect of another cause of the same kind."[66] The causality of reason can be considered a first beginning in this sense as well, since such an intelligible cause, unlike a natural cause, does not follow from any cause of its same type.

In saying all this, however, "we should not be asserting that the effects in the sensible world can begin of themselves" [A541/B569]. Rather, the token-token identity thesis allows us to say of that causally unconditioned, absolute beginning that it is tokened by an event that always has merely a subordinate beginning. Hence, the atemporality and lack of information relevant to establishing empirical causal connections between events, which characterize the content of action descriptions, do not lead, as is often thought, to the atemporality or to the

---

[65]*Prolegomena to Any Future Metaphysics*, p. 94; Ak. Ed. 4:346; see also 4:347.
[66]*Religion within the Limits of Reason Alone*, trans. T. M. Greene and H. H. Hudson (New York: Harper and Row, 1960), p. 34; Ak. Ed. 6:39.

causally unconditioned nature of the objects that fall under those descriptions.

Our present analysis also leaves us with a way to deal with a notoriously difficult passage in the *Critique of Practical Reason*, the "wretched subterfuge" passage. I have here suggested that, as in his early *Nova dilucidatio*, Kant locates freedom in the type of the determining ground of an action that is also causally necessitated. Specifically, he locates freedom in the applicability of a nondetermining description concerning a pro-attitude, propositional determination of a will through imperatives furnished by practical reason, which, as it happens, is token-token identical to some natural event.

Apparently against exactly this, Kant now writes, it is "a wretched subterfuge to seek escape" with reference to "the kind of determining grounds of [an agent's] causality." He labels this notion the concept of a 'free effect', meaning "that of which the determining natural cause is internal to the acting thing." Even worse, along these same lines, Kant seems to argue against freedom as determination by laws of reason as well: "If these determining conceptions themselves have the ground of their existence in time, and more particularly, in the antecedent state . . . then it is natural necessity after all and not transcendental freedom."[67] This wretched subterfuge, he maintains, yields only the freedom of a clock, a projectile, or a turnspit: provided that it is wound up, launched, or cranked, it carries out its further motions without influence from any other external forces.

In this passage Kant argues against what he takes to be a Leibnizian theory of freedom [Ak. Ed. 5:97], but careful attention to his text shows that what he says is not also a rejection of the view I have attributed to him. What he objects to in this passage is the claim that freedom obtains when "the determining natural cause is internal to the acting thing." On the present reconstruction, though, freedom is not accounted for in terms of natural causes at all, whether internal or external to the acting thing. Rather it is found in the applicability of an *intelligible* cause, independent of natural causes. Again, he objects to the view of freedom's consisting in being determined by reason, "*if* these determining conceptions themselves have the ground of their existence in time or in the

---

[67]*Critique of Practical Reason*, p. 100; Ak. Ed. 5:96–97.

antecedent state." But the present reconstruction, as shown in our answers to the problems of absolute beginnings and atemporality, denies just this. Nondetermining descriptions of the sort appropriate for the pro-attitude, propositional determination of the causality of reason do not yield temporal determination of their objects, and therefore no "antecedent state" or law is such as to determine the causality of reason [see Ak. Ed. 5:97–98].

Nevertheless, misreadings of the wretched subterfuge passage have been quite successful in supporting rejections of the sort of compatibilism I have attributed to Kant. One recent example that deserves special mention and some extended discussion is Henry Allison's attack on compatibilist readings of Kant. In his treatment of Kant's theory of freedom, Allison repeatedly advances the thesis that the concept of transcendental freedom is an explicitly incompatibilist conception of freedom, and therefore that Kant cannot properly be read as adhering to a compatibilism between freedom and causal determination of the Humean, Leibnizian, or even contemporary Anglo-American stripe. Allison acknowledges that Kant does argue for a reconciliation of some sort, though, and he follows Allen Wood's description of this project by saying that Kant wants "to establish the compatibility of compatibilism and incompatibilism."[68] In other words, on Allison's view, Kant wants to hold both a genuine compatibilism between freedom and causal determinism and, in some sense, an incompatibilist theory of freedom.

The problem with such an approach is that Allison repeatedly and mistakenly treats "indeterminist" and "incompatibilist" synonymously in the descriptions he uses to characterize Kant's conception of transcendental freedom. Allison rightly argues that the concept of transcendental freedom is a nonempirical or indeterminist one precisely because it involves an act of (practical) spontaneity performed by the agent which, *insofar as* it is regarded as an expression of intelligible character, is nonexperienceable, unknowable, and thus indeterministic. Nevertheless, one may respond that this indeterminist conception can make for an incompatibilist conception only to the extent that a given compatibilist theory depends on a notion of freedom that is determinist in this

[68]Allison, *Kant's Theory of Freedom*, pp. 5, 28, 34. See also Wood, "Kant's Compatibilism," p. 74.

sense—for example, the one we have just seen Kant attribute to Leibniz, in which freedom is located in the right kind of natural determining cause, internal to the acting thing.

As should now be clear, though, not all the types of compatibilist theory Allison hopes to rule out of consideration as approximating Kant's view do depend on such a determinist conception of transcendental freedom, thereby identifying it with a special kind of empirical or natural cause. In brief, Allison is mistaken to group the Humean, Leibnizian, and various contemporary Anglo-American compatibilist positions together. His arguments work only against ascribing to Kant a compatibilism that takes an empirical or determinist conception of freedom (i.e., they work against an ascription of Leibnizian compatibilism to Kant), but they say nothing against a compatibilism that takes a nonempirical or indeterminist conception of freedom.

When Allison considers these contemporary approaches, he suggests that they presuppose a "naturalistic framework" and that they try to show that rational agency can somehow be "naturalized."[69] According to Allison, such views suggest that rational agency is to be explained on the familiar belief-desire model, with the resulting reason for action being identified with the empirical cause of the rational activity. But this achievement, Allison would protest, addresses only the empirical character of rational agency by identifying the empirical, psychological causes (some belief-desire pair) of action, and hence it fails altogether to address the intelligible character of rational agency. As we have seen, however, stating that a reason is identical to a cause is not at all equivalent to stating that reason descriptions are identical or even reducible to empirical or causal descriptions.

Hence, once again, the contemporary compatibilist can claim to have located the empirical cause of an action with a determining description regarding an agent's coming to have a certain belief-desire pair functioning as a reason for action (i.e., in a certain neurophysiological event that tokens the reason) but can also claim to have satisfied the Kantian demand for an intelligible character of the action in virtue of the applicability of a reason description to that token, a nondetermining description that employs a nonempirical, indeterminist conception of

[69]Allison, *Kant's Theory of Freedom*, pp. 34, 81.

transcendental freedom, complete with its notion of (practical) spontaneity. Furthermore, since reason descriptions are not a species of empirical or causal descriptions, spontaneity, the ground of imputation, is not thereby analyzed in a naturalistic, causal framework, and neither is the freedom signaled by such spontaneity accounted for in terms of any special kind of natural determining ground. Thus the present view is not subject to Allison's criticism.

Whether or not the resulting compatibilistic theory is immune from other standard criticisms is another question and remains to be investigated in the next chapter. But for the moment we may safely conclude that Kant's indeterminist conception of freedom does not prohibit his adopting an ancestor of certain versions of contemporary Anglo-American types of compatibilism. Indeed, the fact that Kant adopts an indeterminist conception of freedom is largely responsible for making him such a distinctive figure in the history of thought regarding different species of compatibilism and incompatibilism, and clarifying that indeterminist conception of freedom does justice to the significance of Kant's incompatibilist insights by making explicit their target: Kant argues against a certain brand of compatibilism; he does not give up on compatibilism in general.

Incomprehensibility

How can Kant say that actions are fully explicable and predictable as events in nature and yet rise from unknowable and incomprehensible grounds? This problem is slightly easier to deal with than the previous three. In the second *Critique*, actions are tokened by natural events that we could predict with certainty, if we knew all the relevant empirical facts and the causal laws [Ak. Ed. 5:99; see also A549–550/B577–578], since nature is subject to a thoroughgoing causal determinism. Nevertheless, we may still regard actions as arising from intelligible causes, causes which are thought apart from conditions of spatial and temporal determination and which, to this extent, are not regarded as objects of experience or as knowable for us, since they are not subject to any intuition in the absence of these conditions [Ak. Ed. 5:56–57]. For Kant, if an object is unintuitable, it is unknowable as well. The unknowability or incomprehensibility of these grounds, however, does not cast any doubt on their status as intelligible causes. Instead it simply underscores a traditional Kantian thesis: only natural causality produces explanations [Ak. Ed. 5:30]. Or, as Kant declares in the *Foundations*, "we can explain nothing but what we can reduce to laws whose object can be given in some possible experience."[70] Put simply, the ground of any action is knowable and explicable as an event under an empirical, determining description, but it is unknowable (but nonetheless thinkable) under an intelligible, nondetermining description.

In conclusion, my reconstruction of Kant's compatibilism has not been obstructed by the four problems that have led commentators to incompatibilist readings, to two-worlds distinctions, and to such dubious rescue attempts as calling on the doctrine of timeless agency or the reduction of constitutive, categorial principles to regulative Ideas. On the strength of a two-descriptions interpretation of Kant's distinction between things in themselves and appearances, that is, on the strength of his theory of token-token identity and type-type irreducibility, we have a compatibilistic reading that accommodates the various texts often thought to threaten any imputation of a serious compatibilism to Kant, and we have discovered an interesting philosophical thesis: whereas at any moment of time the entire world at that time and the laws of nature together determine a unique future, the human will, independent of pathological necessitation, is capable of both autonomous and heteronomous spontaneity of action. Or, if one prefers, human action is both causally determined and transcendentally free.

[70]*Foundations of the Metaphysics of Morals*, p. 77; Ak. Ed. 4:459.

Chapter 3

Kant and the Contemporary Metaphysics of Freedom and Determinism

Not all commentators are sympathetic with attempts to discuss Kant in a contemporary context, or with attempts to construe Kant as anticipating some current and fashionable view. One good example of this tendency can be found in Henry Allison's book on Kant's ethics. Allison reports that a certain interpretive strategy has become popular which "consists in rehabilitating Kant's views on mind and agency by seeing them as anticipations of popular contemporary forms of compatibilism or nonreductive versions of materialism." And in the parting sentence of his book he strikes out against this strategy by announcing that, even if his own treatment of the issues fails to convince readers "of the profundity and overall coherence of Kant's position," he hopes that "it will at least convince would-be defenders of Kant of the folly of trying to gain a hearing for his views by depicting him as anticipating contemporary forms of compatibilism."[1]

I detect two general sorts of objection on this score. The first is that in order to construe Kant as a proto-proponent of some contemporary theory, one has to suppress or ignore certain features of his account which are peculiar to his system and era, and thus that aligning him with contemporary positions invariably involves misconstruing his own position. The second is that it is somehow degrading to associate Kant with contemporary thinkers, and that it is preferable to approach Kant's position without attempting to engage his views with modern, analytic terminology and methods.

Neither objection strikes me as particularly compelling. By way of response, let me first note that occasionally, in literature sympathetic to Kant's views, I have noticed a tendency in commentators to downplay Kant's faults as a writer and philosopher, sometimes suggesting that there is hardly any real need to supplement or clarify Kant's views with comparisons to other writers and thinkers. Although I risk committing heresy by saying so, it is all too obvious that Kant's writings suffer from various defects. Kant is (by his own admission) a terrible stylist; his books are dry and obscure, suffer from excessive repetition, and are overflowing with complicated terms and phrases that are repeatedly misapplied. Also, it seems to me, Kant's virtue as a thinker is not that he managed to produce intricate, meticulous constructions of his philosophical positions, exhaustively working out the details of his philosophical views and the interconnections among his philosophical views. (Often, one wishes that this *had* been more prominent among his virtues.) Rather, much of the profundity of Kant's writings derives from his exceptional insights into and subsequent attempts at answering traditional philosophical problems in an astoundingly broad range of areas, even though the insights and solutions are frequently marred by his manner of exposition.

I do not find it in the least degrading or insulting to Kant to look to later writings on the same topics, frequently revealing his influence, for a clearer and often more refined version of the theories he gave initial

[1]Allison, *Kant's Theory of Freedom*, pp. 76, 249. Allison primarily seems to have in mind the work of commentators such as Ralf Meerbote, Patricia Kitcher, and Wilfred Sellars.

expression to. Allison's warning can be heeded at least this far: if one is searching for Kant's considered opinion on some matter, ascribing some twentieth-century position to him which utilizes concepts with which he was not and could not have been familiar is surely a mistake. But to show on rational reconstruction of his views that Kant anticipated some such theory, that the theory is broadly Kantian in its foundations, that it is consistent with and is a reasonable extension and appropriate refinement of Kant's general system, is of great interest in Kant studies and certainly does not require misrepresenting his original views. In fact, such comparisons, based on rational reconstruction, constitute one of the best means of discovering just how developed (or undeveloped) his original views really were, while holding out the promise of improving contemporary theory by uncovering and clarifying his original insights.

As the previous chapter makes clear, I believe that Kant developed a compatibilist position that is philosophically sophisticated, but a position that has probably found better expression (in both lucidity and detail) in its descendants, among the writings of certain contemporary philosophers who study problems of human freedom and mind-body identity. I do not wish to claim that any of the later views is Kant's view, or even that the contemporary theorists would claim to be developing and refining Kant's view, since I imagine that many of them would decline to take a stand regarding just which views Kant endorsed. I do claim, however, that their positions are Kantian in character, that their views are developed along the lines provided by the Kantian insights into the problems of free will and determinism. Also, I think we do Kant a service if we admit (when it is true) that his views resemble certain contemporary views in certain respects and treat them as the sort of thing that can be improved and refined in the light of contemporary analysis, without thereby doing violence to his original intentions, rather than treat them merely as wonders to be unearthed and marveled at. Accordingly, in the first and second sections of this chapter I offer a few remarks on some of the current work in philosophy of mind which I see as Kantian in character.

Whereas sympathetic Kant commentators are often somewhat reticent (if not apologetic) about arguing for a serious and prominent place for Kant in the context of current debates, Kant critics do not tend to be similarly shy about criticizing his views from the standpoint of the most recent discoveries and results of the contemporary philosophical scene. This is particularly true with respect to Kant's views on causality, freedom, and compatibilism. For example, two popular problems in the contemporary metaphysics of freedom and determinism concern the ability to do otherwise. One prominent issue is whether the ability to do otherwise can be properly regarded as a necessary condition on free action. Another prominent issue is whether the ability to do otherwise (regarded as a necessary condition on free action) is compatible with causal determinism. Not only are our intuitions likely to be in favor of incompatibilism here, but also quite powerful arguments have surfaced which seem to make an incompatibilist verdict on these matters unavoidable. A common scenario, then, involves a commentator (who adopts such an incompatibilism) either criticizing Kant's compatibilistic views for failing to appreciate the alleged insights supporting the incompatibilist position or "improving" Kant's position by making him appear to say something in agreement with these alleged incompatibilist insights after all. Lewis White Beck's interpretation of Kant's compatibilism, examined in the previous chapter, is an example of both approaches.

In the third and fourth sections of the present chapter I address these two problems and attempt to reveal their impact on the Kantian position developed in Chapter 2. In the third section I argue that, despite an ingenious proposal to the contrary, we do not have compelling counterexamples to the claim that freedom requires the ability to do otherwise. In the fourth section I argue that the most plausible versions of the argument in favor of incompatibilism have been refuted, nonetheless, and that the strategy employed in those arguments exhibits a general defect likely to frustrate any related attempt to demonstrate the truth of incompatibilism.

Token-Token Identity and Type-Type Irreducibility

A rapidly growing area of interest in contemporary philosophy of mind is directed toward theories of mind-body identity.[2] Widespread worries, largely based on the undesirability of certain ontological com-

[2]For a recent overview of this literature, see Cynthia MacDonald's *Mind-Body Identity Theories* (New York: Routledge, 1989).

mitments, have shifted the focus of the discussion from attempts to demonstrate the identity of mental substances and physical substances to attempts to demonstrate the identity of mental events and physical events.

There are immediate difficulties in defining the phrases 'mental event' and 'physical event' without automatically ensuring identity claims by definition. Donald Davidson gives an account of mental events which relies on what is known as the intentionality criterion: "'event x is m' is a mental description if and only if the expression that replaces 'm' contains at least one mental verb essentially," and "an event is mental if and only if it has a mental description,"[3] mental verbs being those that express intentionality—for example, believing, hoping, wishing, wanting, thinking, regretting, desiring. One good way of picking out which linguistic expressions exhibit intentionality is that the operation of the substitutivity of coreferentials tends to fail when performed on them. Or, more simply, they are those verbs that create nonextensional contexts. As has been frequently pointed out, this account may be generous enough to ensure that *all* events are mental events,[4] but that does not show that all mental events are also physical events, and the latter is the aim of the identity theorist.

Various proposals for defining the phrase 'physical event' have also surfaced, each with its own cluster of problems. One of the more promising is the following: 'event x is p' is a physical description if and only if the expression that replaces 'p' instantiates either the antecedent or consequent of a causal law, and an event is physical if and only if it has a physical description. Whereas some physical events (e.g., a rockslide) may themselves be such a complex series of events that no single causal law governs their occurrences, on the present account they need only be composed of a series of events each of which has an expression that instantiates either the antecedent or consequent of a causal law. Despite

[3]Donald Davidson, "Mental Events," in *Essays on Actions and Events* (Oxford: Clarendon Press, 1980), p. 211.

[4]The trick is to turn any clear example of a physical event (e.g., "Kant's dipping his pen into ink") into a mental event by offering the following sort of description of it: "Kant's dipping his pen into ink, while Fichte hopes for a favorable public recognition of his new manuscript." We have the same physical event, but now we may count it as a mental event as well, under the intentionality criterion, since we have found a mental description true of it.

the difficulties associated with giving an independent account of a physical law, these definitions at least have the virtue of not *guaranteeing* that
every mental event is also a physical event. However, since neither do
they rule out this possible relation, a successful identity theory of mental and physical events would be philosophically interesting and significant for the attempt to argue for compatibilism, rather than merely
being definitionally true.

In the previous chapter, I suggested that Kant was interested in establishing the identity of human actions (or events that arise from freedom)
with natural events that stand under causal laws, but that his compatibilism depended on the irreducibility of either natural descriptions to
action descriptions or of action descriptions to natural descriptions.
Kant's distinction between things in themselves and appearances led us
to investigate and identify this crucial feature belonging to the freedom
of the will in its independence from nature. As we also saw in the
previous chapter, the irreducibility of these description types was established, among other reasons, by the ineliminable presence of the term
'ought' in the imperatives that are essential to those bits of human
behavior that count as human actions—'ought' being a term which, on
Kant's view, has no place in nature or empirical descriptions but which
is essential in all complete action descriptions.

Similarly, in the recent history of the theory of mind-body identity,
one prominent focus has also been the problem of the reducibility or
irreducibility (and even of the identity) of mental and physical event
types. Kant, who was interested primarily in establishing the irreducibility of action descriptions to natural descriptions, grounded his
case with a theory about necessary features of human agency. The most
common, current objections advanced against type-type identity theories, however, are directed at *any* alleged type-type identities between
mental and physical events. So, instead of some specific feature of free
agency bearing the weight of the argument, these objections are
grounded in a theory of necessary identity, in proposals specifying the
appropriate conditions under which we may attribute mental properties
to a subject, in claims regarding essential features of sensation states,
and in "Cartesian" intuitions regarding the separability of phenomenal
states and bodily states. More specifically, two sorts of objection foun-
ded on these considerations have been offered against the identity or

reducibility of mental types to physical types held by theorists such as J. J. C. Smart.[5] Briefly, they can be described as follows:

Phenomenal property objection. Suppose that (i) some type-type identity theory is true and that, say, having pain is identical to the firing of C-fibers. But (ii) if having pain is identical to the firing of C-fibers, then necessarily having pain is identical to the firing of C-fibers, since all such identities are necessary. However, (iii) having pain is such that it is essentially felt, whereas no physical type (including the firing of C-fibers) is such that it is essentially felt. So, (iv) it is possible that there be a having-pain event that is not a firing of C-fibers, and this conflicts with the consequence of (i) and (ii), namely, (v) necessarily, having pain is identical to the firing of C-fibers.[6]

Variable realizability objection. (i), (ii), and (v) are the same as above. If (v), then (vi) it is not possible to have pain without the firing of C-fibers. However, (vii) beings with different physical structures, altogether lacking C-fibers and their firings, might still have pain; that is, we would be justified in attributing pain events to them on the strength of introspective reports and behavioristic evidence, and this conflicts with (vi).[7]

Each reductio argument establishes the untenability of type-type identity theories, and, whereas neither is in any special way Kantian, Kant could welcome the general results of these arguments as an independent buttressing of a specific thesis fundamental to his ethical views.

Mind-body identity can be revived, however, in the manner Kant himself endorses: through a token-token identity thesis of mental and physical events. Contemporary accounts of token-token identity have stirred up an exciting philosophical debate. One philosopher who has contributed to this debate as a proponent of the thesis is Donald Davidson. In a series of essays on freedom, agency, event theory, and the philosophy of psychology, Davidson has sketched a theory of action and

[5]J. J. C. Smart, "Sensations and Brain Processes," in *Modern Materialism: Readings on Mind-Body Identity*, ed. John O'Connor (New York: Harcourt, Brace and World, 1969), pp. 32–47.

[6]For examples of this type of objection, see Frank Jackson, "What Mary Didn't Know," *Journal of Philosophy* 83 (1986): 291–295; and Saul Kripke, *Naming and Necessity* (Cambridge: Harvard University Press, 1972).

[7]For an example of this type of objection, see Jaegwon Kim, "Phenomenal Properties, Psychophysical Laws, and the Identity Theory," *Monist* 56 (1972): 177–192.

a relation between mind and body that, although distinct in several aspects, nevertheless, bears remarkable similarity to Kant's own view.

I have already had occasion to compare Kant to Davidson with reference to how we are to understand Kant's theory of human agency and with reference to how we are to understand the pro-attitude, propositional determination that belongs to a proper analysis of the causality of reason. Davidson treats the relation between the reason for performing an action and the action itself (under one type of description) as a species of causal explanation. Also, like Kant, he construes such a reason, a "primary reason," as composed of the union of a propositional representation of a means-end connection with a desire for the end in question. Davidson, then, advocates a theory of action in which the primary reason on the basis of which an action is performed is its cause.[8] Furthermore, again like Kant, he sees causation as a relation between individual *events* (unrepeatable, dated particulars with a determinate location in time and space), and he argues that a particular causal connection requires some causal, covering law instantiated by some correct descriptions of the events related as cause to effect.[9] For both Kant and Davidson, then, an important consequence of these views is that, whereas causality is a relation between events however described, the instantiation of a causal law is a relation between events relative to a description. These common views contribute to a version of the token-token identity theory which Davidson advances in his essay "Mental Events" and which he terms "anomalous monism."[10] To this influential thesis we may now briefly turn.

Anomalous Monism

Davidson begins his classic "Mental Events" with a quotation from Kant and an expression of agreement with the content of the quoted passage which suggests that philosophical study will reveal a compati-

---

[8]See Davidson, "Actions, Reasons, and Causes," and "Freedom to Act," both in *Essays on Actions and Events*, pp. 3–19, 63–81.

[9]See Davidson, "Causal Relations," in *Essays on Actions and Events*, pp. 149–162.

[10]Again, reprinted in *Essays on Actions and Events*, pp. 207–225. See also "Psychology as Philosophy" (together with comments and replies), and "The Material Mind," in the same collection, pp. 229–244, 245–259.

bilism between freedom and determinism. As is customary in the contemporary discussion, however, Davidson argues for the compatibility of the existence of various sorts of mental events that act as causes (of which the employment of free will is a species) with the anomalousness of mental events in general (which is a feature of free will as well as of rememberings, perceivings, regrettings, etc.).[11]

Davidson directs this Kantian optimism specifically at a reconciliation of three theses: the Principle of Causal Interaction (PCI): "At least some mental events interact causally with physical events"; the Principle of the Nomological Character of Causality (PNCC): "Events related as cause and effect fall under strict deterministic laws"; and Anomalism of the Mental (AM): "There are no strict deterministic laws on the basis of which mental events can be predicted and explained." The apparent worry is that these principles might form an inconsistent triad, since PCI and PNCC seem to imply that AM is false. Davidson suggests that the three theses can be shown to be consistent, though, and he points out that such a demonstration is "essentially the Kantian line."[12]

He is more correct than he might have guessed. Davidson simply assumes the truth of PCI and of PNCC as "undeniable facts" and argues in favor only of AM. Kant, on the other hand, attempts to offer argument for all three, and a brief reminder of the nature of those arguments reveals how serious the issue is for him. When Kant offers his theory of rational agency, he commits himself to PCI—to the view that some mental events cause physical events. In fact, he is committed to a stronger series of theses as well; when he opens the first *Critique* by referring to occasions when objects affect our senses [A19/B33], he also acknowledges that some physical events cause some mental events (e.g., our coming to have sensations). And when he writes that having sensations "stirs the understanding" (prompts the activity of concept formation and application), he admits that some mental events cause other mental events. Also, as I argue in Chapter 4, Kant's proof of the Law of Universal Causation in the Second Analogy has as a corollary that the causal

---

[11]Whether Kant can ultimately claim that it is also a feature of sensations is a troublesome issue. For a discussion of the problems involved here, see Ralf Meerbote, "Kant's Functionalism," in *Historical Foundations of Cognitive Science*, ed. J. C. Smith (Dordrecht: Kluwer, 1990), pp. 161–187.

[12]Davidson, "Mental Events," pp. 208–209.

connection is generalizable, that is, that there are covering laws, and that causal connections are not singular. Accordingly, I also argue that Kant has reason to regard PNCC not merely as a regulative principle but rather as a constitutive a priori principle governing the very possibility of experience. Finally, Kant's notions of transcendental and practical freedom require a sense in which the will is independent from nature. This requirement, which proves both to be an essential feature of his ethical theory and to play a crucial role in his compatibilistic analysis, also involves a clear affirmation of AM.[13] Davidson is right, then, to note that he and Kant are working on the same problem, Davidson with its general form and Kant with its specification, the relation of causal determinism to free will.

Davidson's project is to argue from PCI, PNCC, and the absence of any psychophysical laws (which justifies AM) to the truth of a token-token identity theory he classifies as anomalous monism. He hints that this argument is weak, since he does not offer any support for PCI and PNCC beyond their own self-evidence. As just noted, though, Kant believes the principles can be supported by argument. Kant's defense of these principles relies heavily on his causal theory of time, and whether or not one believes that theory to be well developed in Kant's writings, at the very least Kant succeeds in showing the relevance of the theory to the truth of PCI and PNCC. Perhaps, then, in the contemporary advocates of a causal theory of time, Hans Reichenbach and Adolf Grünbaum, one could find grounds for a more compelling Kantian argument in favor of PCI and PNCC than Davidson offers himself.[14]

Davidson's strategy in arguing for AM is first to argue for a position which (together with some other less problematic assumptions) entails it, namely, that there are no psychophysical laws. This claim, (AM), together with his token-token identity, captures the dual thesis of anom-

---

[13]Kant's claims about the predictability of human actions [e.g., A550/B578] seem to contradict this. The reason they do not is illuminating, and I return to address this potential problem in what follows.

[14]In Chapter 4, I will defend the claim that Kant endorses a causal theory of time. For contemporary versions of this thesis see Hans Reichenbach, *The Philosophy of Space and Time*, trans. M. Reichenbach and J. Freund (New York: Dover, 1958); and Adolf Grünbaum, *Philosophical Problems of Space and Time*, 2d ed. (Dordrecht: D. Reidel Pub. Co., 1973).

alous monism.[15] Monism for Kant and Davidson is a version of token physicalism, with any mental event being identical to some physical event, but it is a nonreductive version of token physicalism. By the anomalousness of the mental, Davidson sometimes writes as if he just means a denial of psychophysical and correlation laws, but it would seem that he also intends (and needs) to deny strict psychological laws as well. Kant is once again in agreement on both counts: as Davidson correctly points out, "Kant believed freedom entails anomaly," and as is well known Kant denied that psychology could be a science because it lacked both the requisite mathematical structure and the strict laws necessary for explanation and predictability of psychological occurrences.[16]

Before I consider the arguments against psychophysical and psychological laws further, it would be worthwhile to sketch the precise argument for the identity theory offered by Davidson in "Mental Events" and elsewhere.[17] Some mental events interact causally with physical events (from PCI). When a mental event stands in a causal relation with a physical event, there is some strict law they instantiate (from PNCC). But there are no psychophysical laws (strict laws subsuming a mental event and a physical event under mental and physical descriptions), nor are there any psychological laws (strict laws subsuming two mental events under mental descriptions), nor are there any bridge laws (claims to a necessary coextension between a mental and a physical predicate on the basis of which a reduction can be accomplished) (from AM). So, by elimination, these events instantiate a strict physical law. Therefore, since the only events that instantiate strict physical laws are physical

[15]Ralf Meerbote has recognized and commented on the similarities between Kant's position in the resolution to the Third Antinomy and Davidson's anomalous monism in "Kant on the Nondeterminate Character of Human Actions" and elsewhere.

[16]Davidson, "Mental Events," p. 208, and see the Preface to the *Metaphysical Foundations of Natural Science*, Ak. Ed. 4:467–479.

[17]Davidson, "Mental Events," pp. 223–224. In this regard, Brian McLaughlin's "Anomalous Monism and the Irreducibility of the Mental," in *Actions and Events: Perspectives in the Philosophy of Donald Davidson*, ed. Ernest LePore and Brian P. McLaughlin (New York: Basil Blackwell, 1985), pp. 331–368, is remarkably helpful in its clear summarization and reconstruction of the views Davidson offers in several of his essays.

events, any mental event that interacts causally with a physical event is itself a physical event.

It is only fair to point out that this argument, if successful, establishes merely that all mental events that stand in causal relations with physical events are themselves physical events, and Davidson shies away from the prospect of showing that all mental events have such causal relations. But it also seems fair to point out that the argument establishes the identity thesis for those mental events we are likely to care about. Although this argument leaves conceptual room for some special sort of being that has psychological states with no causal history or future in virtue of which they are related to the physical world (e.g., a being who does not perceive), we are certainly not such beings ourselves. To borrow a line from Kant, for us "there can be no doubt that all our knowledge begins from experience" [B1], and all our subsequent mental events thereby possess the appropriate causal history, grounded in perceptual encounters, to be proper targets for the present argument. In addition, an alternative Kantian argument for the claim that *all* mental events stand in causal connections to physical events can be drawn from the fact that any two events (whether mental or physical) are temporally related; this fact together with Kant's theory of the time determination of events in the Second Analogy guarantees a thoroughgoing causal connectedness between the mental and the physical.

As before, the important move in Davidson's argument is from events as the relata of causal connections to events under certain descriptions as instantiating a strict physical law. In other words, whereas events, however described, are the relata of causal connections, only certain descriptions of those events are relevant for *explaining* the causal connection. Thus, instantiating a causal law is something events undergo only relative to certain of their descriptions. Hence, we are to understand the two principles at work in this argument with the following important italicized qualifications: (PNCC) "events related as cause and effect [*have descriptions in virtue of which they*] fall under strict deterministic laws," and (AM) "there are no strict deterministic laws on the basis of which mental events can be predicted and explained [*which subsume events under mental descriptions*]." Consequently, whereas AM seems to mean that we cannot "explain and predict human behavior with the kind of precision that is possible in principle for physical phenomena," we can in principle predict and explain the occurrence of a human action, but only insofar as we can in principle predict and explain the physical event with which it is identical. What we cannot do with strict precision is explain or predict the event in terms of a mentalistic vocabulary.[18] I submit that this is also the reading to adopt with respect to Kant's own claim that human actions are as predictable as an eclipse of the sun or moon [A549–550/B577–578]. One should note that Kant claims that we can do the latter only when considering those actions in the field of appearance, that is, as physical events under natural, determining descriptions, and he explicitly contrasts this with predicting them as human, mental actions, that is, in their relation to reason and to an intelligible character.

One may note that Davidson's argument strategy for the identity theory is also employed in Kant's compatibilistic resolution, and that we may substitute "free will" for "mental event" and draw the corresponding conclusion, that all instances of an exercise of free will are also physical events: Kant, who is committed to PCI due to his theory of action, to PNCC due to his argument for causal determinism, and to AM due to his views on psychology and to his theory of a type of freedom essential for rational, human agency, also argues to a token-token identity of actions and natural events in the resolution of the Third Antinomy.

The key premise for both Kant and Davidson is the denial of strict psychophysical, psychological, and bridge laws, which prevents this version of token-physicalism from becoming a reductive materialism. Davidson defends the premise by (i) denying strict psychophysical and psychological laws on the grounds that psychology is not a closed theory and cannot be nomologically reduced to a closed theory (psychology is not and cannot be reduced to a theory which, like physics, has no causes or effects that are not of the same type), and by (ii) denying bridge laws on the grounds that there are irreducible differences in the constitutive principles characterizing the domains of psychological and physical predicates.[19]

[18]Davidson, "Psychology as Philosophy," p. 230.
[19]Davidson, "Psychology as Philosophy," p. 231. See McLaughlin, "Anomalous Monism and the Irreducibility of the Mental," pp. 342–359, for an extended discussion.

I close these observations on Davidson's (Kantian) identity theory with a brief discussion of Kant's arguments for (i) and (ii) and the relation of those arguments to Davidson's defense of the same theses. Against psychological laws, Kant argues that psychology is not a science and is not reducible to a proper science such as physics, precisely because it lacks the required mathematical structure to support lawlike generalizations subsuming events under mentalistic descriptions.[20] Moreover, psychology, unlike physics, offers no well-defined contrariety relations to support scientific investigation. Against psychophysical laws, Kant can also offer an argument grounded in his ethical views. As we discover in Chapter 5, Kant argues from a consciousness of the moral law, characterized as the necessary determination of the power of choice by pure practical reason, to a sense of freedom of the will involving independence from nature. Kant could, then, argue from that particular feature of his theory of free will to the absence of any psychophysical laws that would otherwise violate the sort of independence required for rational, human agency. There is no circularity here, for though the absence of psychophysical laws is a necessary condition for Kant's compatibilism, which is a necessary condition for an attribution of freedom to a subject, on Kant's view the argument for the denial of such laws begins with an independent justification for the moral law which in turn guarantees the freedom of independence with which Kant can deny such laws.

Finally, against bridge laws (claims to the necessary coextension of a physical and a mental predicate), Kant would share with Davidson the approach that relies on distinguishing non-interchangeable constitutive principles of the physical and mental conceptual schemes and non-interchangeable standards of application for the respective concept types. The argument, then, is that no bridge laws are possible, since the concepts from the two essentially different conceptual schemes, which would thereby be made necessarily coextensive, have incompatible standards of construction and application.[21] The constitutive principles

---

[20]*Metaphysical Foundations of Natural Science*, Ak. Ed. 4:467–479.

[21]This specific argument is analyzed at some length in McLaughlin, "Anomalous Monism and the Irreducibility of the Mental," pp. 354–359. What follows is partially drawn from that discussion.

in question occupy a normative role in concept formation and application, and those underlying the mental conceptual scheme are in general rationality requirements. Davidson writes, "If we are to intelligibly attribute attitudes and beliefs, or usefully to describe motions as behavior, then we are committed to finding, in the pattern of behavior, belief, and desire, a large degree of rationality and consistency." These conditions express how one ought to behave and what one ought to believe, given certain background evidence and beliefs, in order to conform to the standards of rationality and consistency.[22] Since no principles underlying physical conceptual schemes can manage to do this, the conditions for mental concept formation and application cannot be stated with purely physical terminology. In short, then, since mental concepts can have only rational conditions of application, and since physical concepts can have only nonrational conditions of application, and since bridge laws would require that mental concepts have nonrational conditions of application, there cannot be such laws.

Similarly, Kant believes that there are rational conditions of mental concept formation and application. Talk of purposes and reasons for action invokes teleological, nondetermining, reflective judgments which may be contrasted with those causal, determining judgments required for empirical knowledge which do invoke concepts taken from the physical conceptual domain. In the specific subclass of such mental concepts Kant is interested in, the conditions required for the application of action descriptions apply to expressions of the pro-attitude, propositional determination at work in the causality of reason. And, as is now obvious, the nondetermining descriptions serving as the relevant action descriptions are not reducible to any determining descriptions. One sufficient reason for this, among others, is that the former offer no causal connections or determinability of their objects in space or in time, and the latter require such connections and determinability. Consequently, Kant would deny the existence of bridge laws for exactly the same reasons Davidson offers: because any claim to a necessary coextension of a physical predicate and a mental predicate would require the lawlike union of concepts from essentially incompatible conceptual domains.

[22]Davidson, "Psychology as Philosophy," pp. 237, 231.

Freedom and the Ability to Do Otherwise

Let us now turn our attention to a pair of puzzles regarding the ability to do otherwise. The first problem (the topic of the present section) threatens to render the Kantian compatibilist position superfluous, since it appears to undermine a thesis held by both the compatibilist and the incompatibilist we have been considering; specifically, it appears to undermine the thesis that freedom requires the ability to do otherwise. The second problem (the topic of the following section) threatens to refute the Kantian compatibilist position by denying that we have any good counterexamples to the thesis that freedom requires the ability to do otherwise and by then attempting to demonstrate the incompatibility of causal determinism and the ability to do otherwise.

As we saw in Chapter 2, in his defense of Leibniz and Wolff against Crusius, Kant characterized the "freedom of indifference" as an illusion, conceding the claim that an agent cannot do otherwise than the agent in fact does, yet he continued to argue for compatibilism nevertheless. In other words, early in his precritical period Kant did not regard the ability to do otherwise as a necessary condition on free action. A remarkably short way with a standard style of incompatibilist argument suggests itself: if the ability to do otherwise is not a necessary condition on free action, then a demonstration of the incompatibility of that particular ability and causal determinism should not by itself worry the theorist who maintains the compatibility of free will and causal determinism.

In his *Nova dilucidatio*, Kant was willing to analyze freedom merely with reference to the source of the necessity behind the performance of an action. The favored type of necessity turned out to be an internal determination of an agent's will through reason, a determination requiring the spontaneous inclination of his will. Moreover, Kant went to some pains to emphasize that he was not suggesting that, in the case of a freely performed action, the will could have inclined otherwise.[23] In his critical period, however, Kant retracts this universal claim and clearly endorses the view that human agents possess the ability to do otherwise. Most notably, when an agent freely transgresses the moral law, he

[23]*Nova dilucidatio*, Ak. Ed. 2:402.

does something different from what he ought to have done, and, Kant argues, if he ought to have done otherwise, then he was capable of doing otherwise [A554–556/B582–584].[24]

One might observe that this defense of the ability to do otherwise, if it shows anything, only shows that the agent has the ability to do otherwise on *some* occasions when he freely performs an act, namely, on those occasions when he does something which he should not have done. Furthermore, one may observe, this is hardly equivalent to the claim that freedom of action invariably requires the ability to do otherwise.

Still, during his critical period, Kant seems quite willing to hold this stronger thesis as well. According to him, on any given occasion in which we act freely, not only are we always able to carry out the prescriptions of the moral law, we are also always able to refrain from carrying out those prescriptions.[25] As we discover in Chapter 5, Kant believes that human agents possess a special type of will, an *arbitrium liberum*. Two consequences of possessing this type of will are that we are never simply pathologically necessitated to perform the action that most appeals to our sensuous nature, the fate of those with an *arbitrium brutum*, nor are we intellectually necessitated to perform only those actions that are required by moral law; we have neither an animal will nor a holy will.[26] On the contrary, we have a will which may aspire to goodness but which is always subject to rational deliberation regarding moral, morally neutral, and immoral means and ends, and we have a will which may spontaneously adopt any of several maxims through which we can attempt to secure those ends through our rational agency.

A controversial essay by Harry Frankfurt, though, suggests that Kant

[24]In addition to the malicious-lie passage from the first *Critique*, see also the second *Critique*, Ak. Ed. 5:30, 36–37, 101, 159; and *Religion within the Limits of Reason Alone*, Ak. Ed. 6:41.

[25]See the *Critique of Practical Reason*, Ak. Ed. 5:25, 37. See also the *Foundations of the Metaphysics of Morals*, Ak. Ed. 4:412–413.

[26]In addition to the passage in the first *Critique* in which Kant draws his distinction between an *arbitrium brutum* and an *arbitrium liberum* [A534/B562], see also his *Lectures on Ethics*, trans. Louis Infield (Indianapolis: Hackett, 1963), p. 28, for a further remark on the *arbitrium liberum* and the ability to do otherwise. I take these matters up in some detail in Chapter 5.

may well have made a mistake when he relinquished his precritical view that freedom of action does not require the ability to do otherwise.[27] Actually, Frankfurt addresses a related principle regarding the alleged necessity of the ability to do otherwise for moral responsibility, but I intend to adapt the considerations Frankfurt offers on that score in order to investigate the alleged necessity of the ability to do otherwise for free action.

Frankfurt observes that the principle that moral responsibility requires noncoercion is both widely held and extremely plausible. This plausible principle, is, however, routinely confused with another principle, and failing to distinguish between the two may have led many of the adherents of the first principle into error. Frankfurt christens the offending second principle the Principle of Alternate Possibilities (PAP): "A person is morally responsible for what he has done only if he could have done otherwise." Now, if we accept the first principle about noncoercion, we are likely to accept PAP as well, because when we think about scenarios in which some agent cannot do otherwise we tend to think only of cases in which whatever circumstances prevent the agent from doing otherwise also compel or constrain or coerce the agent to perform those acts he actually performs. Consequently, since we think that coercion interferes with moral responsibility, so too we tend to think that the inability to do otherwise interferes with moral responsibility. After offering this assessment of our reasons for accepting PAP, Frankfurt proposes a counterexample to PAP which turns on specifying a case that separates these two features. He asks us to consider a case in which the circumstances that prevent some agent from doing otherwise play no role whatsoever in bringing about the action the agent actually performs. Consequently, he suggests, we can show that PAP is false without endangering our view about the relation between moral responsibility and coercion.[28]

---

[27]Harry Frankfurt, "Alternate Possibilities and Moral Responsibility." This is not to suggest that Kant had any good reasons to justify his precritical belief on these matters, just that the principle that he originally endorsed may have been true after all.

[28]In other words, Frankfurt is still willing to endorse the principle that "a person is not morally responsible for what he has done, if he did it only because he could not have done otherwise."

To adapt Frankfurt's discussion to our present purpose, let us devise a principle similar to PAP which deals explicitly with free action rather than with moral responsibility (PAPF): "An agent performs an action freely only if he could have done otherwise." The considerations noted above which seem to speak in favor of PAP also seem to speak in favor of PAPF. We probably tend to think that the inability to do otherwise interferes with moral responsibility for something like the following series of reasons: (i) because the inability to do otherwise invariably results in coercion, (ii) because coercion interferes with free will, and (iii) because free will is necessary for moral responsibility. Frankfurt challenges our belief in PAP by providing reasons for rejecting (i). Of course, (i) and (ii) are just what we need to motivate PAPF; hence, to the extent that Frankfurt's challenge constitutes an objection to PAP it also seems to constitute an objection to PAPF.[29]

One can construct a Frankfurt-style counterexample with reference to human agents, or to machines, or to blind forces of nature, or to evil demons. I think, though, that invoking some (imaginary) powerful, supernatural entity best precludes certain irrelevant objections to these attempted counterexamples. Consider, then, the following Frankfurt-style counterexample to PAPF.

Suppose that we have just joined our heroes shortly after their race around the walls of Troy, and suppose that Achilles is right on the verge of delivering the blow that will bring an end to Hector's life. Furthermore, suppose that among the various gods who are enjoying this spectacle there is one who is absolutely determined to see Achilles kill Hector. This god has a plan. If for some reason Achilles should falter or lose his resolve and decide not to act in such a way as to deliver the fatal blow to Hector by a certain time t, then this god will intervene and

---

[29]It is worth noting that the other steps in the argument are open to dispute as well. Many philosophers have denied the notion that coercion genuinely interferes with freedom, and, surprisingly, some theorists have even argued that moral responsibility does not require free action; see Michael Slote, "Understanding Free Will," *Journal of Philosophy* 77 (1980): 136–151. In any event, I suspect that there are objections and replies relevant to PAP which are not relevant to PAPF. I do not wish to enter into these problems here. Let us simply note that Frankfurt's remarks about the initial plausibility of PAP also seem to favor the initial plausibility of PAPF, and let us now direct our attention to PAPF itself. I do, however, now talk about Frankfurt-style counterexamples to PAPF, since Frankfurt addresses himself only to PAP.

manipulate Achilles in some fashion that results in Achilles delivering
the fatal blow to Hector by t. Moreover, whatever sort of manipulation
one thinks would be required (e.g., instilling false beliefs, neurophysiological tinkering), suppose that this god is just powerful enough
to carry this plan out. Fortunately for our scheming god, however,
Achilles does not hesitate or lose his resolve, and consequently, he
delivers the fatal blow to Hector by t. Well, this pleases our god to no
end, since he never, in fact, has to intervene in any way whatsoever in
order to witness the killing of Hector by Achilles (an event which de-
lights him), and since he does not have to face any punishment from the
other gods for intervening, and so forth.

Initially, at least, it appears that we here have a genuine objection to
PAPF. What should we say about the action performed by Achilles in
this example? First, could Achilles have done otherwise than deliver the
fatal blow to Hector by t? It seems not, since every possible future open
to Achilles is a future in which Achilles delivers the fatal blow to Hector
by t. Admittedly, in some of those possible futures, Achilles does so
because he is caused to do so by the god, and perhaps these are cases
where his doing so is unfree. It is not clear, however, how this fact
makes any important difference. After all, the point at issue is not one
about the freedom of Achilles in interference cases, but rather about the
freedom of Achilles in non-interference cases that would have been
interference cases had Achilles acted differently. Second, did Achilles
freely deliver the fatal blow to Hector by t? Once again, it seems that he
did, since all the facts about the scheming god in this example are facts
about unrealized causal powers of the objects that constituted Achilles'
environment at the time of his action, and there is no reason to think
that facts of that sort (facts that in no way help us to explain why or how
someone acted as he did) could affect ascriptions of freedom to agents.[30]
It appears, then, that we have a counterexample to PAPF: Achilles both
freely delivers the fatal blow to Hector by t, and could not have done
otherwise than deliver the fatal blow to Hector by t.

---

[30] I borrow the language I utilize in responding to the two questions just posed from
van Inwagen's discussion of Frankfurt's article in *An Essay on Free Will*, p. 163. Also, I
assume that there are no other circumstances (independent of the facts about the
scheming god) which jeopardize Achilles' freedom. If this assumption is in conflict
with something in the *Iliad* (which is entirely likely), suppose that I am here talking
about some other remarkably similar story without that troublesome feature.

If this were a successful counterexample, it would seem to divorce free will from the ability to do otherwise, and it would seem to eliminate incompatibilist threats to freedom that are aimed merely at the incompatibility of causal determinism and the ability to do otherwise. As I mentioned before, though, Frankfurt counterexamples to PAP are controversial, and so I next argue that Frankfurt-style counterexamples to PAPF are highly suspect as well.

Peter van Inwagen has offered one response questioning the significance of Frankfurt's attack on PAP by way of providing an intriguing line of defense for a trio of principles that are distinct from, but related to, PAP.[31] Like Frankfurt, van Inwagen addresses principles that deal directly with moral responsibility rather than principles that deal directly with free will, and his position depends crucially on distinguishing between various types of things for which agents might be held morally responsible. He suggests that we do not tend to hold people responsible for their actions or inactions but rather for the consequences of their actions or inactions.[32] In short, we might reasonably hold agents morally responsible for those things we call events or for those things we call states of affairs. Van Inwagen then further inquires into the nature of these types of entities, asking whether they are to be construed as particulars or as universals. With this question in mind, his overall strategy is to demonstrate the truth of the following two claims: (i) when we treat the object of moral responsibility consistently as a particular (say, as an event particular), then whenever an agent is morally responsible for the occurrence of such an event, the agent is also capable of preventing the occurrence of that event; in other words, he maintains, "a person is morally responsible for a certain event (particular) only if he could have prevented it." (ii) when we treat the object of moral responsibility consistently as a universal (say, as a state-of-affairs universal), then whenever an agent is incapable of preventing the obtaining

[31]In van Inwagen, "Ability and Responsibility"; and again in *An Essay on Free Will*, pp. 162–182. Whereas he is (charitably) willing to grant that Frankfurt's counterexamples show the falsity of PAP, he argues that this does not have any consequence that undermines the compatibilist-incompatibilist debate, since the related principles van Inwagen substitutes for PAP are not subject to Frankfurt's type of counterexample.

[32]Van Inwagen, *An Essay on Free Will*, pp. 166–167. This turns out to be the motivating feature of his discussion. However, since I am ultimately concerned with PAPF, a principle that talks about free actions rather than about moral responsibility, my discussion inevitably diverges from van Inwagen's in important respects.

of that state of affairs, the agent is also not morally responsible for the obtaining of that state of affairs; in other words, he maintains, "a person is morally responsible for a certain state of affairs only if (that state of affairs obtains and) he could have prevented it from obtaining."

Although it requires a slightly different analysis, I believe that one can exploit this same basic strategy to investigate the success of the present Frankfurt-style counterexample to PAPF. We may begin by raising a similar initial question. What are the various types of things agents might be said to do freely? The obvious answer is "perform actions" (or perhaps in Kantian terminology, "spontaneously adopt a maxim governing the performance of actions"), but then, as in the former discussion, we need to know whether these actions are to be construed as particulars or as universals. When an agent freely does x, is x an "act particular" (a species of event particular with a special genesis involving volition) or is x the obtaining of an "act universal" (something that could be done by a different agent, or which could be done by the same agent at a different time, or which is capable of being instantiated by distinct event particulars each of which has a special genesis involving volition)?

It seems to me that free actions are best construed as act particulars; that is, the things we do freely are token-token identical to unrepeatable event particulars, with spatiotemporal determinations and empirical, causal histories. It is worth noting, however, that when van Inwagen briefly turns his attention from the distinction between event particulars and state-of-affairs universals to the distinction between act particulars and act universals he suggests that the things for which we are *morally responsible* are the obtainings of act universals and not simply act particulars.[33] But this view does not seem to conflict with the claim that the specific things we *do freely* are act particulars rather than act universals. One might be inclined to say that, although free actions are act particulars (e.g., the particular event actually denoted by the phrase "Achilles kills Hector"), these free actions instantiate act universals (e.g., "the act of causing Hector's death") for which an agent may or may not be morally responsible.[34]

[33]Or, at least, this is how he interprets Frankfurt's discussion of PAP; see van Inwagen, *An Essay on Free Will*, pp. 179–180.

[34]Van Inwagen does not offer his reasons for denying that we hold agents morally responsible for act particulars as well; he simply calls the view uninteresting. Inciden-

Furthermore, van Inwagen expresses reservations about simply trans-
ferring his remarks regarding state-of-affairs universals to act universals, since he is worried about how to characterize the latter precisely.
But this worry is troublesome only when we treat the objects of moral
responsibility as the obtainings of act universals and when we are dealing with a principle that addresses moral responsibility such as PAP.
Since I am interested instead in free actions (in act particulars) and in
dealing with a principle that addresses free action such as PAPF, I can
simply overlook the lack of a precise analysis of an act universal. I trust
that this omission may be excused on the grounds that any such analysis would not bear the weight of the argument against the Frankfurt-
style counterexample to PAPF anyway, given that the most reasonable
account of the things we do freely is to be provided with an analysis of
act particulars rather than of act universals.

Let us now return to our example involving Achilles and Hector. If we
apply our distinction to this case, we discover that we have equivocated
in the attempt to provide a Frankfurt-style counterexample to PAPF. The
phrase "Achilles delivers the fatal blow to Hector by t" is ambiguous.
When we said that Achilles *freely* delivers the fatal blow to Hector by t,
we treated the phrase as if it denoted an act particular; but when we said
that Achilles *could not have done otherwise* than deliver the fatal blow to
Hector by t, we treated the phrase as if it denoted the obtaining of an act
universal.

Suppose that we treat the phrase as consistently denoting a specific
act particular.[35] Then it is simply false that Achilles could not have done
otherwise than deliver the fatal blow to Hector by t. Suppose that,
instead of deciding to deliver the fatal blow to Hector by t, Achilles had
decided to rush over and embrace Hector at t. Well, the scheming god
certainly would have intervened, and an event would have occurred
that we would denote with the phrase, "Achilles delivers the fatal blow

---

tally, it would seem that Kant, for one, would be willing to hold just such an "uninteresting" view, insofar as an agent is morally responsible for (the act particular of)
spontaneously adopting a maxim designed to violate the moral law, whatever the
consequences may be.

[35]Given the fact that the example requires that this phrase refer to a free act performed by Achilles, and given the fact that free actions are best construed as act
particulars, this is how we *should* treat the phrase.

to Hector by *t*." But the event we would *then* denote with that particular phrase would be a different act particular from the event we actually denote with that phrase. This follows simply from the fact that act particulars are a species of event particulars and from a plausible principle of event individuation: *x* is the same event as *y* if and only if *x* and *y* have the same causes.[36] Since any case in which the scheming god interfered with Achilles would be a case in which Achilles was caused by the god to deliver the fatal blow to Hector by *t*, any such case would fail to result in an act particular identical to the one actually performed by Achilles. But then it is not true that every possible future open to Achilles is one in which "he delivers the fatal blow to Hector by *t*" (since, by hypothesis, we are regarding this phrase as denoting an act particular), even though it is true that every possible future open to Achilles is one in which we denote some event or other by the phrase "Achilles delivers the fatal blow to Hector by *t*."

Consequently, if we construe free actions as act particulars, then even though it is true that Achilles freely delivers the fatal blow to Hector by *t*, it is not true that Achilles could not do otherwise than deliver the fatal blow to Hector by *t*. For instance, his deciding to embrace Hector at *t* and the subsequent interference of the scheming god would count as Achilles doing otherwise in our example, since Achilles would thereby (freely) perform an action sufficient for the nonoccurrence of the act particular actually denoted by the phrase "Achilles delivers the fatal blow to Hector by *t*." Hence, our alleged counterexample fails.

Suppose now that someone treats the phrase as consistently denoting the obtaining of a certain act universal. Then it is simply false that Achilles freely delivers the fatal blow to Hector by *t*. It is certainly still true that all the facts about the scheming god in this example are facts about unrealized causal powers of the objects that constituted Achilles' environment at the time of his action. But if we are asked to regard the action as the obtaining of an act universal, the presence of those powers becomes relevant, whether or not they are unrealized. Recall that, insofar as we regard Achilles' action as the obtaining of an act universal, we

---

[36]Van Inwagen persuasively argues for this quasi-Davidsonian (and Kantian) principle of event individuation in *An Essay on Free Will*, pp. 167–169. It is crucial to understand that this principle maintains that the causal history of an event is an essential property of that event.

regard it as the sort of thing that could be done by the same agent at a different time, or as something capable of being instantiated by distinct event particulars each of which has a special genesis involving volition. In other words, it is the sort of thing that happens whether Achilles delivers the fatal blow to Hector by *t* as a result of his own beliefs and desires or whether he does it as a result of being caused to do so by the scheming god. But if *this* is what we mean when we refer to Achilles' action (if we really mean to refer to the obtaining of a universal), then I see no good reason to affirm that Achilles freely delivers the fatal blow to Hector by *t*, since that act universal could have and would have been instantiated no matter what Achilles decided to do.

Now, one might be tempted to think that Achilles still does something freely: he freely does *something* that instantiates that universal. But to put the matter this way is to abandon our construal of Achilles' free action as an act universal. When we treat actions as the sort of things that might be construed either as act particulars or as act universals, we want to distinguish between saying that an agent freely does *something* (which instantiates a universal) and saying that an agent freely instantiates a universal. The former construal is just an admission that Achilles freely performs an act particular, after all. I do not think that I can say much more in favor of this intuition, since I am not able to offer any precise analysis of an act universal that can be uncontroversially subjected to the same style of criticism van Inwagen brings against what I have called state-of-affairs universals. Once again, though, I see no real need to say much more, since the present case depends on the implausible assumption that free actions are to be construed as the obtainings of act universals.[37]

Consequently, if we construe free actions as the obtainings of act universals, then, even though it is true that Achilles could not do otherwise than deliver the fatal blow to Hector by *t*, it is not true that Achilles freely delivers the fatal blow to Hector by *t*. Hence, once again, our alleged counterexample fails.

On the strength of this discussion, I conclude that no short way with

[37]I would, however, direct anyone who still thinks that Achilles acts freely in our example (when his acts are construed as the obtainings of act universals) to van Inwagen's discussion of state-of-affairs universals in *An Essay on Free Will*, pp. 171–178.

the incompatibilist argument sketched at the beginning of this section is available, either for Kant or for the contemporary theorist. Hence, one cannot successfully avoid the contemporary attempts to demonstrate the incompatibility of causal determinism and free will by way of demonstrating the incompatibility of causal determinism and the ability to do otherwise simply by denying that the ability to do otherwise is a necessary condition on free will.

Causal Determinism and the Ability to Do Otherwise

We now reach a stumbling block for interpretations of Kant's compatibilism. In this section I defend the compatibilistic position I have attributed to Kant from an exceedingly popular objection, attempted answers to which are largely responsible for the diverse readings of Kant's compatibilism to be found in the literature. I argue that this objection (which appears particularly threatening to the reading I have endorsed in Chapter 2) is unsuccessful, and that Kant's position (as construed in Chapter 2) emerges unscathed.

Recall that, like Leibniz, the critical Kant believes that human agents have free will and that this means they also have the ability to do otherwise than they in fact do. Unlike Leibniz, however, the critical Kant believes that such freedom is not to be analyzed in terms of any special type of natural cause; rather, it is to be analyzed in terms of an intelligible cause. To this extent, Kant finds the Leibnizian analysis of freedom unsatisfactory, and he gives up on the Leibnizian brand of compatibilism. This move takes advantage of Kant's distinction between things in themselves and appearances (under a two-descriptions interpretation), and the resulting account of intelligible causality is provided through nondetermining descriptions, expressing the pro-attitude, propositional determination of an agent's will. We then have an intelligible story to tell regarding episodes of the exercise of transcendental freedom, a story not related in any lawlike manner to an empirical story (Kant's type-type irreducibility thesis). We also thereby preserve the efficacy of intelligible causes, without introducing any supernatural powers of will into nature, by way of affirming an identity claim between an intelligible cause and a natural event (Kant's token-token identity thesis).

Since any exercise of a causal power of will can thereby be identified with some natural event that is the effect of a sufficient, empirical cause, a resolution of this sort allows Kant to preserve the universality of the scope of the causal principle and to retain his general thesis of causal determinism. Nevertheless, generations of Kant commentators have maintained that this version of a two-descriptions reading compromises his theory of freedom. As Terence Irwin puts it, "now if an event is determined, it is true of it under all true descriptions that it is determined, even though only some true descriptions, those referring to the relevant laws, show why it is determined. Hence, if an event is phenomenally determined under its phenomenal description, it is also phenomenally determined under its noumenal description."[38]

True enough. The mere applicability of noumenal descriptions (of whatever specific sort) to phenomenal events does not alter the fact that such events retain all their phenomenal properties. At most, it attributes to them additional properties. But there is no reason to think that the two-descriptions interpretation must be understood as an attempt to find some point of view from which a natural event (which is also a free action) fails to be causally determined. The whole point of Kant's compatibilism is that free actions *are* causally determined, but that such determination does not interfere with the fact that they are also free; it is not to show that some particular event both has a property (e.g., 'being causally determined') and fails to have that property if we just consider it from two different points of view. Moreover, this is true even if we are talking about properties a thing has simply in virtue of its relation to the conditions governing human cognition. When we regard a thing as it is in itself, we happen to think it apart from those particular relational properties relevant to our knowledge of it, but the thing we thus regard in this special manner does not thereby somehow lose those properties in virtue of which it also can be regarded in relation to human cognition. On the contrary, even though we abstract from those relational properties when we consider it as it is in itself, it continues to have those properties nevertheless; otherwise, it could not appear to human cognizers.[39]

[38]Terence Irwin, "Morality and Personality: Kant and Green," in *Self and Nature in Kant's Philosophy*, ed. Allen Wood (Ithaca: Cornell University Press, 1984), p. 38.

[39]Furthermore, Irwin's point does not seem to me to be a claim about the essential properties of events. To the extent that I understand Henry Allison's discussion invoking possible-world semantics (in which he apparently suggests that "the phe-

The unlikely task of finding a point of view from which an event is not causally determined, as opposed to finding a point of view from which an event can be regarded as free despite causal determination, was never the purpose of Kant's two-descriptions view. Rather, Kant's two-descriptions view plays a vital role in the explanation and defense of his theory of the anomalousness of mental events (including the exercise of free will), in his theory of a thoroughgoing causal determinism, and in his subsequent nonreductive, token physicalism.

We might, then, grant Irwin's observation noted above. But in the same spirit, let us also take note of the following: now, if an event is free, it is true of it under all true descriptions that it is free, even though only some true descriptions, those referring to the relevant intelligible concepts, show why it is free. Hence if an event is transcendentally free under its noumenal description, it is also transcendentally free under its phenomenal description.[40] In other words, the Kantian compatibilist maintains that some natural events (which are also free actions) are both causally determined and transcendentally free, no matter how exhaustive a list of their true descriptions is available, although only one type of true description shows why they are causally determined and only another type of true description shows why they are transcendentally free.

But is this good enough? If this is really Kant's view, can he consistently maintain that human agents are free? Or, more specifically, can he consistently maintain that human agents enjoy the ability to do otherwise, a necessary component of free agency? The received opinion is that he cannot, and that therefore, in order to preserve Kant's consistency, some element in the version of compatibilism I have ascribed to him must be rejected.

An example of the type of criticism that would try to reject the version of compatibilism I have ascribed to Kant, then, employs some variation

---

nomenal world" and "the intelligible world" can be construed as different possible worlds), I think that he goes thoroughly wrong in his answer to Irwin on this issue in *Kant's Theory of Freedom*, pp. 43–44.

[40]By the phrase "some true descriptions show why an event is a free action" I here simply mean that some types of true descriptions (and not others) serve to provide us with the right sort of intelligible concepts to play a role in imputational and justificatory contexts. It does not mean that we thereby give an explanation of freedom, something Kant repeatedly denies we can do.

of the following argument. Suppose that we sufficiently "impoverish" the notion of transcendental freedom so that it no longer threatens the universal scope of the causal principle, and that we do so with the naive device of regarding the efficacy of intelligible causality as nothing more than the efficacy of natural causality under another description. But, a rose by any other name would smell as sweet, and no matter how we may truly portray the activity of the will with this description, and no matter what we might say about the irreducibility of the relevant description types, it remains the case that free actions turn out to be identical to natural events, and that they therefore have *all* the properties correctly attributable to these natural events. Consequently, they are sufficiently determined by the laws of nature and empirical causes after all. But if they are thus causally determined, then they are not free, since (i) if they are causally determined under one description, they remain causally determined regardless of whatever other descriptions happen to be true of them, and since (ii) causal determinism is incompatible with the ability to do otherwise, and since (iii) freedom requires the ability to do otherwise.

I think that this argument, or something very much like it, is largely responsible for the apprehension one might feel when presented with the reading of Kant's compatibilism developed in Chapter 2. It seems that, if the above argument (which is directed at precisely such a reading) is sound, then that reading of Kant's compatibilism leaves him with a wholly unsatisfactory theory of free will, if it leaves him with a theory of free will at all.

I also think that attempts to deal with this argument, or something very much like it, by theorists who accept the truth of (i), (ii), and (iii) are largely responsible for the wealth of interpretations we currently have of Kant's compatibilism. Disputing some feature or other of the particular construal of Kant's position which is the target of this argument results in distinct readings of Kant's compatibilism. And, of course, there are plenty of features to dispute, producing readings that may lead to a two-worlds interpretation of Kant's distinction between things in themselves and appearances, or to a thesis of intelligible efficacy (distinct from the efficacy of an empirical, natural cause), or to a doctrine of timeless agency, or to a regulative reading of the category of causality, and so forth.

On the strength of my discussion in Chapter 2, though, I think that the position briefly characterized in the argument above *is* Kant's position, and I also think that to answer this popular objection we do not need to take refuge in one of these other assessments of Kant's compatibilism, assessments which I have already argued are unsatisfactory. Furthermore, I do not think that Kant is simply confused or inconsistent. Accordingly, I reply to the argument both in order to defend the claim that he can remain consistent when his compatibilism is understood as I have construed it and in order to defend the philosophical significance of his view.

Three obvious strategies come to mind: the soundness of the argument depends, at least, on the truth of propositions (i), (ii), and (iii); so, either deny (i) or deny (ii) or deny (iii). Given Kant's explicit, critical views on the matter, and given the discussion of Frankfurt-style counterexamples to PAPF in the preceding section, I do not think that one can or should want to deny (iii). Also, I see no good reason to deny (i).[41] Fortunately, however, I believe that one can successfully deny (ii).

According to (ii), causal determinism is incompatible with the ability to do otherwise, and in one way or another reactions to this proposition have had an influence on every alternative reading of Kant's compatibilism I have thus far investigated. For instance, one could accept proposition (ii) but still want to preserve the freedom of indifference or the ability to do otherwise. Accordingly, one might suggest that intelligible, free actions are not identical to phenomenal, causally determined actions, but rather that they condition these natural events in some fashion. Hence one could avoid saying of one and the same action both that it was causally determined and yet that the agent who performed it could have done otherwise. This is just the approach that ultimately led to the puzzling doctrine of timeless agency that occupied Wood.[42] Again, one could accept proposition (ii) but still want to preserve the freedom of indifference or the ability to do otherwise. This time, though, rather than deny the relevant identity claim, one might instead

---

[41]Although, once again, to the extent that I understand his discussion invoking possible-world semantics, this is the route I believe Henry Allison to take in *Kant's Theory of Freedom*, pp. 43–44.

[42]See Wood's "Kant's Compatibilism," pp. 85, 89–93, and Bennett's "Commentary: Kant's Theory of Freedom," pp. 102–112.

suggest that, although intelligible, free actions are indeed also phenomenal events, they happen to be identical to those phenomenal events that lack a sufficient, natural cause. This is just the strategy underlying the dilemma that motivated Beck's and Butts's regulative interpretation of the category of causality.[43]

If proposition (ii) is true, however, then it appears that the views I have attributed to Kant are false, since on my reading one and the same event/action both is causally determined and is such that the agent who freely performs it could have done otherwise than perform it. Moreover, if proposition (ii) is demonstrably true, then it appears that the views I have attributed to Kant are demonstrably false. Since I think those are in fact the views he held, if proposition (ii) is demonstrably true, it appears that one can prove that Kantian compatibilism is an unsuccessful doctrine.

There is nothing like a proof of this proposition offered in the interpretations of Kant's compatibilism we have thus far considered. Indeed, the discussions seem simply to begin with the (admittedly initially plausible) assumption that causal determinism is incompatible with the ability to do otherwise and then to continue by devising readings of Kant's compatibilism that make him consistent with at least this version of incompatibilism. But there are reasons to doubt that this initial assumption is warranted.

First, one might think that Kant could not have accepted the view that causal determinism is compatible with the ability to do otherwise (unless we interpret that claim in the manner of Wood or of Beck and Butts), since that was just the Leibnizian position he so soundly rejected. Undoubtedly, Kant's views constitute an advance on Leibnizian compatibilism, since his distinction between things in themselves and appearances allows him to replace the Leibnizian determinist conception of freedom with his own indeterminist conception of freedom and thereby to explicate his thesis of the anomalousness of the mental (a crucial feature of his theory of free will), simultaneously to preserve his thesis of causal determinism, and to defend the subsequent version of nonreductive, token physicalism. But none of these advantages comes at

[43]See Lewis White Beck, *A Commentary on Kant's Critique of Practical Reason*, pp. 191–192; and Robert E. Butts, *Kant and the Double Government Methodology*, pp. 260, 271–272.

the expense of a denial of the thesis of the token-token identity of transcendentally free actions and natural events (a thesis Kant shares with Leibniz); rather, they all depend on such token-token identity, but they also depend on an affirmation of type-type irreducibility regarding the descriptions relevant to transcendentally free actions and the descriptions relevant to natural events (the thesis with which Kant goes beyond Leibnizian compatibilism). I grant, then, that Kant does have genuine incompatibilist insights, and that these insights properly lead him to reject a Leibnizian compatibilism, a compatibilism that crucially fails to distinguish between two types of descriptions. Happily, though, they are incompatibilist insights wholly consistent with a thesis of token-token identity. In short, they are incompatibilist insights that permit Kant both to hold the view that causal determinism is compatible with the ability to do otherwise and to renounce Leibnizian compatibilism.[44]

If not because of his quarrel with Leibniz, then, one might think that Kant would not have accepted the view that causal determinism is compatible with the ability to do otherwise (unless we interpret that claim in the manner of Wood or of Beck and Butts), because that proposition is just so obviously false. Since there does seem to be genuine disagreement about the truth of the matter, however, and since it is highly uncharitable to suggest that those in favor of affirming the view are simply not being attentive enough to see how obvious it is, perhaps we should investigate an argument allegedly refuting the position once and for all.[45]

In the remainder of this section, then, I investigate the best argument designed to show the incompatibility of causal determinism and the ability to do otherwise I know of. I maintain not only that this argument can be refuted but also that its strategy exhibits a general defect, likely to frustrate related attempts to argue in favor of this type of incompatibilism. Consequently, I conclude that the criticism brought against the

[44]The method of defense that I employ below against contemporary attempts to demonstrate the truth of the incompatibilism of causal determinism and the ability to do otherwise could be used consistently by either a Leibnizian or a Kantian compatibilist. But this observation should not detract from the fact that Kantian compatibilism constitutes a significant improvement over Leibnizian compatibilism.

[45]As the old story goes about Nicolai Hartmann, the professor was fond of bringing the following remark to the attention of his students: "It may be obvious to common sense, but it is certainly not obvious to a philosopher."

present reading of Kant's compatibilism, a criticism that seems to necessitate adopting one of the alternative, problematic interpretations we have considered thus far, is ultimately unsuccessful. Finally, I submit that the Kantian compatibilist position has not been rendered obsolete by contemporary demonstrations of the truth of incompatibilism.

We need to concentrate on a particular case in which an agent is allegedly free despite causal determinism, so first a brief anecdote. Once, when Kant was an old man, he slipped and fell in the streets of Königsberg. Two women who were passing by stopped and helped him stand. After he regained his footing, he presented each of the women with one of the roses he was carrying.[46] Now, consider the gift of that first rose. According to the reading of Kant's compatibilism advocated in Chapter 2, we here have an intelligible, free action, but an action that is identical to a phenomenal, causally determined event. Consequently, since the phenomenal event is causally determined, so too is the free action with which it is identical, even though the intelligible descriptions utilized in expressing or describing the free action do not show us *why* it is causally determined. Moreover, according to that reading, despite the fact that his free action is causally determined, Kant nevertheless could have done otherwise than present each of the women with one of the roses he was carrying.

The demonstration of incompatibilism I propose to examine is roughly modeled on an argument developed at length in the writings of Peter van Inwagen.[47] Intriguing variations on the general style of incompatibilist argument I have in mind, though, can be found in the essays of Carl Ginet, James Lamb, and David Wiggins as well.[48]

Recall that according to causal determinism, at any moment of time,

[46]I do not know that this story is true, but it is a nice story. For the purposes of the argument, let us at least pretend that it is true.

[47]First in "The Incompatibility of Free Will and Determinism," *Philosophical Studies* 27 (1975): 185–199, and then in *An Essay on Free Will*, esp. pp. 55–105.

[48]For examples of this general type of argument, see Carl Ginet, "Might We Have No Choice?" in *Freedom and Determinism*, ed. Keith Lehrer (New York: Random House, 1966), pp. 87–104, and again in "The Conditional Analysis of Freedom," in *Time and Cause: Essays Presented to Richard Taylor*, ed. Peter van Inwagen (Dordrecht: D. Reidel, 1980), pp. 171–186; James Lamb, "On a Proof of Incompatibilism," *Philosophical Review* 86 (1977): 20–35; David Wiggins, "Towards a Reasonable Libertarianism," in *Essays on Freedom of Action*, ed. Ted Honderich (London: Routledge and Kegan Paul, 1973), pp. 31–61.

the entire world at that time and the laws of nature together determine a unique future. To facilitate the discussion, let us further say that, if causal determinism obtains, then (i) "for every instant of time, there is a proposition that expresses the state of the world at that instant", and (ii) "if p and q are any propositions that express the state of the world at some instants, then the conjunction of p with the laws of nature entails q."[49]

Now consider three propositions:

H = a proposition expressing the state of the world at some instant a billion years ago.
L = a proposition that is the grand conjunction of all the propositions that are (or that express) laws of nature.
P = a proposition expressing the state of the world at a certain time t, the very time at which Kant presents a rose to a woman who has just helped him up from a fall.

Given the above definition of causal determinism and our three propositions, we may assert that

(1) If causal determinism obtains, then (H and L) entail P.

Also, given that (among other truths) P expresses that a "rose-giving action" was actually performed by Kant at t, it is impossible both that P is true and that Kant did otherwise than perform that rose-giving action at t. Thus,

(2) It is not possible that Kant have done otherwise than perform a rose-giving action at t and P be true.

To state the next premise, I make use of a particular phrase, namely, that "the agent could have rendered it false that x," where x is some proposition. I say more about the meaning of this phrase below, but intuitively the idea behind one important use of this phrase is that an agent could

---

[49]Van Inwagen, *An Essay on Free Will*, p. 65. Van Inwagen distinguishes causal from physical determinism, but I do not add that complication here. Once again, Kant's views on causal determinism are the focus of Chapter 4, where I return to a discussion regarding the problems with this thesis.

have done otherwise than perform a certain action if the agent could
have falsified the appropriate proposition corresponding to that action.
Let us also say that an event (or action) A falsifies a proposition x if and
only if, necessarily, if A occurs, then x is false.[50] Thus,

(3) If (2) is true, then if Kant could have done otherwise than perform a
rose-giving action at t, then Kant could have rendered it false that P.

But clearly,

(4) If Kant could have rendered it false that P, and if (H and L) entail P,
then Kant could have rendered it false that (H and L).

But, once again, clearly,

(5) If Kant could have rendered it false that (H and L), then either Kant
could have rendered it false that H or Kant could have rendered it
false that L.

But, the way the world was some instant a billion years ago is not up to
any human agent, not even to a great philosopher such as Kant. Accordingly,

(6) It is not the case that Kant could have rendered it false that H.

Similarly, which propositions are (or express) the laws of nature is not
up to any human agent. Accordingly,

(7) It is not the case that Kant could have rendered it false that L.

It follows from (1)–(7) that

(8) If causal determinism obtains, then Kant could not have done otherwise than perform a rose-giving action at t.

[50]Equally suitable devices (which require reference to events or states of affairs
instead of to propositions) can be had with the phrases "x is avoidable for the agent,"
or "x is within the agent's control," or "whether or not x obtains is up to the agent,"
and so forth.

Moreover, since the example is perfectly general, no human agent ever has the ability to do otherwise (and therefore no human agent ever is free) if causal determinism obtains.

I do not intend to speculate whether or not Kant ever seriously considered an argument of this sort,[51] and I do not intend to suggest that he offered (or even considered) the type of reply I endorse against this argument. Rather, I simply maintain that this argument is unsound and cannot serve as an adequate criticism of Kant's compatibilistic stance, if it should turn out (as I think it does) that a proponent of that stance must claim that one and the same event/action can be causally necessitated and yet that the agent who performs that act could have done otherwise. The significance of this result is considerable, since it undermines straightforward incompatibilist critiques of Kant, a paradigm of which is Beck's dilemma, and since it thereby removes the need for revisionist (and unacceptable) strategies of interpretation such as the regulative reading of the category of causality. Moreover, it also provides us with a far less perplexing defense of the liberty of indifference or the ability to do otherwise than does a thesis of timeless agency. I know of no arguments for the incompatibilist's conclusion superior to the present one, and until such an argument is developed with the same degree of sophistication van Inwagen offers I see no reason to believe that this species of incompatibilism is true.[52]

The incompatibilist argument presented above is a valid one, and the compatibilist who is unsatisfied with the conclusion had better either find a reason to reject one of the premises or prepare to enter into the debate between the hard determinists and the libertarians after all. An ingenious style of response to this type of argument has been suggested by contemporary compatibilists, compatibilist sympathizers, and in-

---

[51]Although it bears some resemblance to Kant's argument in the *Critique of Practical Reason*, Ak. Ed. 5:96.

[52]One route to reviving this sort of incompatibilism, however, might be devised by construing it as an essential component in a certain theory of human agency. This sort of approach has been associated with the names of Roderick Chisholm and Richard Taylor, and I return to this matter in Chapter 4 when I discuss the thesis of agent causation (construed as substance causation) in the context of an inquiry into Kant's theory of causal determinism.

compatibilists alike, in the writings of David Lewis, John Martin Fischer, Jan Narveson, Richard Foley, John Turk Saunders, and Thomas Flint.[53]

The incompatibilist argument seems unassailable, since it appears that to contest its premises the compatibilist would have to maintain that we can sometimes act in such a way that either the past would not be what it was or the laws of nature would not be what they are. But, as David Lewis has wittily remarked, "if we distinguish a strong and weak version of this incredible consequence, I think we shall find that it is the strong version that is incredible and the weak version that is the consequence."[54] The point is that the phrase "an agent could have rendered it false that x" is ambiguous. It seems that either the phrase is used inconsistently, in which case the argument is guilty of equivocation, or the phrase is used consistently, in which case the argument has at least one false premise (although just which premise is false depends on just how the phrase is used consistently).

Suppose, for example, that we are asked to consider the following pair of potential definitions for this problematic phrase, one causal and one noncausal reading:

(D1) An agent could have rendered it false that $x =_{df}$ There is some action the agent could have performed such that, if the agent had performed that action, then either that action or a causal consequence of that action would have falsified x.

(D2) An agent could have rendered it false that $x =_{df}$ There is some action the agent could have performed such that, if the agent had performed that action, then something would have falsified x.

[53]One of the clearest explications of this style of rebuttal is offered in Thomas P. Flint's, "Compatibilism and the Argument from Unavoidability," *Journal of Philosophy* 84 (1987): 423–440. But also see David Lewis's classic "Are We Free to Break the Laws?" *Theoria* 47 (1981): 113–121; John Martin Fischer's somewhat technical "Incompatibilism," *Philosophical Studies* 43 (1983): 127–137; Jan Narveson's "Compatibilism Defended," *Philosophical Studies* 32 (1977): 83–86; Richard Foley's "Compatibilism and Control over the Past," *Analysis* 39 (1979): 70–74; and for an early version, John Turk Saunders's "The Temptations of Powerlessness," *American Philosophical Quarterly* 5 (1968): 100–108.

[54]Lewis, "Are We Free to Break the Laws?" p. 113.

If the argument uses the phrase in the sense of D1, then premises (6) and (7) are true but premise (4) is false. Recall that premise (4) states, If Kant could have rendered it false that P, and if (H and L) entail P, then Kant could have rendered it false that (H and L). To see why premise (4) is false under the causal interpretation of the phrase provided by D1, note first that there *is* an action Kant could have performed (pressing the roses to his chest and hurrying off down the street) such that had he performed that action it would have falsified P. Certainly, there is no reason to deny the compatibilist this point, since the argument does not reject the claim that Kant could have done otherwise; it is rather designed to show that Kant could have done otherwise only if causal determinism does not obtain. But, as we have just seen, when we understand the phrase under the causal interpretation provided by D1, whether or not (H and L) entail P, Kant still could have rendered it false that P.

Hence, the antecedent in premise (4) is true. But the consequent in premise (4) is false. In other words, there is not an action Kant could have performed such that, had he performed that action, either that action or a causal consequence of that action would have falsified (H and L). Not even a great philosopher such as Kant could have done anything as incredible as that. It follows that premise (4) should be rejected when interpreted under D1, since, when so interpreted, its antecedent is true and its consequent is false.

If the argument uses the phrase in the sense of D2, then premise (4) is true after all, but then either premise (6) or premise (7) is false. Recall that premise (6) states, It is not the case that Kant could have rendered it false that H, and that premise (7) states, It is not the case that Kant could have rendered it false that L. To see why either premise (6) or premise (7) is false under the noncausal interpretation of the phrase provided by D2, note that once again there is an action Kant could have performed (pressing the roses to his chest and hurrying off down the street) such that, had he performed that action, either something would have falsified H or something would have falsified L.

It is crucial to understand that this is not the preposterous claim that Kant could have done something such that, had he done it, either that action or a causal consequence of that action would have falsified H or would have falsified L; *that* claim is not required by D2. Rather, the compatibilist simply says that Kant could have done otherwise than perform a rose-giving action at t, and if he had done otherwise, then either the past would have been different than it was or the laws would have been different than they are; the compatibilist does not say that Kant has any causal power over the past or any causal power over the laws.

Considerations like these have given rise to two somewhat similar species of compatibilism: theorists sometimes designated "altered-past" compatibilists are likely to deny premise (6), and theorists sometimes designated "altered-law" compatibilists are likely to deny premise (7).[55] The altered-past compatibilist maintains that Kant could have done otherwise than perform a rose-giving action at t, and if he had done otherwise then the past (relative to t) would have been different than it in fact is. The altered-law compatibilist maintains that Kant could have done otherwise than perform a rose-giving action at t, and if he had done otherwise then some "miracle" would have occurred (sometime shortly before t). Initially, this latter approach may sound outlandish, but the apparent absurdity quickly vanishes when the notion of such a miracle is properly clarified. Lewis, a principle advocate of altered-law compatibilism, clearly does not think that miracles or law-breaking events actually occur, and thus when he says that a law is broken he means simply that some generalization is broken in another possible world and is not a law in that world, although it is a law in the actual world.[56]

Whether one responds to D2 as an altered-past compatibilist or as an altered-law compatibilist may well depend on one's view of what it takes for one possible world to be more like the actual world than another possible world. One might think that possible worlds with a

[55]See Fischer, "Incompatibilism." For more on "altered-past" compatibilism, see Foley, "Compatibilism and Control over the Past," and Saunders, "The Temptations of Powerlessness." For more on "altered-law" compatibilism, which might also be christened "divergence-miracle" compatibilism, see Lewis, "Are We Free to Break the Laws?"

[56]See Lewis, "Are We Free to Break the Laws?" Various aspects of Lewis's general position on these matters are developed and defended in his book *Counterfactuals* (Cambridge: Harvard University Press, 1973), and in his essays "Counterfactual Dependence and Time's Arrow," and "Postscripts to Counterfactual Dependence and Time's Arrow," in *Philosophical Papers* (Oxford: Oxford University Press, 1986), 2:32–52, 52–66.

different past but the same set of laws are closer to the actual world than are possible worlds with a different set of laws but the same past. If so, one is likely to respond as an altered-past compatibilist; if not, one is likely to respond as an altered-law compatibilist. In either event, however, it seems that either premise (6) or premise (7) may be rejected when interpreted under D2.

Finally, if premises (6) and (7) are interpreted under D1 and all of the other premises are interpreted under D2, then the argument has all true premises. It acquires them at the expense of its validity, however, since it now generates its conclusion only through equivocation. Plainly, then, if the argument is to be persuasive, we need to find another definition of the phrase "an agent could have rendered it false that x."

It must be acknowledged that merely by showing two potential definitions of this key phrase to be inadequate I have not shown that the phrase cannot be given an adequate definition. As Thomas Flint has argued, though, the prospects for an adequate definition are not promising. He maintains that any such definition has to pass three tests: it must be devised in such a way that the resulting incompatibilist argument (i) is valid, (ii) has true premises, and (iii) generates a conclusion relevant to a denial of freedom.[57] The test of relevance becomes important when we examine a definition that is not open to the type of objections raised here against D1 and D2. Suppose that someone attempts to block the altered-past and altered-law compatibilists' replies with the following definition:

(D3) An agent could have rendered it false that $x =_{df}$ There is some action the agent could have performed such that it is jointly possible that (i) the agent does perform that action, (ii) the past and the laws of nature are just as they are in the actual world, and (iii) x is false.

The idea here is that we "hold fixed" the past and the laws, that we build them into what we mean by the phrase "an agent could have rendered it false that x."[58] Interpreted under D3, the argument is valid

[57]Flint, "Compatibilism and the Argument from Unavoidability," esp. p. 428.
[58]Van Inwagen's definition of the key phrase is one in which he "holds fixed" the past (*An Essay on Free Will*, p. 68); and Wiggins's definition of the key phrase is one in which he seems to "hold fixed" both the past and the laws ("Towards a Reasonable

and the troublesome premises (4), (6), and (7) are all true. Nevertheless, D3 fails the test of relevance. Under D3, the compatibilist grants that Kant cannot render it false that P but also insists that this inability must be strictly interpreted in the sense provided by D3. And, the compatibilist asks, why should that type of inability be a threat to Kant's or to anyone's freedom? Since the compatibilist believes that if Kant had done otherwise then something would have been different either in the past or in the laws, and since the incompatibilist has simply built the fixity of the past and the laws into the definition in question, the compatibilist can respond that most assuredly Kant cannot do otherwise in the sense provided by D3 but that the resulting sense of "cannot do otherwise" is simply not relevant to the compatibilist's notion of freedom.[59]

As one might expect, the compatibilist is now likely to reject premise (3) in the argument for incompatibilism. Recall that (3) reads, If (2) is true, then if Kant could have done otherwise than perform a rose-giving action at t, then Kant could have rendered it false that P. The compatibilist is surely ready to grant the truth of premise (2) and is naturally happy to reaffirm her conviction that Kant could have done otherwise than perform a rose-giving action at t. But, given the compatibilist's conception of freedom, she denies that this commits her to the view that there is some action Kant could have performed such that it is jointly possible that Kant does perform that action, the past and the laws of nature are just as they are in the actual world, and P is false. The reason for the denial is straightforward: when the compatibilist says that Kant could have done otherwise, she simply means that Kant had an ability that is such that, if he had exercised it, then either the past or the laws of nature would have been different than they in fact are.

Flint has made a case for the significant claim that the compatibilist and the incompatibilist are likely to disagree over a fundamental princi-

---

Libertarianism," pp. 45–46). If one is an altered-law compatibilist, then, one can respond to van Inwagen by denying premise (7) in the same manner employed under D2, and if one is an altered-past compatibilist, one can respond to van Inwagen with the charge that his definition fails the test of relevance. Either type of compatibilist can respond to Wiggins with the charge that his definition fails the test of relevance.

[59]In other words, an altered-law compatibilist might say, of course, Kant could not do otherwise, *if* you stipulate that the laws are held fixed; but since according to my conception of freedom, if Kant did do otherwise, then the laws would be different than they are, *that* admission is no threat to Kant's freedom after all.

ple, a principle motivating definitions such as D3. Retaining our account of the propositions H and L, the controversial principle can be stated as follows:

(CP) For any agent S and any action A (if S could have performed A, then it is possible that (H and L and S does perform A)).[60]

Given the different intuitions regarding freedom exhibited by the altered-past compatibilist, the altered-law compatibilist, and the incompatibilist, it is improbable that they will come to any sort of an agreement about the truth of this principle. In fact, this is precisely what the compatibilist denies and precisely what the incompatibilist purports to prove. It appears that any valid proof that makes use of a definition such as D3, a definition that precludes the objections from the altered-past and altered-law compatibilists, must assume the truth of CP and thereby must also assume the very point at issue.[61]

This general difficulty, I believe, is likely to frustrate any attempt to demonstrate the truth of incompatibilism in the manner we have been investigating. Of course, the incompatibilist may insist that the compatibilist is simply being obstinate and pretending not to see that CP just *does* state a limiting condition on the ability to perform actions, but that sort of debate does not seem to do much to advance the discussion.

I conclude, then, that this argument, an argument in favor of rejecting an essential component of the position that I have ascribed to Kant, does not offer us any compelling reasons to believe that his form of compatibilism is unpalatable. For that reason, the original criticism brought against the present reading of Kant's compatibilism, a criticism that seemed to necessitate adopting one of the alternative, problematic interpretations of Kant's compatibilism considered in Chapter 2, is ultimately unsuccessful. Finally, then, I submit that the Kantian compatibilist position has not been rendered obsolete by contemporary demonstrations of the truth of incompatibilism.

---

[60]Flint, "Compatibilism and the Argument from Unavoidability," pp. 432–440.

[61]For instance, our D3 seems to assume the truth of CP. Flint has also argued, not surprisingly, that incompatibilism falls out of CP immediately; see "Compatibilism and the Argument from Unavoidability," p. 438.

Chapter 4

Kant's Theory of Causal Determinism

The Leibnizian-Wolffian school of rationalism dominated German metaphysical thought in the early eighteenth century. Both Leibniz and Wolff maintained the following two principles regarding causality: (i) every event has its cause (a truth following from the Principle of Sufficient Reason), and (ii) the denial of a given causal connection leads to an implicit self-contradiction. Furthermore, they agreed that particular causal judgments are provable a priori (although, according to Leibniz, finite minds may be wholly incapable of providing the requisite proofs). Kant, too, thought that principle (i), also known as "the Law of Universal Causation," was knowable a priori. Dissatisfied, though, with Wolff's alleged derivation of the Principle of Sufficient Reason (and of its specification, the Law of Universal Causation) from the Law of Contradiction, Kant eventually produced his own reasons in favor of that doctrine. Moreover, although he had once been an adherent of principle (ii) as well, he subsequently abandoned it and joined many of his contemporaries in the charge that reason alone is powerless to reveal any hidden partial-identity relation between the subject and predicate concepts in the statement of a particular causal connection or to reveal any ontological condition referred to in the subject of the judgment which would ensure the reality of the predicate.[1]

Leibniz holds the doctrine that there are truths of reason and truths of fact. The former are logically necessary, certain, and provable a priori. The latter, though logically contingent, are also certain and provable a priori. According to Leibniz, the provability of the former rests on the logical Law of Contradiction, and the provability of the latter rests on the Principle of Sufficient Reason.[2] Wolff, following Leibniz, made explicit the derivative relation of causal judgments from the Principle of Sufficient Reason but, parting company with Leibniz, he attempted to derive this principle itself from the Law of Contradiction.[3]

Under the influence of Crusius, the Kant of the middle 1750s attacked this derivation, yet he simultaneously produced his own rationalistic defense of causation in his *Nova dilucidatio* published in 1755, the very same work that contained his initial compatibilistic defense of Leibnizian-Wolffian theories of freedom against Crusius.[4] During the next decade, however, he separated himself permanently from his rationalistic predecessors' modes of proof, but he could not separate himself from his desire to endorse their first principle of causality, the Law of Universal Causation.[5]

[1]Whereas Leibniz believes that a true causal judgment signals a logical relation between the subject and predicate concepts, Wolff believes that it signals an ontological relation in which the subject itself (and not merely its concept) contains the condition of the predicate, since the subject and predicate both refer to the same essence.

[2]Gottfried Wilhelm Leibniz, *Discourse on Metaphysics* (1686), sec. 13; *Monadology* (1715), secs. 32–33.

[3]In accordance with his twofold distinction between types of truth, Leibniz had denied that the Law of Contradiction entailed the Principle of Sufficient Reason, but for Wolff's attempt to argue against Leibniz on this point, see Christian Wolff, *Vernünftige Gedanken von Gott, der Welt, und der Seele der Menschen, auch allen Dingen überhaupt* (1729, 4th ed.), sec. 142; *Philosophia prima sive ontologica* (1730), secs. 27–78, 886.

[4]For a brief history of the phases of Kant's development in his treatment of the causal principle, see Lewis White Beck's *Early German Philosophy*, pp. 424–425, 451–453, 465–467.

[5]For a general overview of Kant's philosophical maturation during his precritical

During the 1760s, primarily in two essays, "An Attempt to Introduce the Concept of Negative Quantities into Philosophy" and "Dreams of a Spirit-Seer," Kant acknowledged the logically contingent character of all causal judgments, admitting that such judgments do not follow from the applications of logical laws to relations between objects, and he relinquished his own attempts to establish the logical force of the causal relation. In accordance with these new views, he also admitted that knowledge of specific causal laws is merely probabilistic and not certain.[6] The result of these admissions is that, inasmuch as Kant now saw all particular causal judgments as synthetic, a posteriori claims, he held a distinctly different view from that of Leibniz or Wolff.

Nevertheless, Kant still remained sympathetic with the Leibnizian-Wolffian commitment to the Law of Universal Causation. In the 1770s and 1780s, Kant developed and eventually published arguments that would secure this principle and simultaneously serve as his response to the rationalists who had attempted to purchase this principle at the cost of reducing causality either to logical principles or to the Principle of Sufficient Reason. His classical treatment of the issue is contained in the Second Analogy of Experience in the *Critique of Pure Reason*; as is well known, he there maintains that, whereas particular causal judgments are always synthetic and a posteriori, the judgment that every event has a cause is a synthetic, a priori condition of the possibility of such particular causal judgments. Thus, Kant's treatment of causation can be seen partially as a response to the rationalists with whom he shared the belief that the causal principle is a priori, but against whom he urged the claim that it is also a synthetic proposition, not an analytic truth of reason.

---

period, see Frederick C. Beiser's "Kant's Intellectual Development: 1746–1781," in *The Cambridge Companion to Kant*, ed. Paul Guyer (Cambridge: Cambridge University Press, 1992), pp. 26–61.

[6]*Versuch den Begriff der negativen Grössen in die Weltweisheit einzuführen* (1763), Ak. Ed. 2:165–204; *Träume des Geistersehers* (1766), Ak. Ed. 2:315–373. Beck argues that in this "quasi-Humean" phase Kant may have been led away from his former position by Crusius and other German philosophers rather than by reading Hume's *Enquiry concerning Human Understanding* in German translation; see his "A Prussian Hume and a Scottish Kant," in *Essays on Kant and Hume* (New Haven: Yale University Press, 1978), pp. 111–129.

The Causal Principle and the Precritical Kant

Although Kant's treatment of the causal principle has most often been characterized by his German commentators as a response to Leibniz and Wolff under the influence of Crusius, traditionally this has not been the approach emphasized by Kant's Anglo-American commentators. Rather, by his Anglo-American commentators Kant is primarily read as answering a challenge allegedly issued by Hume in *A Treatise of Human Nature*.[7] Both approaches should be taken into consideration, though, since Kant's long history of uneasy flirtation with Leibnizian-Wolffian rationalism prompted him to reflect seriously on Hume's challenge to the causal principle (or, at least, to reflect on what he thought was Hume's challenge to the causal principle), and since through that reflection Kant was able both to answer that challenge and to reconcile himself with his previous rationalistic tendencies.

The vexed question of Kant's answer to Hume's account of causality has a long and illustrious history. In the following, I concentrate on just those aspects that have direct bearing on the task of developing a Kantian theory of causal determinism. To this end, distinguishing between a "Scottish Hume" and a "German Hume" is profitable. Let the Scottish Hume's account correspond to Hume's analysis of causation as it appears in English in *A Treatise of Human Nature*, and let the German Hume's account correspond to the fragments from the *Treatise* of Hume's analysis of causation as they were made to appear in a German translation to which Kant had access.

Now, the question of whether Kant successfully answered the German Hume, thus construed, is somewhat easier to answer than is the question of whether he successfully answered the Scottish Hume. Ironically, Kant once defended Hume from his English critics by writing, "Hume suffered the usual misfortune of metaphysicians, of not being understood."[8] But Kant's own misunderstanding of Hume was not a result of having merely read through the *Treatise* and not having thought through it, his diagnosis of those who had misunderstood the first *Critique*; rather, it was a result of having only the German Hume to

---

[7]All citations in the text to this work are from David Hume, *A Treatise of Human Nature*, ed. L. A. Selby-Bigge (Oxford: Clarendon Press, 1964).

[8]*Prolegomena to Any Future Metaphysics*, p. 6; Ak. Ed. 4:258.

read or, more specifically, of having only a translation of James Beattie's reconstruction of Hume's position in the *Treatise*.[9] Hence, Kant charges the German Hume with borrowing the argument advanced against the view that particular causal judgments are justifiable on the basis of reason alone and applying it against the causal principle itself. Consequently, Kant believed that "Hume was therefore in error in inferring from the contingency of our determination *in accordance with the law* the contingency of the *law* itself" [A765–768/B793–796]. Kant's assessment of the German Hume's mistake, then, is that, whereas Hume properly restricted the understanding's insight into particular causal relations and rightly denied any a priori knowledge in that area, he crucially failed to define the limits of the understanding. This latter endeavor, Kant optimistically believes, would have prompted Hume to discover the synthetic a priori conditions of experience which account for the possibility of particular judgments, the very conditions Kant appeals to and argues for in defense of the causal principle in the Second Analogy.

Postponing for the moment an elaboration of this approach to answering the German Hume, let us turn to the more controversial and philosophically interesting question of whether Kant could have successfully answered the Scottish Hume. I prefer to separate this question from the debates regarding Kant's ability to read the *Treatise* for himself in English, and whether Kant ever came to fully appreciate the Scottish Hume's analysis of causality in that work. As becomes clear in the course of my discussion, however, the strategy in Kant's answer to the German Hume capitalizes on a feature that is shared by the accounts of the German Hume and the Scottish Hume: Kant demonstrates that the causal principle obtains by showing that it is implied by a necessary condition of (either) Hume's analysis of causation. Interestingly enough, then, Kant may have answered the Scottish Hume without ever being completely aware of the nature of his challenge.

Just which answer one believes Kant would need to give to a Scottish Hume depends on whether one interprets the Scottish Hume as espousing a subjectivist view of events, which merely requires repeating patterns of subjective sense impressions, or an objectivist stance, which

---

[9]From a German translation (1772) of James Beattie's *Essay on the Nature and Immutability of Truth*. For this tenuous connection to Hume, see Beck, "A Prussian Hume and a Scottish Kant," pp. 117–120.

requires repeating patterns of the objective events we recognize in experience. Moreover, with respect to the objectivist reading, it also depends on whether one reads the Scottish Hume as a realist or as instead maintaining that, whereas we have knowledge of objective events, they need to be phenomenalistically reduced.[10]

Kant certainly did not intend to answer a subjectivist Hume in the Second Analogy. If that had been his intention, then he would not have repeatedly begged the question in his arguments by continually assuming that we possess knowledge of objective events. A subjectivist Hume would have denied this, and consequently no proper answer would have been furnished by Kant. This is not to suggest that Kant was incapable of providing an answer to a subjectivist Hume. Such an answer would no doubt refer the subjectivist Hume to the Transcendental Deduction, to the First Analogy, and to the Refutation of Idealism, in order to argue that, if one grants the fact that some subject actually recognizes repeating patterns of subjective sense impressions, then one is also forced to grant the existence of empirically real substances and of objective events that are constituted by alterations in the states of those substances. Then, once Kant had secured this conclusion, he would be faced with answering an objectivist Hume after all. The question need never arise, though; as Lewis White Beck has argued, Hume cannot be consistently read as a subjectivist if he is to utilize the notion of an objective event in order to draw his distinction between sense perceptions that are of an object and those that are of a succession of states in an object, a distinction required for his own inductive argument and analysis of causation.[11] Furthermore, in Hume's own analysis of causation, especially in his treatment of contiguity and succession, he clearly adopts an objectivist approach.

Finally, then, our question is, Could Kant have answered an objectivist, Scottish Hume? and the answer depends on just which questions

[10]On this point, see William Harper and Ralf Meerbote's introduction to the numerous difficulties surrounding the interpretation of Kant's answer to Hume and of the arguments in the Second Analogy titled "Kant's Principle of Causal Explanations," in *Kant on Causality, Freedom, and Objectivity*, ed. William Harper and Ralf Meerbote (Minneapolis: University of Minnesota Press, 1984), pp. 3–19.

[11]Beck, "A Prussian Hume and a Scottish Kant," pp. 127–128.

this Hume investigated and on exactly what problems he raised for a proper analysis of causation.

In his *Treatise*, Hume explains what he believes is generally understood by causation, and he provides an analysis of that concept. Causation is thought to be a connection by means of which we can infer the existence or action of a particular kind of object which is given to the senses [1.3.2; pp. 73–74]. In his well-known investigation, though, Hume searches in vain for this connection *in the objects*. He fails to find the connection in the qualities of the objects, and in their relation he finds only spatial contiguity and temporal succession. This failure to find a necessary connection in the objects leads him to pose two questions:

(a) For what reason we pronounce it *necessary*, that everything whose existence has a beginning, shou'd also have a cause?
(b) Why we conclude, that such particular causes must *necessarily* have such particular effects; and what is the nature of that *inference* we draw from the one to the other. and of the *belief* we repose in it? [1.3.2; p. 78]

Examining Hume's discussion of these questions, then, should yield the content of his challenge to philosophers such as Kant. Beck reads the questions in the following way, and his reading is seconded by Henry Allison:[12]

(a*) "Why every event necessarily has some cause" (alternatively, (a**) "every-event-some-cause")
(b*) "Why the same cause necessarily has the same effect" (alternatively, (b**) "same-cause-same-effect")

Beck wants to show that the Scottish Hume is more like Kant than one might have thought and that, whereas (b*) is the product of inductive inferences, (a*) cannot be similarly regarded but rather is used to defend (b*) from potential refutation in experience.[13] Perhaps this is a reason-

[12]Beck, "A Prussian Hume and a Scottish Kant," p. 120; Henry Allison, *Kant's Transcendental Idealism*, p. 216.

[13]This is a primary thesis in both "A Prussian Hume and a Scottish Kant,"

able interpretation of Hume's considered view of the relation between (a*) and (b*), but (b*) does not seem to be the appropriate reading of Hume's (b). Hume uses the phrases "particular causes" and "particular effects," suggesting that he is referring to instances of a type, and this is at least prima facie in conflict with Beck's phrases "same [type of] cause" and "same [type of] effect," which, on the contrary, suggest that Hume is referring to the type itself. But after one acknowledges that there is at least a serious ambiguity in Hume's phrasing, one should note that there are more substantial reasons to suspect that (b*) does not capture the meaning of Hume's (b).

As a way of seeing why, note that Beck has misplaced the modal operator in his (a*). Hume's (a) is a question concerning a de dicto ascription of necessity, a question concerning the status of the Law of Universal Causation, but Beck's (a*) is a question concerning a de re ascription of necessity, a question concerning the essential features of events. Now, Hume's (b) has the same modal structure as Beck's (a*); it asks why we (mistakenly, in Hume's opinion) ascribe a de re necessity to something, and it makes sense to inquire whether that something is more reasonably regarded as causal types or as the individual causes themselves. To put the matter a little differently, Beck, in a later essay, concedes that there is an ambiguity in Hume's (b): it states either that a particular cause necessitates its effect or that "like causes necessarily have like effects," and in the present discussion Beck opts for the second of these alternatives.[14]

Although Beck is right to believe that Hume's full analysis of causation must take account of (b*) at some point, and that, according to Hume, (b*) is the result of inductive inferences, Hume's own treatment of this second alternative (that like causes have like effects) and his separation of it by nearly a hundred pages from the explicit discussion

---

pp. 121ff., and in "Kant on the Uniformity of Nature," *Synthese* 47 (1981): 449–464. It remains to be seen, however, whether Beck is correct in thinking that Hume would be more like Kant, if this turned out to be his position.

[14]Beck, "Kant on the Uniformity of Nature," p. 449. Due to the prima facie conflict noted above, I have a more difficult time in finding plausible the second alternative of the ambiguity here, and I believe that, whereas Hume is quite obviously concerned with the second alternative in his *Enquiry concerning Human Understanding*, that alternative plays little if any role in the discussion of the *Treatise*.

of his questions (a) and (b) count significantly against the suggestion that (b*) is the correct interpretation of Hume's (b). Indeed, it is only after Hume has completed his inquiry that he explicitly draws attention to the rule that "the same cause always produces the same effect, and the same effect never arises but from the same cause" [1.3.15; pp. 173–174]. Rather, Hume is concerned from the outset with whether there is ever a ground for affirming the relation of necessary connection between any particular cause and its specific effect. He expressly states that his questions (a) and (b) are posed to further *this* investigation, and the bulk of Book 1, Part 3, is given over to analyzing just this relation.

Finally, and perhaps most important, Hume's own resolution to his question (b) constitutes a proper answer only if the question is taken in the first sense of the ambiguity noted above, and it is an answer that presupposes a prior answer to the question taken in the second sense. At the beginning of the fourteenth section of the third part of Book 1, "Of the idea of a necessary connexion," Hume announces that he has answered both parts of his own question (b). As he succinctly puts his answer, "the necessary connexion betwixt causes and effects is the foundation of our inference from one to the other. The foundation of our inference is the transition arising from the accustom'd union. These are, therefore, the same" [1.3.14; p. 165].

In short, then, (b) does not ask the question, Why do we conclude that the same causes have the same effects? Rather, this is the question that occupies Hume in the *Enquiry concerning Human Understanding* when he argues that the conclusion that every instance of type A will be accompanied by an instance of type B is inferred from the fact that, in experience, an instance of type A has always been accompanied by an instance of type B. But this inference, he goes on to argue, is based not on reasoning but on custom.[15] Instead, (b) asks, Why do we say that a particular cause is necessarily connected to its effect? We do *this* in Hume's opinion, because the habit formed from our inductively generated belief in the rule that the same causes have the same effects psychologically compels or determines the mind to pass from the presentation of a particular cause to the belief in the existence of its particular effect. It

[15]David Hume, *Enquiry concerning Human Understanding*, 3d ed., ed. L.A. Selby-Bigge (Oxford: Clarendon Press, 1975), pp. 32–39.

is exactly because we grant Beck's (b**), that we are led to engage in the inferences Hume inquires into in his question (b). Hence, answering (b*) gives us only the foundation for answering (b), not an answer to (b) itself.

Against these inferences Hume pleads, "Let men be once fully persuaded of these two principles, That there is nothing in any object, consider'd in itself, which can afford us a reason for drawing a conclusion beyond it; and, That even after the observation of the frequent or constant conjunction of objects, we have no reason to draw any inference concerning any object beyond those of which we have had experience" [1.3.12; p. 139]. First, Hume denies necessary connection in the objects, and then he denies the legitimacy of the inference we are psychologically determined to make from the existence of one object to the existence of another based on their necessary connection in the mind. This is not, of course, a denial of practical necessity, but only of objective necessity.

Let us now turn to the impact these Humean reflections have on Kant's theory of causation and to the difficulties they raise for a Kantian argument for causal determinism. Reading the Scottish Hume in this manner allows us to describe one aspect of this Hume's challenge to philosophers such as Kant. According to the Scottish Hume, there are no grounds for saying that an object necessitates its effect or has a necessary connection with its effect on the basis of which an inference of existence from one to the other can be properly grounded. If Kant is to answer the Scottish Hume, then, he has to argue that a cause does in some sense necessitate its effect, such that in granting the reality of the former one grants also the existence of the latter. If Kant is successful in this endeavor, this will not only constitute a partial answer to the Scottish Hume and uphold one feature of the causal relation so important to his rationalist predecessors but will also serve as justification for the premise of the necessity of the causal connection, a premise that is essential to the Argument for Causal Determinism, which is my focus in the following sections.

The other part of Hume's challenge is found in his question (a). Here I agree with Beck: after arguing against the possibility of establishing the Law of Universal Causation by reason alone, Hume suggests that experience gives rise to this principle of causation and then discusses this proposal no further.[16] Perhaps his attack on the method of providing rationalistic proofs in its defense is a sufficient challenge, though. By what right, Hume can demand, do we claim that this principle is necessary and universal, that is, a law governing experience, if we cannot establish it as a truth of reason? So, if Kant is to answer the Scottish Hume, he must also argue for the Law of Universal Causation, but without running afoul of Hume's demonstration that this argument cannot be based on reason alone. If Kant is successful in this endeavor, he will have provided a complete answer to the Scottish Hume and upheld another feature of causality so important to his rationalist predecessors; moreover, his answer will also serve as justification for the premise of the universal validity of the causal connection, a premise that also figures prominently in the Argument for Causal Determinism.

If I am correct in the above discussion against Beck's reading of this portion of the *Treatise*, then it appears not to be an essential part of Kant's answer to Hume in the Second Analogy to show the third presupposition of a thoroughgoing causal determinism, the premise of the generalizability of the causal connection, from the Argument for Causal Determinism. Naturally, Kant must eventually address issues related to this premise, including inductive generalization and the existence and nature of particular causal laws, if only to reconcile his account with Newtonian physics. It is quite clear, though, that Kant is willing to endorse this premise (which asserts that similar causes have similar effects) as well. And, as I intend to show in the course of this chapter, despite the fact that it would not properly constitute part of his answer to the Scottish Hume of the *Treatise*, Kant *can*, nevertheless, establish this premise in exactly the same manner in which he argues for the Law of Universal Causation.

Three features of a conception of causality have thus emerged in our

[16]Shortly after Hume sinks the question, How does experience give rise to question (a)? into question (b), he says "'Twill, perhaps, be found in the end, that the same answer will serve for both questions" (1.3.3; p. 82). Beck takes this to mean that the same answer will serve for how experience gives rise to (a) and for an answer to (b), and he is then puzzled at why Hume should think so; "A Prussian Hume and a Scottish Kant," p. 121; "Kant on the Uniformity of Nature," p. 450. However, given the nature of Hume's answer to (b), one might take his remark as referring instead to the two questions that make up (b) itself and not as a promise to further investigate (a). Beck omits the second question in his restatement of Hume's (b).

discussion of Leibnizian-Wolffian rationalism and of Humean skepticism: the universality, the necessity, and the generalizability of the causal relation. In the *Critique of Pure Reason*, Kant works with this conception of causality, and he there endeavors to show that this conception has a priori application to the objects of experience.[17] Before we turn our attention to the Argument for Causal Determinism supported by this rich conception of causality, though, a reminder of Kant's treatment of the causal principle in the *Critique of Pure Reason* is worthwhile.

The Development of the Causal Principle within the *Critique of Pure Reason*

In what has come to be known as the Metaphysical Deduction of the Categories, Kant argues that in general logic there are four genera of the function of thought in a judgment, each of which contains three species [A70/B95]. Judgments of Relation, the third of these genera, are either categorical, relating a subject and predicate (utilizing two concepts only), or hypothetical, relating a ground and a consequent merely in terms of their logical sequence (utilizing two judgments), or disjunctive, relating many subject-predicate combinations to one another in terms of their logical opposition (utilizing at least two judgments) [A73–74/B98–99]. Transcendental logic has the advantage over general logic in taking account of the immediate intuitions given in space and time which may serve as the content of a meaningful empirical judgment, and which are made possible by the a priori forms of sensibility introduced and established in the Transcendental Aesthetic [A76–77/B102–103]. This advantage is that, since "the same function which gives unity to the various representations in a *judgment* also gives unity to the mere synthesis of various representations *in an intuition*" [A79/B104–105], the very same acts of the understanding that revealed no synthetic knowledge about

---

[17]There exists a substantial controversy over treating the generalizability of the causal relation as a feature of Kant's conception of causality and over regarding it as among his prospective conclusions for the proof offered in the Second Analogy. I argue in the closing section of this chapter that it does belong to that conception and that he does intend to demonstrate it in the Second Analogy. A recent paper by Michael Friedman contains an excellent discussion of this issue; see his "Causal Laws and the Foundations of Natural Science," in *The Cambridge Companion to Kant*, ed. Paul Guyer (Cambridge: Cambridge University Press, 1992), pp. 161–199, esp. secs. 1–3.

their objects (in general logic) can now be regarded as applying pure concepts a priori to objects of experience (in transcendental logic), thereby making possible empirical knowledge.

Under the genus of Relation, then, in transcendental logic, Kant gives the following three pure concepts or categories of the understanding whose counterparts from the logical table of judgments were just described above: corresponding to categorical judgment is the pure concept or category of 'inherence and subsistence'; corresponding to hypothetical judgment is the pure concept or category of 'causality and dependence'; and corresponding to disjunctive judgment is the pure concept or category of 'community' [A80/B106]. Once the Metaphysical Deduction has shown *what* concepts belong to the list of categories and (once it, at least, claims to have shown) the necessity and systematic completeness of that list, the Transcendental Deduction is carried out to show *that* the categories (most notably, for our purposes, the category of causality and dependence) are objectively valid (i.e., hold of all possible objects of cognitive experience) since, with the assistance of some additional premises, they are thus derived from our very forms of judgment.

Finally, it is left to the chapter on the schematism of concepts to show *how* the categories are applied to objects. The homogeneity of an individual with the concept under which it is subsumed is a requirement of subsumption in general, but the category itself is not homogeneous with an intuition. Kant believes, however, that the categories and the intuitions to which they are applied can be mediated by the transcendental determination of time, and this, he maintains, serves as their schema [A137–139/B176–178]. The three categories under investigation receive their individual schemata as follows: "the schema of substance is the permanence of the real in time"; "the schema of cause, and of the causality of a thing in general, is the real upon which, whenever posited, something always follows" (a succession subject to a rule); and finally, "the schema of community . . . is the coexistence, according to a universal rule of the determinations of the one substance with those of another" [A144/B183]. So, the condition of applying these categories of relation to possible objects of experience is that they be schematized, and, considering all three of the schematized categories of relation together, this requires "the connecting of [all possible] perceptions with one another at all times according to a rule of time determination" [A145/B184].

This temporal connection of all possible objects of experience in accordance with rules of time determination is the subject matter of Kant's investigation into the principles he terms the Analogies of Experience. These principles are the synthetic a priori judgments that are the ground of empirical judgments and can be proven by showing their connection to "the subjective sources of the possibility of knowledge of an object in general" [A149/B188]. In the B edition the general principle of the Analogies is as follows: "experience is possible only through the representation of a necessary connection of perceptions" [B218]; in the A edition Kant makes it clear that this necessary connection is one that governs their relations to one another in time [A177]. Hence, Kant believes that, if we are to have experience at all, then every possible object of experience must have a determinate location in time.

Since there are three modes of time—permanence, succession, and coexistence—there are three rules by means of which every possible object can be determined in time. These three rules are the specific principles of the Analogies: corresponding to the schematized category of substance is the First Analogy's Principle of Permanence of Substance: "in all change of appearances substance is permanent; its quantum in nature is neither increased or diminished" [B224]; corresponding to the schematized category of cause is the Second Analogy's Principle of Succession in Time, in accordance with the law of causality: "all alterations take place in conformity with the law of the connection of cause and effect" [B232]; and corresponding to the schematized category of community is the Third Analogy's Principle of Coexistence, in accordance with the law of reciprocity or community: "all substances, in so far as they can be perceived to coexist in space, are in thoroughgoing reciprocity" [B256]. Each of these principles receives what Kant calls a transcendental proof. The transcendental proof, then, of the rule given in the Second Analogy is Kant's attempt to demonstrate the synthetic, a priori principle underlying experience known as the Law of Universal Causation.

An Argument for Causal Determinism

Despite the fact that the Law of Universal Causation is not equivalent to the thesis of causal determinism, the particular style of proof produced by Kant in the Second Analogy which demonstrates this synthetic a priori principle underlying experience also provides him with the tools to demonstrate the more complex thesis of causal determinism as well.

Intuitively, causal determinism is the thesis that, at any moment of time, the state of the world at that time and the laws of nature together determine a unique future.[18] I can now set forth an argument for this thesis consisting of seven propositions, the seventh of which follows from the first six.

Argument for Causal Determinism
  (1) Every event has a cause.
  (2) If event A causes event B, then it cannot happen that both A occurs and B fails to occur.
  (3) Causes of the same type have effects of the same type.
  (4) Every cause is itself an event that has a cause.
  (5) Any series of causes which has no earliest member is such that, for every time t, some event in that series happens prior to t.
  (6) If (1)–(5), then causal determinism obtains.
  (7) Causal determinism obtains.

Premise (1) is just the Law of Universal Causation, and it may also be titled the premise of "the universal validity of the causal connection." This premise is Kant's chief concern with respect to his theory of causation, but to see why the additional premises are necessary to establish the more complex thesis of causal determinism, consider the following explanations.

Premise (2) may be titled the premise of "the necessity of the causal connection," and it denies the view that there is merely a productive, rather than a necessary, connection between events in a causal relation. If causes merely produced their effects, then one unique future would not be determined by the state of the world at a time and the laws of

---

[18]As in Chapter 3, I can offer the following more precise definition: causal determinism $=_{df}$ (i) for every instant of time, there is a proposition that expresses the state of the world at that instant, and (ii) if p and q are any propositions that express the state of the world at some instants, then the conjunction of p with the laws of nature entails q. For a discussion of this definition, see Peter van Inwagen, *An Essay on Free Will*, p. 65.

nature, since the all-important necessity would be missing in the transition from cause to effect. Hence, causal determinism would not obtain.

Premise (3) may be titled the premise of "the generalizability of the causal connection," and it denies the view that there are instances of causal connections without covering laws; in other words, it asserts that every causal relation is governed by some particular causal law. For, in the absence of this strict association of causal laws and individual episodes of causation, one unique future would not be determined by the state of the world at a time and those very laws of nature. Hence, once again, causal determinism would not obtain.

Premise (4) denies that substances are causes, it denies that states of substances are causes, and it denies that agents are somehow *directly* the cause of events (i.e., that the cause is simply the agent rather than some change or event to be found in the agent's mind or brain). If an agent qua agent could be such a direct cause, then since nothing is such as to cause the *agent*, so construed, one unique future would not be determined by the state of the world at a time together with the laws of nature, and causal determinism would not obtain.[19]

Premise (5) denies the view that any series of causes which has no earliest member might yet be causally unrelated to some prior state of the world (e.g., when event A's cause occurs at 12:30, event A's cause's cause at 12:15, event A's cause's cause's cause at 12:07.30, but no causal ancestor of A occurs before 12:00). This condition may seem to guard against a problem that would not trouble Kant, although it might trouble others, since Kant would not countenance the notion of a *completed* infinity in a series of causes. However, if violated, (5) poses similar problems even for Kant's finitistic, constructivist views on these matters. Therefore, without this premise guaranteeing that there is no time prior to every member of the causal series, one unique future would not be determined by the state of the world at a time and the laws of nature, and again, causal determinism would not obtain.

---

[19]Contemporary defenders of versions of agent causation include Roderick Chisholm and Richard Taylor. See Chisholm, "Freedom and Action," in *Freedom and Determinism*, ed. Keith Lehrer (New Jersey: Humanities Press, 1966), pp. 11–44, and *Person and Object* (LaSalle, Ill.: Open Court, 1976); and Taylor, "Determinism and the Theory of Agency," in *Determinism and Freedom*, ed. Sidney Hook (New York: Collier Press, 1958), pp. 224–230, and in *Action and Purpose* (Englewood Cliffs, N.J.: Prentice-Hall, 1966).

Premise (6) asserts that (1)–(5) are jointly sufficient for causal determinism.[20] Hence, according to our statement of causal determinism, if (1)–(5) are true, then at any moment of time the world at that time and the laws of nature together determine a unique future.

I do not wish to suggest that Kant ever formulated an argument like this one, or even that he ever considered each of the premises separately. Kant was preoccupied with establishing what he took to be most controversial about his theory of causation, namely, the Law of Universal Causation, and consequently he concentrated his efforts in an attempt to prove (1). Kant occasionally even seemed to indicate that causal determinism follows from (1) alone, and since he believed himself to have secured that premise he tended to regard his position as one of a thoroughgoing causal determinism. Now, causal determinism is not simply a consequence of (1), since someone could consistently affirm (1), deny any of (2)–(5), and thereby reject that doctrine; and thus, if Kant's position turns out to be inconsistent with any of (2)–(5), he would have been mistaken in regarding his position as one of causal determinism, no matter what his views on (1) happened to be. Perhaps Kant can be excused for his confidence in (1), however, since (if my interpretation of his position on these matters turns out to be successful) he also thought the transcendental argument used to defend (1) immediately establishes (2) and (3) as well. In the remainder of this chapter, then, I show how and why Kant explicitly or implicitly endorses all the premises in the Argument for Causal Determinism.

Subjectivism, Phenomenalism, Realism, and the Irreversibility Argument

In his statement of the causal principle in the B edition, Kant shifts from the phrase "everything that happens" to the phrase "all alter-

---

[20]Depending on the interpretation one gives to (2), (3) may be superfluous, but for purposes of later discussion regarding the Second Analogy it is worthwhile at this stage to state (3) independently. I take (2) and (4), with modifications, from van Inwagen's discussion of what must be conjoined with the Law of Universal Causation in order to deduce physical determinism, see *An Essay on Free Will*, p. 4. Remarks on the importance of (3) can be found, among other places, in Beck's discussion of the features of a thoroughgoing causal determinism in "Kant on the Uniformity of Nature," pp. 449–450. Proposition (5) is due to a consideration noted by Jan Łukasiewicz in "On Determinism," in *Polish Logic* (Oxford: Clarendon Press, 1967).

ations," and he declares that "all alterations take place in conformity
with the law of the connection of cause and effect" [B232]. This shift
does not indicate a change of mind with respect to the scope of the
causal principle, as if "everything that happens" were a broader category than "all alterations." Rather, both locutions simply serve to pick out
all events that occur in time. Moreover, one can immediately observe
that, if it should turn out that free actions are events that occur in time,
then these events are subject to the causal principle as well and cannot
be considered as "somethings which happen" but which are somehow
exempt from this causal principle. As is shown in the first of the two
new introductory paragraphs to the Second Analogy added in B, the
shift in terminology is simply the result of Kant's bringing the language
of the Second Analogy into agreement with that of the First Analogy, in
which Kant argues that all change, all events, all successions in time, are
alterations of permanent substance.

Kant assumes that it is possible for us to have veridical cognitive
experiences, and in the second introductory paragraph added in B he
makes clear his intention to show that this is possible only if all alterations are subject to the law of causality [B234]. Thus, given his assumption and this conditional, the Law of Universal Causation follows. This
seems easy enough. Nevertheless, the actual structure of his argument
to support this conditional is vigorously debated. One approach stems
from Kant's remarks in the third through sixth paragraphs in B, in
which Kant introduces some of the notions that become significant in
his account.[21]

"The apprehension of the manifold of appearance is always successive" [A189/B234]. Kant has taken criticism for holding this view. Both
H. J. Paton and Lewis White Beck regard it as demonstrably incorrect,
and Paton even suggests that it might mean that "we never directly
apprehend even the subjectively coexistent or simultaneous."[22] Wheth-

---

[21]Lewis White Beck has provided a gloss on this third paragraph in "A Reading of
the Third Paragraph in B," in *Essays on Kant and Hume*, pp. 141–146. Paragraphs 3–6
constitute what Paton has called the second proof (he claims to find six) in which
"Kant develops the argument as a whole"; H. J. Paton, *Kant's Metaphysic of Experience*
(London: Allen and Unwin, 1936), 2:159–331.

[22]Paton, *Kant's Metaphysic of Experience*, 2:231; Beck, "A Reading of the Third Paragraph in B," p. 144. For a partial defense of Kant from these criticisms, see William

er or not apprehension is always successive, Kant's point is that at least some occasions of successive apprehension are apprehensions of objective coexisting states of affairs and other occasions are apprehensions of objective succession, that is, an alteration in a permanent substance consisting of a temporally ordered pair of contrary determinations of that substance. The thrust of this observation is that the mere temporal order of perceptions does not entail whether the perceptions are perceptions of an objective coexisting state of affairs or of a succession of states in an object.

So, to take a variation on a Kantian example: consider a sinking ship, *The Queen of Rationalist Metaphysics*, and consider the Rock of Königsberg, which has just cracked the ship's hull. Now, as I watch this spectacle, I might perceive first the west face and then the north face of the Rock of Königsberg, and then I might perceive the deck of *The Queen of Rationalist Metaphysics* sink into the depths of the Baltic Sea.[23] With respect to my first series of observations, my perceptions, though successive, are perceptions of a coexisting state of affairs; but with respect to my second series of observations, my perceptions, though successive, are perceptions of an objective succession. Kant continues his remarks, though, with a more startling observation: in the former case I might have had my series of perceptions of the Rock of Königsberg in the order north face first, west face last; in other words, the ordering of my perceptions of the very same objective coexisting state of affairs is not a necessary ordering. In the latter case, however, my perception of the submerged position of the ship's deck follows on my perception of its position above the surface of the water, and it is impossible that in the apprehension of this event the ship's deck should first be perceived below the surface of the water and then above the surface of the water [A192–193/B237–238]. This is not to suggest that it is impossible that the ship might have had a different history (say, in which it sank much earlier after an encounter with the treacherous Humean Reef while sailing past Scotland) and thus that it could have been refloated at the time at which I saw it sinking. That might have happened, but that would

---

Harper, "Kant's Empirical Realism and the Distinction between Subjective and Objective Succession," in *Kant on Causality, Freedom, and Objectivity*, pp. 108–137.

[23] I owe thanks for the idea behind this amusing variation to one of my students, Samuel Ruhmkorff.

have been a different event.[24] Kant merely maintains that, if some series of perceptions is a series of perceptions of an objective succession (i.e., of some specific event), then those perceptions are "bound down" or determined in a necessary temporal order.

In what immediately follows, I adopt the following notation: $<a,b>$ = a subjective succession of perceptions, a temporally ordered pair of perceptions which when taken together constitute either the apprehension of an objectively coexisting state of affairs or the apprehension of an objective succession of contrary determinations of a substance; $<A,B>$ = an objective succession (an event), a temporally ordered pair of contrary determinations of a substance.[25]

Kant concludes that, "in this case [of event perception], therefore, we must derive the subjective *succession* of apprehension from the *objective succession*" [A193/B238], and this "derivation" amounts to the claim that $<a,b>$ is a perception of $<A,B>$ only if the temporal order of $<a,b>$ is irreversible. For instance, Kant would claim that my apprehension of the event constituted by the sinking of the ship was such that the temporal order of my perceptions could not have been reversed and have remained an apprehension of the same event. Unfortunately, Kant leaves himself vulnerable when he later begins his indirect proof of the principle of causation by stating, "let us suppose that there is nothing antecedent to an event, upon which it must follow according to a rule [i.e., grant some uncaused event]. All succession of perception would then be only in the apprehension, that is would be merely subjective, and would never enable us to determine objectively which perceptions are those that really precede and which are those that follow" [A194/B239]. It appears as if Kant is here saying that it would follow that perceptions of that event would not be irreversible. Emphasizing this

[24]It seems that Jonathan Bennett makes the mistake of confusing distinct events in this way in his counterexample to Kant's principle in *Kant's Analytic*, p. 222.

[25]Note once again that with respect to this notation Kant does not want to show that state A causes state B, but rather that for any such pair $<A,B>$ there is some other event $<X,Y>$ such that $<X,Y>$ causes $<A,B>$. In other words, all causes and effects are events, not states. This point, which is necessary for but not equivalent to (4) in the Argument for Causal Determinism, is not always readily granted as an expression of Kant's own view. But for an explicit endorsement, see *Prolegomena to Any Future Metaphysics*, Ak. Ed. 4:343–344.

inference, P. F. Strawson has reconstructed Kant's argument and charged Kant with committing "a *non sequitur* of numbing grossness."[26] We may now briefly look at two of Strawson's reconstructions.

Strawson's Argument I
   (1) Conceiving <A,B> as necessary [i.e., as an objective succession] requires conceiving <a,b> as necessary [i.e., as irreversible].
   (2) Conceiving <a,b> as necessary [i.e., as irreversible] is equivalent to conceiving <A,B> as causally determined.
   (3) Hence, conceiving <A,B> as necessary [i.e., as an objective succession] requires conceiving <A,B> as causally determined.

In this argument, the reconstruction Strawson devotes the most time to presenting, (2) is false, and the argument establishes a conclusion different from the one Kant claims to establish. Strawson suggests that it is an analytic truth that all perceptions of objects whose existence is independent of our awareness of them are effects caused by those objects.[27] Proposition (2) is false, though, for even if the mere conception of <a,b>-irreversibly in some instance *analytically* involves a reference to an objective succession <A,B> that stands as the cause of those perceptions, this conception does not specify whether that objective event <A,B> itself has a cause. Moreover, even if it did, this would serve to show only that we *conceive* <A,B> as being causally determined, and Kant has claimed to establish the stronger claim that <A,B> in fact *is* causally determined [B168].

Strawson's next argument is presented as a summary of what preceded it, and his critics regard it as Strawson's main formulation. Neither of these seems to be the case, but this version (with the following charitable elaboration) is the reconstruction offered by Strawson which has received the most attention in the literature, and it is the reconstruction to which Strawson's own criticisms most naturally apply.

[26]P. F. Strawson, *The Bounds of Sense* (London: Methuen, 1966), pp. 133–140. Actually, Strawson's reconstructions are somewhat less unified than he is usually given credit for. In the span of two pages he gives what appears at first glance to be four different versions of the same argument but which on closer inspection turn out to be four different arguments, none of which, I believe, is Kant's.

[27]Strawson, *The Bounds of Sense*, p. 136.

Strawson's Argument II

(1) If <a,b> is a perception of an objective succession <A,B>, then (granted perceptual isomorphism[28]) <a,b> is irreversible.

(2) If <a,b> is irreversible, then the objective succession <A,B> is necessary (causally determined).

(3) Hence, if <a,b> is a perception of an objective succession <A,B>, then <A,B> is necessary.

Notwithstanding the vast amount of support Strawson has received in first attributing this argument to Kant and then in damning him for it, a simple point needs to be stressed: although there is the one piece of evidence from the indirect proof noted above, the remainder of the text of the Second Analogy shows that this is simply not Kant's intended demonstration. Throughout the Analogy, Kant unambiguously declares that perception does not determine objective relations between objects of experience [e.g., A189/B233–234]. Nor is Kant arguing from our *knowledge* of the irreversibility of those perceptions, something that certainly could never be revealed in experience or through the perceptions themselves [A177/B219]. As Paton warned thirty years before Strawson's critique, "It is absolutely vital not to misunderstand this crucial statement": Kant does not argue from the awareness of the irreversibility of one's perceptions to the necessity in an objective succession; he merely argues from the assumption of an objective succession to the irreversibility of the perceptions of that succession.[29] And thus, if the argument can be reconstructed in a manner that better conforms to the text, and does not force Kant to blatantly contradict himself on these matters, that reconstruction is to be preferred.

Finally, it is worth noting that this argument perpetrates exactly the non sequitur Strawson accuses it of. Proposition (2) moves from <a,b>-irreversibly to <A,B>'s being causally necessitated. The mistake is that (granted perceptual isomorphism), even if the objective succession

---

[28]This is James Van Cleve's term for the following conditions: (a) an effect cannot precede its cause in time; (b) the perception of an item is the effect of that item; (c) *a* is a perception of A and *b* of B; (d) there is no relevant difference in the modes of causal dependence of *a* on A and of *b* on B. Condition (d) is the important one for our purposes. See Van Cleve, "Four Recent Interpretations of Kant's Second Analogy," *Kant-Studien* 64 (1973): 71–87.

[29]Paton, *Kant's Metaphysic of Experience*, pp. 239–240.

<A,B> were to occur without being caused, the sequence of percep-
tions <a,b> would be irreversible all the same, and hence <a,b>-
irreversibly does not require that <A,B> is causally determined.[30]

In summary, neither of Strawson's reconstructions turns out to be
Kant's argument, and neither is successful on its own. There is still the
temptation, though, to try to find a crucial role for the irreversibility of
event perceptions to play in Kant's argument. One manner of salvaging
the premise without endorsing the non sequitur is to follow James Van
Cleve and note that Strawson treats Kant as a realist, whereas Kant's
position might be better presented assuming that he is a phenomenalist
or a subjectivist.[31]

The subjectivist approach is a non-starter. This view of empirical objects is such that they are constituted by actual perceptions, thereby
identifying <a,b> with <A,B>. Since our apprehension is successive,
however, this interpretation would make objective coexisting states of
affairs impossible, and it would turn Kant's distinction between these
and objective successions into nonsense.[32]

The phenomenalist approach has it instead that empirical objects are
such that they are constituted by sets of actual and possible perceptions
connected in accordance with a rule, where possible perceptions receive
a counterfactual analysis; that is, they are what a subject would perceive

[30]It is interesting to note the argument does not commit the other fallacy Strawson
says it does, namely, of equivocating on 'necessity'. Strawson maintains that logical
necessity is at work in (1) but that causal necessity is at work in (2), and thus that (3) is
had by equivocation. To see why Strawson is incorrect in this charge, see Van Cleve,
"Four Recent Interpretations of Kant's Second Analogy," p. 82.

[31]Van Cleve, "Four Recent Interpretations of Kant's Second Analogy," p. 84. Van
Cleve himself characterizes Kant's profession of transcendental idealism as an uneasy
mixture of ontological and analytical phenomenalism, with the analytical variety
predominating in Kant's better moments; see his "Another Volley at Kant's Reply to
Hume," in Kant on Causality, Freedom, and Objectivity, pp. 42–57, esp. pp. 43–44. His
later objection to Kant (p. 48), namely, that Kant's view that objects and events are
causes of internal perceptions is incompatible with his analytical phenomenalism,
might better be treated as a reason to suspect Van Cleve's interpretation of Kant's
transcendental idealism than as a criticism of Kant's consistency. For a volley at Van
Cleve and other straightforward phenomenalist interpretations of Kant in the Second
Analogy, see Allison, Kant's Transcendental Idealism, pp. 226, 233–234.

[32]See Van Cleve, "Four Recent Interpretations of Kant's Second Analogy," pp. 76–
78. This subjectivist interpretation seems to be defended by A. C. Ewing in Chapter 4
of his Kant's Treatment of Causality (London: Kegan and Paul, 1924).

if she were placed in the appropriate circumstances. An example of a reconstruction along these lines is provided by Beck.[33]

In examining Beck's argument, I suspend the current use of my terms <A,B> and <a,b> and now use A and B to represent distinct events and *a* and *b* to represent perceptions of distinct events. Doing so permits me to present Beck's position more fairly and accurately by adhering to the terminology he adopts in his own writings. This version of Beck's argument is motivated by what he takes Kant's strategy to be in answering Hume: Hume believes that we know that some perceptions are perceptions of objective events; this requires that we distinguish between objective events and objective coexisting states of affairs, and this implies the causal principle as follows:

Beck's Argument I

(0) We are able to decide that a sequence of representations *a/b* is evidence of a sequence of events A/B (a requirement of Hume's analysis of causation).

(1) We are able to decide that a sequence of representations *a/b* is evidence of a sequence of events A/B only if the order of the representations is such that we believe (rightly or wrongly) that one of the representations must occur before the other.

(2) If the order of representations is such that we believe (rightly or wrongly) that one of the representations must occur before the other, then (interpreting representation *a* as evidence for event A, and *b* for B, and believing, say, that *a* cannot occur after *b*), we believe (rightly or wrongly) that B cannot occur before A.

(3) A condition under which an event B cannot occur before A is that A is the cause of B.

(4) Hence, we are able to decide that a sequence of representations *a/b* is evidence of a sequence of events A/B only if we believe (rightly or wrongly) that A is the cause of B.

Beck concludes more generally with "the experience of something happening is possible only on the assumption that appearances in their succession, that is, appearances as they happen (= events), are determined by the preceding state."[34] Van Cleve has objected that, depend-

[33]Beck, "Once More unto the Breach: Kant's Answer to Hume, Again," in *Essays on Kant and Hume*, pp. 130–135.

[34]Beck, "Once More unto the Breach," p. 133.

ing on the interpretation of the conclusion, either (4) does not follow from the premises or (4) is weaker than Kant's intended conclusion, but he also suggests that this objection can be overcome. In the latter claim, I think he is mistaken.[35] His point is that the premises are about what we believe, and thus the conclusion they yield should also be merely about what we believe. If (4) is read in this way, though, it has the same problem as Strawson's Argument I: Kant wants to show that objective successions *are* causally determined, not just that we think they are. On the other hand, unless we doctor up the premises by "strik[ing] from the argument all occurrences of the words 'we believe that'," this stronger conclusion does not follow.

It is not clear that this removes the difficulty, though. Suppose that the premises are altered in the manner just noted. There is still a problem with (3). Beck simply uses the term 'condition'. If the argument structure is not to be invalid, this must be read as 'necessary condition'. But the premise is true only if it is read as 'sufficient condition'. The argument ought to have the following structure: (1) If P, then Q; (2) If Q, then R; (3) If R, then S; Hence, (4) If P, then S. To make (3) true, however (when it states that, If an event A is the cause of an event B, then B cannot occur before A), the argument has the following invalid structure instead: (1) If P, then Q; (2) If Q, then R; (3) If S, then R; Hence, (4) If P, then S. To see the falsity of the other reading of (3), which would yield the valid argument structure noted above (when it states that, If an event B cannot occur before an event A, then A is the cause of B), note that in any case in which A is identical to B the antecedent is true and the consequent is false.

One way of trying to save (3) is to read it as discussing event types A and B. Van Cleve has persuasively argued that even on this reading, which we might state as (3*) (= If an event of type B cannot immediately precede an event of type A, then an event of type A is the cause of an event of type B), the conditional is still false. Although the antecedent may be true of some event types A and B, that does not guarantee that an instance of A will be followed by an instance of B, for the important reason that B may fail to happen altogether. Since the necessity of the

---

[35]Van Cleve, "Four Recent Interpretations of Kant's Second Analogy," p. 80. Although one certainly could, Van Cleve charitably does not base his objections on problems with the nonextensionality of the term 'believes that'.

causal relationship between instances of A and B is thereby not preserved, the antecedent can be true and the consequent false.[36] I would also add that adopting (3*) has yet another fatal consequence for the argument. Validity would demand a similar change in (2) such that irreversibly temporally ordered representations of a single instance of an event sequence A/B would be alleged to imply that no instance of event type B could immediately precede an instance of event type A. But surely this new (2*) would be wholly implausible.

In summary, we must reject this attempt at reconstructing Kant's argument as well, and on the strength of the above discussions perhaps we should look for another approach to interpreting Kant's argument that does not emphasize the feature of the irreversibility of our perceptions of objective events.

The Argument from Knowledge of Events

One of the attractions of focusing on the irreversibility of perceptions was that it seemed to give us a way of distinguishing objective events from objective states of affairs, and thus it seemed that this information would somehow have to be involved in the sort of inferences we have just inspected and rejected. But in the first of the two new paragraphs in B designed to form a bridge between the First and Second Analogies, Kant explains that all events or "alterations are opposite determinations of one and the same substance which abides throughout the change" [B233]; this was the justification for originally describing our symbol <A,B> as a temporally ordered pair of contrary determinations of a substance. Hence, returning to that symbolization, if I know that, in my sequence of perceptions of some pair of states in a substance, state A is contrary to state B, then I know that that sequence of perceptions is of an objective succession and not of an objectively coexisting state of affairs. Just which objective succession it is, though, is not yet specified. It might be either <A,B> or <B,A>.

A reconstruction of Kant's argument that capitalizes on these observations (and therefore on what knowledge of <A,B> requires) is offered by Beck in his writings against Strawson's interpretation.[37] In examin-

---

[36]Van Cleve, "Four Recent Interpretations of Kant's Second Analogy," p. 80.

[37]Beck, "A *Non Sequitur* of Numbing Grossness?" in *Essays on Kant and Hume*, pp. 147–153.

ing this argument, I use the letters A and B to represent states of a substance, and I write as if (contrary to fact) a state were the cause of another state rather than an event's being the cause of another event. Once again, doing so permits me to present Beck's position in a manner more faithful to the original. Nevertheless, I have something to say about the serious disadvantages of an approach of this sort in what follows. The heart of Beck's reconstruction depends on the following passage: "In order to know, or to have good reason to believe, that <A,B> occurs, given knowledge of <a,b>-irreversibly, I must know or have good reason to believe both that (i) A and B are opposite states of a substance, in order to rule out [that A coexists with B]; and <A,B>-irreversibly, in order to rule out [that <B,A> occurs]."[38] In the spirit of this passage, I present Beck's argument as follows:

Beck's Argument II
  (0) I know that <A,B> occurs. (a requirement of Hume's analysis of causation)
  (1) If I know that <A,B> occurs, then (i) I am able to rule out the case that A coexists with B, and (ii) I am able to rule out the case that <B,A> occurs.
  (2) If I am able to rule out the case that A coexists with B, then I know that A and B are opposite or contrary states of a substance.
  (3) If I am able to rule out the case that <B,A> occurs, then I know <A,B>-irreversibly (i.e., the schema of causation).
  (4) If I know <A,B>-irreversibly, then I know that A is, or contains, a causal condition of B.
  (5) Hence, if I know that <A,B> occurs, then I know that A is, or contains, a causal condition of B.

As with Beck's Argument I, we can (for present purposes) set aside obvious difficulties with the nonextensionality of the term "knows that" which figures so prominently in the structure of the present argument. I have doubts about (2), but it is inessential for the argument and can be left alone. One might also doubt (3); one might wonder why knowledge

---

[38]I have taken the words "I *must* know or have good reason to believe" as the key to my manner of reconstructing Beck's argument. This version of Beck's argument is condensed from his discussion in "A *Non Sequitur* of Numbing Grossness?" pp. 148–150. In his extended discussion, Beck also includes references to <a,b>-irreversible perceptions of <A,B>, but I do not believe that his argument proper in any way requires those references.

of anything as strong as <A,B>-irreversibly would be required to rule out that <B,A> occurs. Anticipating this problem, Beck gives reasons for believing that knowledge of <a,b>-irreversibly does not suffice, since perceptual isomorphism might fail to obtain: "when, for example, I cannot but see an eclipse of the moon before I see the explosion of a nova, even though the nova exploded thousands of years before the eclipse occurred."[39] Beck acknowledges that in this example he has shifted from discussing contrary states of a substance to a discussion of distinct events, but he suggests that there are more cumbersome ways to state the same fact in the terminology we have already employed. I take it, then, that his point comes to this: in some cases when an objective event <B,A> is perceived, due to some peculiarity in the relation between the agent and the event (e.g., a failure of perceptual isomorphism) the order of the agent's perceptions is <a,b> and that order is irreversible.

However, whether (3) is true depends on how we are to understand the occurrence of "<A,B>-irreversibly" in it. Given the nature of (4), Beck clearly intends it to have a sense appropriate to the schema of causation, that is, to "the real upon which, whenever posited, something always follows" [A144/B183]. So we may understand irreversibility in the strong or schema sense in this way: a sequence <A,B> is *strongly irreversible* just in case, whenever a token of A's type occurs, a token of B's type occurs immediately afterward.[40] Hence, (3) says that, in order to rule out the case that <B,A> occurs, I must know that <A,B> is strongly irreversible. One may, however, object that this is not a necessary condition after all, since a weaker sense of irreversibility will do just as well: a sequence <A,B> is *weakly irreversible* just in case a token of B's type never immediately precedes or occurs at the same time as a token of A's type. Now, knowing that <A,B> is weakly irreversible is sufficient for knowing that <B,A> does not occur, since the former is exactly a denial of any such case <B,A>. Moreover, weak irreversibility

---

[39]Beck, "A *Non Sequitur* of Numbing Grossness?" p. 149.

[40]In developing a series of different arguments against alternative reconstructions presented by Beck, Van Cleve has distinguished two, then four, different senses of irreversibility in "Four Recent Interpretations of Kant's Second Analogy," p. 74, and in "Another Volley at Kant's Reply to Hume," p. 46 and n. 17, respectively. The present discussion invokes versions of his 'irreversibly$_3$' and 'irreversibly$_2$'.

need not require strong irreversibility. For instance, $<x$ as a boy, x as a man$>$ is weakly irreversible, but it is not strongly irreversible since, even though no individual is a man immediately prior to being a boy, some individual may suffer a fatal accident as a boy and never reach manhood.[41] Therefore, (3) requires the sense of strong irreversibility, but when so interpreted it is false.

Suppose that, as an amendment, we were to allow (3) to stand as revised, thus foregoing the strong sense of $<A,B>$-irreversibly. Then (5*) would read, If I know that $<A,B>$ occurs, then I know that no token of B's type ever immediately precedes a token of A's type. Two unfavorable consequences would follow from our (5*): (i) I would not know that some common event like $<x$ as drained of beer, x as filled with beer$>$ had occurred, since (happily) I know that on certain occasions this former state of my favorite stein not only precedes but also immediately follows upon this latter state; and (ii) although I could know that many other events had in fact occurred, I would not thereby know that they were caused to occur, a result that is apparently in conflict with Kant's professed aim in the Second Analogy. In other words, I could know that an event such as $<x$ as bread dough, x as baked bread$>$ had occurred, since I know that these are contrary states of a thing x, and since no state of being baked bread ever immediately precedes a state of being bread dough in a substance. But that knowledge does not depend in any way on the alteration in the states of x being caused, and thus knowing the former does not require knowing that the alteration is the effect of some cause.

Beck has fashioned his reconstruction in such a way that it is possible to interpret him as suggesting that in any objective succession $<A,B>$ the first state of the substance, or something contained in that state, causes the second state: A is, or contains, a causal condition of B. In my objections, I have followed this natural reading of the argument, although the resulting model of causation would apply to very few causal relationships in the world. Kant's position is consistent with the occasional case in which an alteration in a substance causes a further alteration in the same substance, but in general he wishes to show that for

[41]Grant some society in which these predicates are not quite as vague as they are in ours: for example, where the transition from boyhood to manhood comes automatically with one's first kill in the wild.

any objective succession <A,B> there is some event <X,Y> such that <X,Y> causes <A,B>. This approach, then, permits cases in which an alteration in one substance stands as the cause of some further alteration in the same substance, but it is not confined to those cases.[42]

Premise (3) can be modified in accordance with this discussion: (3*) If I am able to rule out the case that <B,A> occurs, then I know for some <X,Y>, <<X,Y>,<A,B>>-irreversibly (i.e., the schema of causation). Here we have a sequence of events, but for present purposes we need not regard these events as occurring in the same substance. Substituting the sense of schema or strong irreversibility, then, we have the claim that, if I can rule out the case that <B,A> occurs, then I know that for some <X,Y>, whenever a token of <X,Y>'s type occurs, a token of <A,B>'s type occurs immediately afterward. In other words, "the real [= <X,Y>] upon which, whenever posited, something [= the alteration <A,B>] always follows." As we have already seen, though, knowing that <A,B> is weakly irreversible is sufficient for ruling out the case that <B,A> occurs, but knowing that <A,B> is weakly irreversible does not require knowing that, for some <X,Y>, <<X,Y>,<A,B>> is strongly irreversible. Hence, (3*) is false; I can rule out the case that <B,A> occurs, and knowing that <A,B> has a cause is not a necessary condition of my doing so. Perhaps an example would be useful. I can rule out the alteration consisting in a raisin becoming a grape by knowing that in a substance no state of being a raisin ever immediately precedes or occurs at the same time as a state of being a grape. But this latter knowledge does not involve or require that I know of the transition in a substance from being a grape to being a raisin that *that* transition or alteration itself has a cause.

In summary, we must reject the present reconstruction since, as I have just argued, the modification of (3) into (3*) is unsuccessful, and since in the original reconstruction either (3) is false or the conclusion is not equivalent to, and does not imply, Kant's intended aim, namely, to demonstrate that every event has a cause.

---

[42]When he offers illustrations, Kant himself tends to focus on cases of causation that involve more than one substance [A202–204/B247–249]. Jeffrey R. Dodge, however, gives a defense of a broader reading of Beck's phrase, "A is, or contains, a causal condition of B"; see Dodge's "Uniformity of Empirical Cause-Effect Relations in the Second Analogy," *Kant-Studien* 73 (1982): 47–54, n. 6.

Arguments from the Empirical Determination of Time Position and from the Nature of Time

Commentators often remark that in the series of proofs that constitute the text of the Second Analogy the "fifth proof," which emphasizes the nature of time [A199–201/B244–246], is considerably different from the rest. One virtue of this proof, as Paton suggested, is that it brings the Second Analogy closer to the First Analogy; whereas in the latter, permanent substance represents the unity of the one, homogeneous time in which all intervals of time are parts, in the former, events that are the necessary effects of other events represent the necessary succession of the parts of time.⁴³

In the paragraph immediately prior to the fifth proof, Kant makes clear the purpose of his earlier discussion of all our representations' being successive. It is simply that when merely given perceptions "nothing is distinguished from anything else" [A198/B243]; that is, one cannot distinguish objective coexisting states of affairs from objective successions on perceptual grounds alone. As even Hume conceded, however, we do in fact distinguish these in experience, and so Kant says that "I represent something as an event, as something that happens; that is to say I apprehend an object to which I must ascribe a certain determinate position in time—a position which, in view of the preceding state, cannot be otherwise assigned." Shortly thereafter he adds, "It can acquire this determinate position in this relation of time only in so far as something is presupposed in the preceding state upon which it follows invariably, that is in accordance with a rule" [A198/B243].

Our attention is now drawn away from the muddle of inferences from the irreversibility of perception sequences to objective successions as caused toward the claim that I can represent something as an objective succession only if I empirically determine the time position of that event. Moreover, we are told that this position is necessary relative to a preceding state on which it follows according to a rule in a language strong enough to suggest the schema of causality and to remind us of the premise of the necessity of the causal connection: "If the state which

---

⁴³Paton, *Kant's Metaphysic of Experience*, p. 253. Paton's commentary on the fifth proof can be found on pp. 253–257.

precedes is posited, this determinate event follows inevitably and necessarily" [A198/B243–244].

Arthur Melnick has explored this approach to reconstructing Kant's position in the Second Analogy.[44] His position, roughly, is that the schematized category of causality is required for the complete determinability of all events in time, which in turn is a necessary condition for the empirical determination of the time position of any given event, which in turn is a necessary condition of representing some sequence of perceptions as perceptions of an objective succession.

Initially this analysis calls for a distinction between complete determinability and empirical determination. Melnick argues that all the types of phrases that can be used to determine empirically the time position of some state or event are analyzable in terms of phrases such as "x happened before y or after z or at the same time as w."[45] Such empirical determination, though, is not a determination of a state or event in absolute time (something Kant repeatedly insists cannot be done [e.g., at A189/B233]), but only a determination of a state or event relative to another state or event. So we might empirically determine two contrary states of a substance to have the time position $<A,B>$ relative to one another. But to determine empirically the time position of what we now regard as the event $<A,B>$, again we must be able to determine the time position of this sequence relative to other states or events. In the introductory material on the Analogies, Kant maintains that by means of the three principles or rules of the Analogies "the existence of every appearance can be determined in respect of the unity of all time" [A177/B219]. But we can regard the existence of *every* appearance as so determinable only if the time position of any given state or event can be determined relative to any other state or event. To deny this is to embrace the absurd view that time is not a unified whole but is somehow fragmented into temporally unrelated parts [see also A216/B263].

Consequently, we can understand Kant's point that all alterations are determinable in time as merely asserting that it is possible to determine the time position of any state or event relative to any other, and this

[44]Arthur Melnick, *Kant's Analogies of Experience* (Chicago: University of Chicago Press, 1973).
[45]Melnick, *Kant's Analogies of Experience*, pp. 85–86.

accords with his view that all objects of experience have a definite position in the one, commonly shared, unified time of which all time intervals are parts. So, if Kant is successful in the Second Analogy, then this thoroughgoing determinability of all events is known a priori, but this knowledge needs to be sharply distinguished from any particular case of the empirical determination of the time position of a given event. The empirical determination of the time position of a particular event is always a posteriori, but the possibility of our determining some particular event "in respect of the unity of all time" is provided by the a priori rule that all events are determinable in time, that is, that all events have a rule-governed temporal relation to all other events. It is apparent that Kant has subscribed to this view when at the end of the Analogies he comments on the mode of proof he has employed by writing that "we have found *a priori* conditions of complete and necessary determination of time for all existence in the [field of] all appearance, without which even empirical determination of time[-positions of particular events] would be impossible" [A217/B264].[46] It is worth noting that saying that all events are thus determinable does not mean that, given any two events, we always *succeed* in relating them to one another in time. Although they do have a fixed temporal position, for us to perform the task of determining them relative to one another we also need to know the contingent causal laws connecting them, which, quite obviously, is knowledge we may or may not have. Perhaps the more cautious statement, then, is that in principle we can always determine the temporal position of any two events relative to one another. Alternatively, to hold a thesis of the complete determinability of all events is just to maintain that given *any* two events, if we had sufficient knowledge of the relevant causal laws, we could temporally order them relative to one another via their causal histories.

Melnick attempts a specific reconstruction of Kant's argument utilizing the material sketched above. He first proposes a "skeletal definition" of a causal law "as a rule that enables us to order events temporally as asymmetric on the basis of features of the events (taking into consid-

---

[46]Second bracket additions, mine; I do not think that Kant means to say that we empirically determine time, or even the parts of time, but rather that we empirically determine the time position of the occupants of the time series, namely, states, events, and sequences of states and events.

eration features of the circumstances)."[47] He then argues from the empirical determination of the relative temporal order of events to the necessity of invoking causal laws as follows:[48]

Melnick's Argument

(0) We sometimes represent objective successions (events).

(1) We can represent objective successions only if we can determine the position of an event or state of affairs in time.

(2) "Determining the position of an event or state of affairs in time is always determining its position relative to other events or states of affairs, and always on the presupposition that the position of the event could be determined relatively to all other events."

(3) "This thoroughgoing determinability is not possible by means of perception or by relating events individually to absolute time, or time by itself."

(4) This thoroughgoing determinability is possible either by means of perception, or by relating events individually to absolute time or to time by itself, or by being based on features of the objects of perception.

(5) "Thus, the determinability must be based on features of the objects of perception." (3),(4)

(6) "No features of objects of perception (states of affairs or events) allow us to infer their relative temporal order except in terms of rules that license such inferences. Thus, if x is P and y is P', this in itself tells us nothing about the relative temporal order of x and y unless there is some rule that determines this order on the basis of the fact that x and y are P and P' (in certain circumstances), respectively."

(7) "Thus the determinability of the relative order of events (according to the dimension 'before, after, at the same time') is possible only through rules that license inferences from the features of

[47]Melnick, *Kant's Analogies of Experience*, p. 90.

[48]The following reconstruction is a revised version of Melnick's own presentation in *Kant's Analogies of Experience*, pp. 95–96. I add (0) and (1) to bring the discussion into line with the general approach to answering Hume, on the strength of Kant's comment at A198/B243; I add (4) since it is obviously required in order to infer (5); and although (8) is frequently regarded (even by Melnick) as the conclusion of his argument, it is clearly only another premise based on his skeletal definitions of causal laws and laws of interaction, and thus I add (9) and (10) to complete the argument in the manner suggested by (8).

events to their temporal order. The thoroughgoing determinability of the relative order of all events requires the thoroughgoing connection of events according to such rules." (5),(6)

(8) "But a rule that allows us to infer, on the basis of certain features
of events or states of affairs, that these events or states of affairs
are temporally ordered in a certain way is simply the core notion
of (a) a causal law, if the inferred temporal ordering is that the
events or states are successive, or (b) a law of interaction or
community, if the temporal ordering inferred is that the states
are simultaneous or coexist through time."

(9) Thus the determinability of the relative order of events requires
causal laws and laws of interaction. (7),(8)

(10) Hence, we can represent objective successions only if there are
causal laws and laws of interaction. (1),(2),(9)

I believe that this is the best argument we have encountered so far,
both with respect to Kant interpretation and with respect to its plausibility; nevertheless, there seem to be some difficulties here as well. I
pass over (0), (1), and (2), since they have been treated at some length in
the earlier discussion. Proposition (3) depends on two claims: first, as
we have repeatedly seen, mere perception does not determine objective
temporal order; second, "time cannot be perceived in itself, and what
precedes and what follows cannot, therefore, by relation to it, be empirically determined in the object" [A189/B233, see also A192/B237].

One of Kant's favorite argument strategies is the argument by elimination, and (4) represents, in Melnick's terminology, his alternatives.
Very infrequently does Kant ever supplement one of his arguments
by elimination with a reason to think that his list of alternatives is
exhaustive, even though he carries on the discussion as if this were to be
understood. Barring other significant candidates for alternatives, though,
the problem with (4) as it stands is found in Melnick's consistent (but
misleading) use of the phrase "being based on features of the objects of
perception." Strictly speaking, he needs to phrase this alternative as one
in which a thoroughgoing determinability is based on *rules* that temporally order events based on features of the objects of perception. One of
Kant's main points is exactly that these rules themselves are *not* "features of the objects of perception." This, then, is partially clarified in (6),
which finally yields an important result of Melnick's proof, (7), through

which we now secure the sought-after connection between the complete determinability of events and the rules (of some type or other) which relate all events temporally. It remains to be seen whether these rules are causal laws.

Proposition (8) is the crucial move. In (8) Melnick analyzes these rules in terms of causal laws and of laws of interaction. Melnick expresses doubts about Kant's belief that he can show that causal laws are uniquely responsible for determining the time order of appearances as successive and that laws of interaction are uniquely responsible for determining the time order of appearances as simultaneous or coexistent.[49] As William Harper and Ralf Meerbote have suggested, this doubt may give Melnick "a rationale for stopping short of Kant's full causal principle," a reason for him to "embrace mere irreversibility laws, in place of Kant's own account of causal laws, in which an earlier state necessitates an effect that follows."[50] Melnick's worry is that the Third Analogy can simply be reduced to a corollary of the Second Analogy, but I am not sure that such a reduction is plausible.

One way to challenge the plausibility of this suggestion is to focus on Melnick's observation that "Kant wishes to distinguish causal connection from mutual interaction; *i.e.*, he wishes to distinguish cases in which one would say that x is the cause of y from cases where x and y are in mutual interaction."[51] Kant, however, would insist that x and y are placeholders for two different types of thing is this sentence: in the case where x causes y, x and y are events; and in the case where x is in mutual interaction with y, x and y are substances. Consequently, Kant does not wish to distinguish cases where the same x and y are considered as cause and effect from cases where they are considered as mutually interactive any more than he wishes to conflate the notions of event and substance. Now, Melnick seems to be led to his skeptical position by his inability to understand what might underlie a law of interaction, if it is not a causal law, and to that extent he seems to be entirely correct. But the following suggestion, which draws on the distinction between events and substances, grants that laws of interaction are dependent on causal laws but does not grant that they are thereby reducible to causal

[49]Melnick, *Kant's Analogies of Experience*, pp. 96–110.
[50]Harper and Meerbote, "Kant's Principle of Causal Explanations," p. 14.
[51]Melnick, *Kant's Analogies of Experience*, p. 102.

laws: causal laws pertain only to relations between events, that of the objective succession of events in time. Interaction laws pertain only to relations between substances, that of the coexistence of substances in time. Admittedly, the latter do so in virtue of reciprocal causal relations between the substances *insofar as* the events or alterations that stand in the causal relationships in question are alterations of the substances in question. As Kant writes in the Third Analogy, "when each substance reciprocally contains the ground of the determinations in the other, the relation is that of community or reciprocity" [A211/B257–258].

Now, we may ask whether causal laws are able to do the work of the laws of interaction, and thus whether Melnick is correct in his suspicion that interaction laws ultimately can be eliminated. In the Third Analogy, Kant argues that two substances are coexistent only if each contains some event that stands as a cause of some subsequent event in the other. A causal law, at best, establishes only one half of this reciprocal relation. But in that case, a law of interaction would need to be quite different from a causal law, in virtue of applying not just to a type of event sequence but instead to a rather complex type of series of event sequences, specified as occurring between two or more substances. Interaction laws, which thus would make reference to substances in their formulation, are not reducible to causal laws, since causal laws need only make reference to event types or alteration types, and since they do not involve any direct or indirect reference to the substances in which these alterations occur which could provide a rule for the instantiation of this reciprocal relation.[52] In short, only interaction laws could provide a means of determining the time order of substances as coexistent.

Whether or not this type of response to Melnick's worries will prove successful, one can still object to Melnick's step (8) in a more important way. First, strictly interpreted, (8) asserts that a causal law is a rule that allows us to infer, on the basis of certain features of events or states of affairs, that the events or states are temporally ordered as successive. This is far too generous a notion. Any rule that merely stated that,

---

[52]Causal laws do make reference to substances indirectly, insofar as they make reference to event types and insofar as any event involves contrary determinations of the states of a substance. But this fact does not yield the reciprocal relation required for laws of interaction.

"given some contrary pair of states in a substance, they cannot be coin-
stantiated" would be sufficient to ensure that the temporal ordering of
the states would be successive, but this rule would not be a causal law.
Proposition (8) can be embellished, though, along the lines of (6) and
with Melnick's earlier skeletal definition of a causal law. The new assertion, (8*), then stipulates that a causal law is a rule that allows us to infer
that events or states are temporally ordered as *asymmetrically* successive.
However, a rule might be strong enough to guarantee temporal asymmetric successiveness but not strong enough to capture the necessity of
the causal connection. Hence, some rule (analogous to the sense of
weak irreversibility from my earlier investigation into Beck's Argument
II) that would ensure that, whenever two events A and B both occurred,
B never preceded A, would satisfy Melnick's description of a rule in (8*).
But to achieve the status of a causal law we need something stronger; we
need a rule (analogous to our sense of schema or strong irreversibility)
that would ensure that any instance of A's type would be followed by an
instance of B's type. Unless this sort of necessity is preserved in the rule-
governed relation from the occurrence of some event (the causal condition) to the subsequent alteration in a substance (the effect), there is no
justification for terming the connection a causal one or the rule a causal
law. Hence, I think we should reject Melnick's version of the argument
for Kant's principle in the Second Analogy.

This does not mean, though, that we should reject Melnick's general
approach or fail to follow through on his insights into the argument
structure of the Second Analogy. Adopting a certain line of interpretation regarding Kant's theory of time (compellingly presented by
Gordon G. Brittan, Jr., in his work on Kant's philosophy of science)
provides us with the means to modify and strengthen the argument
strategy suggested by Melnick.[53] Brittan argues that Kant endorses a
causal theory of time similar to that advocated by Hans Reichenbach.[54]
Brittan does not, however, take full advantage of this insight in his own
reconstruction of the argument for the causal principle, which moves
once again from the necessary order of our perceptions to the order of

[53]Gordon G. Brittan, Jr., *Kant's Theory of Science*, pp. 165–208.
[54]Hans Reichenbach, *The Philosophy of Space and Time*, trans. Maria Reichenbach and
John Freund (New York: Dover, 1958), sec. 21, pp. 135–143.

change in the object of those perceptions as caused. In other words, he resurrects a version of the Strawsonian reading of the Second Analogy, which he introduces with the words, "in my view, the argument of the Second Analogy should be set out in the following way":[55]

Brittan's Argument
(1) We perceive that contrary appearances follow one another in time.
(2) Time order cannot be determined with respect to time itself (we need an empirical, objective criterion of time order).
(3) The mere order of our perceptions does not provide such a criterion.
(4) The necessary order of our perceptions does provide an adequate, empirical, objective criterion.
(5) "But to say that the ordering of our perceptions is necessary, is to say that the order of change in the object perceived is causally determined."
(6) "Thus the fact that some of our perceptions are perceptions of events entails that changes in objects be causally determined."

Given his interpretation of Kant's theory of time, Brittan's reconstruction is somewhat surprising: (1), (2), and (3), though true, do not do any work in the argument as reconstructed; (4) seems to be incompatible with Brittan's chief insight that according to Kant causal relationships are the sole empirical, objective criterion of temporal order; another premise would be required in addition to (5) to generate the conclusion; and, as far as I can tell, (5) just is Strawson's non sequitur of numbing grossness. To be fair to Brittan, he has developed an intriguing argument in a later chapter of his book in which he provides a Kantian derivation of the Law of Universal Causation that takes as a starting point Hume's puzzles concerning induction. On the basis of Kant's lectures on logic (especially sections 9–11) and the Appendix to the Transcendental Dialectic, Brittan ascribes to Kant a Goodman-style resolution to the problem of induction, a resolution that turns on regarding projectability as necessary for inductive inference, and he argues by

[55]Brittan, *Kant's Theory of Science*, p. 170. The numbering of the premises in the following argument is Brittan's.

way of the Kantian notion of an empirical object to the claim that all alterations in these objects are causally governed.[56] Consequently, Kant's overall position can be viewed as a response to Hume's analysis of induction and to his analysis of inferential knowledge, rather than merely as a response to his analysis of causation. This is not the argument of the text of the Second Analogy, however, and Brittan does not attempt to suggest that it is. Rather, that argument, as Melnick recognizes, is from the empirical determination of the time position of events, and, as Brittan recognizes, from the nature of time. Let us combine certain features of their approaches, then, and let us recall that Kant's strategy is to derive the Law of Universal Causation from something necessary for Hume's analysis of causation. Accordingly, we may formulate our final reconstruction of Kant's argument for the causal principle as follows:

(0) We sometimes represent objective successions (events).

This premise, once again, is a requirement of Hume's own analysis of causation.

(1) We can represent an objective succession only if we can empirically determine the position of the event in time.

This premise is understood throughout the Second Analogy and is stated explicitly at A198/B243.

(2) We can empirically determine the time position of an event only if we can empirically determine its position relative to any other state or event.

This premise presupposes a thoroughgoing determinability of all states or events in time, that is, it presupposes that the time position of any state or event could be empirically determined relative to any other state or event. Melnick seems to be right in his discussion about this claim. Empirical determination of the time position of a state or event is exe-

---

[56]Brittan, *Kant's Theory of Science*, pp. 188–208. See also Nelson Goodman, *Fact, Fiction, and Forecast*, 4th ed. (Cambridge: Harvard University Press, 1983), pp. 72ff.

cuted exclusively under the alternatives of x happening before y or after z or simultaneously with w. Also, as can be seen from Kant's statements of the general principle of the Analogies (especially in A), all events are subject to such empirical determination of time position, but only relative to one another [A176–177/B218]; otherwise, we could not claim that "the existence of every appearance can be determined in respect to the unity of all time" [A177/B219], and we would be faced with the absurd view that some occupants of the parts or intervals of time are temporally unrelated to other occupants of other parts or intervals of time.

(3) We can empirically determine the time position of an event relative to any other state or event only if we can do so either on the basis of mere perception, or by relating the state or event to time itself, or by recognizing it as the consequence of a previous event and a rule.

Kant, as usual, argues by elimination to his conclusion, and this premise lists the alternatives he considers again and again [e.g., A177/B219].

(4) We cannot empirically determine the time position of an event relative to any other state or event on the basis of mere perception, nor can we do so by relating the state or event to time itself.

This premise brings us back to Kant's discussion of the irreversibility of perceptions of events which has been so frequently misinterpreted. His claim is that in a sequence of perceptions (something common both to perceptions of objectively coexisting states of affairs and to perceptions of objective successions) "nothing is distinguished from anything else," and that even though our perceptions of events are irreversible we do not make an inference from this fact to caused sequences of states but rather require a rule that orders the states [A198/B243]. The remaining disjunct is disqualified since time cannot be perceived in itself, and so no empirical determination of the time position of a state or event is possible with respect to perceptions of time itself [A189/B233, A192/B237].

(5) Hence, we can represent an objective succession only if we can empirically determine the time position of an event relative to

any other state or event by recognizing it as the consequence of a previous event and a rule. (1),(2),(3),(4)

Premise (5) amounts to the claim that representing events requires employing the schematized category of causality, that is, a succession subject to a rule (a causal law) such that when the real (an instance of the previous event type) is posited, something (an instance of the event type in question) always follows. Brittan's inquiry into Kant's theory of time gives us a new way to support this argument, since it provides us with a defense of the crucial premise (3), the premise that identifies the conjunction of a causal law and a previous event as one of the alternatives for empirically determining the time position of some given event.

According to Brittan, Kant holds the view that the causal order provides the sole, empirical, objective criterion of time order.[57] This might be expressed, following Reichenbach, as follows: (CT) If an event E_2 is the effect of an event E_1 or is the effect of an event simultaneous with E_1, then E_2 is later than E_1. To say that the causal order is the sole empirical criterion, though, is to assert a necessary condition as well as a sufficient condition. Perhaps in an attempt to convey this biconditional, Brittan reformulates the view: (CT*) "An event E_1 is earlier than an event E_2 just in case E_1 causes, or is simultaneous with the cause of, E_2."[58] Although this is closer to what we need, it is still incorrect (or at least misleading). To see why, assume that there is some event $E_{1.5}$ which is caused by E_1, which is the cause of E_2 and is not simultaneous with either E_1 or E_2. Then, we have a chain of nonsimultaneous cause-effect relations $\{E_1, E_{1.5}, E_2\}$, and in this chain (by hypothesis) E_1 should be earlier than E_2. Brittan's formulation would, however, maintain that E_1 is earlier than E_2 only if it either causes E_2 or is simultaneous with the cause of E_2, neither of which here obtain. Hence, Brittan's formulation is mistaken (or at least misleading). I propose the following modification, which avoids the type of problem just mentioned: (CT**) An event E_1 is earlier than an event E_2 just in case E_1 either causes, or is a causal ancestor of, or is simultaneous with a causal ancestor of E_2.

Next, Brittan makes some crucial observations about the relation of a cause to a causal law according to Kant: "To say that E_1 causes E_2 is to

[57]Brittan, Kant's Theory of Science, pp. 171–180.
[58]Brittan, Kant's Theory of Science, p. 180.

say that there is a law or, in Kant's terminology, rule, which taken together with a description of E_1 allows us to infer a description of E_2."[59] The evidence for this claim is quite good: "Every efficient cause must have a *character*, that is, a law of its causality, without which it would not be a cause" [A539/B567]; and again, "every cause presupposes a rule according to which certain appearances follow as effects; and every rule requires uniformity in the effects" [A549/B577].[60]

One significant consequence of this observation is that, when Kant declares that the event follows from the previous event in accordance with a rule, the 'following from' is logical and not merely temporal. E_2's following from E_1 by means of a rule would require a particular, causal law. Suppose that we represent the simplest case of such a law by the universal generalization of a conditional—For all x, if Fx, then Gx—and thus that we regard the claim "If E_1, then E_2" as one instantiation of this law. This rule, then, together with the occurrence of E_1 would logically necessitate the conclusion that E_2 also occurs. This certainly does not mean that the existence of E_2 is logically necessary, but just that a logically contingent, but physically necessary, universalized conditional, together with the occurrence of an instance of its antecedent, permits a deductive inference to an instance of its consequent. Thus, we can define a strict causal order between events which orders them in accordance with inferences involving causal laws asserting connections between the events. Then, given the causal theory of time, we can also order the events temporally, that is, we can empirically determine the time position of the events relative to one another. Since the thoroughgoing determinability of all events in time relative to one another thus requires that every event follow (deductively as well as temporally) some other event and a rule (which stand as the cause and the causal law, respectively), then, provided that we can represent objective successions (given the starting point granted even by Hume), every event has a cause. Once again, note that maintaining the thesis of a thoroughgoing determinability of all events in time does not require that we have knowledge of *which* previous event is in fact the cause of some given event, or of *which* universal generalizations are in fact the causal laws

---

[59]Brittan, *Kant's Theory of Science*, p. 173.

[60]For an in-depth discussion of this and related issues, see Friedman, "Causal Laws and the Foundations of Natural Science," esp. secs. 1–3.

governing the necessary relations between events. Rather, we only need assert that there is something real, an instance of some event type or other, which when posited is followed by an instance of another specific event type in accordance with some particular causal law or other.

Kant's Causal Determinism

In the preceding discussion, I have presented Kant's reasons for holding (1), "the universal validity of the causal connection," from the Argument for Causal Determinism. The consequence of this result is that according to Kant all events, all happenings, all alterations of a substance in time have a cause.

As we have seen above, Kant regards an event as an efficient cause only insofar as it has a character, only insofar as it presupposes a law of causality that allows it to stand in a rule-governed connection to other events [A539/B567, A549/B577]. Hence, he has grounds for holding (2), "the necessity of the causal connection," from the Argument for Causal Determinism as well: If an event A is the cause of an event B, then there is some particular, causal law such that, given that A occurs as an instance of its antecedent, B is causally necessitated as an instance of its consequent. And, once again, this amounts to the claim that it is impossible for both A to occur and B to fail to occur. As Kant puts the point in this Third Postulate of Empirical Thought, "now there is no existence that can be known as necessary under the condition of other given appearances, save the existence of effects from given causes, in accordance with laws of causality" [A227/B279]; and again, "this necessity of the existence of [the states of substances] we can know only from other states which are given in perception, in accordance with empirical laws of causality" [A227/B280].

It is a matter of some controversy whether or not Kant has reasons, given the Second Analogy, also to adopt (3), "the generalizability of the causal connection," from the Argument for Causal Determinism. Allison, for example, has distinguished what he terms the strong interpretation of the Second Analogy from the weak interpretation (roughly) as follows: the strong interpretation states that all succession of states in an object must be lawlike, and that necessarily causes of the same type have effects of the same type; the weak interpretation states only that, given "some antecedent condition," necessarily some particular cause has its particular effect, and "there are no additional assumptions regarding the repeatability of the sequence and its relevance to other objects of [the cause's] type that are either required or licensed by this presupposition."[61] Similarly, Brittan suggests that (what he terms) "the principle of induction—[that] the course of nature continues always the same—is not implied by the conclusion of the Second Analogy—[that] everything that happens, that begins to be, presupposes something upon which it follows according to a rule." Brittan argues that this principle would "guarantee more than contingent status for the laws or generalizations that fall under it."[62] I believe we can agree that, if regarding the principle that causes of the same type have effects of the same type as a consequence of the Second Analogy is found either to guarantee a priori that certain causal conditions or sequences will be repeated, as Allison suggests, or to provide a deductive justification of particular laws or inductive generalizations, as Brittan suggests, then we can argue that this principle is not an a priori one and we can cite Kant himself as one theorist who does not accept the consequences. Fortunately, though, we do not have to believe that regarding the principle as a priori leads to either of these unacceptable results.

Before I suggest why not, let us first ask why one might think the principle *is* an a priori one, bound up with the argument and conclusion of the Second Analogy.[63] Aside from Kant's previously quoted remarks about the intimate relation of an efficient cause to a causal law, which seem to me to settle the matter, I believe that we already have enough

[61]Allison, *Kant's Transcendental Idealism*, pp. 230–231. Allison opts for the weak interpretation, pp. 228–229.

[62]Brittan, *Kant's Theory of Science*, p. 189. For additional variations on the argument for a general separation of the principle of the Second Analogy and questions regarding the nature and existence of particular causal laws, see Friedman, "Causal Laws and the Foundations of Natural Science," esp. pp. 161–164, and n. 7.

[63]Dodge has argued, on other grounds than those about to be presented here, that the principle of the generalizability of the causal connection could be a proper conclusion of the Second Analogy, if we recognize that our (and Hume's) distinction between what Dodge calls "causal pairs" and "causal half-pairs" presupposes it. See his "Uniformity of Empirical Cause-Effect Relations in the Second Analogy," esp. pp. 49–53.

additional information to show that, even if Kant did not explicitly affirm the latter principle as a constitutive condition of the possibility of experience, he certainly could have done so. As I have argued above, the principle that every event has a cause follows from the claim that we sometimes represent objective successions or events. In that analysis, we discovered that one can empirically determine the time position of a given event relative to another event only by presupposing a causal order between the two events, for example, that E_2 follows from E_1 in accordance with a rule. We also saw that, if the causal theory of time is to permit us to explain how the causal order provides a criterion for relative temporal ordering, then we may understand the term 'follows from' in a deductive sense, which then makes possible the temporal reading as well. But to say that E_2 follows from the conjunction of E_1 and a rule of this sort is to straightforwardly commit oneself to rules of this sort, to particular, empirical causal laws.

The prior discussion of Kant's Third Postulate of Empirical Thought and the explanation of the necessity in a causal connection which is had between cause and effect by means of the rule which governs their relation show that Kant regards the rules mentioned in the Second Analogy in precisely this fashion. Accordingly, it is worth noting that, since Kant claims that the necessity of the causal connection is a physical or empirical necessity provided by causal laws (which are discovered empirically and are the rules in question in these rule-governed connections), there is no good reason to think that the term 'rule' in the statement of the causal principle in the A edition refers to *itself*. That is, when Kant says that some particular event follows from another in accordance with a rule, he means in accordance with some particular, causal law; this, then, is to be distinguished from the claim that any event follows from some other event in accordance with some rule or other, which thesis is itself the rule or principle of the Second Analogy. Moreover, the repeated emphasis on necessity also indicates that Kant intends to convey the sense of 'rule' as "without possible exceptions" as opposed to the sense of 'rule' as "generally, but with occasional exceptions."[64]

This is all we require in order to endorse (3), "the generalizability of

---

[64]See Beck's discussion of the ambiguities in Kant's use of the term 'rule' in "Kant on the Uniformity of Nature," pp. 453–454, 460–461, and n. 11.

the causal connection." To see why, suppose we deny (3). Then some instance of a causal type (say, Fx) occurs but does not have an instance of the effect type (say, Gx) had by other instances of that causal type (hence, some Fx is not Gx.) However, when we committed ourselves to a rule necessarily connecting those types (say, for all x, if Fx, then Gx) on the grounds that we could not empirically determine the time position of some given event without presupposing the existence of that rule, we ruled out the possibility of any such case. Hence, causes of the same type have effects of the same type, and we can argue for this in precisely the same way that we can argue for the principle that every event has a cause, namely, that both principles are required if we sometimes represent objective successions or events.

Furthermore, the apriority of this principle does not have either of the consequences Allison and Brittan have cautioned us against. Causal laws assert a connection between events, but they do not thereby somehow imply the existence of any contingent individual. Hence, they do not stipulate that their antecedent (causes) obtain, and a fortiori they do not involve assumptions about the repetition of the sequences of events they govern. In other words, a causal law would state that necessarily, whenever Fx, then Gx, but not that Fx, and not that Fx then Gx repeatedly.

It may well be true that for us to discover (or to have good grounds for claiming knowledge of) a causal law empirically there must be some frequency in the cause-effect relations it governs; otherwise, we would have no grounds for our inductive inference that some statement is a law governing our experience. This, however, is a problem concerning how we come to have knowledge of particular, causal laws. It does not endanger the claim that there are particular, causal laws governing experience. Whereas we may be empirically shown to have been mistaken in what we believed to be a veridical causal law by encountering a disconfirming case in experience, that merely shows that we were wrong when we judged some proposition to be (or to express) a causal law, but not that some causal types do not invariably give rise to the same effect types. For Kant, then, the claim that there exist particular, causal laws is no more empirically refutable than is the principle that every event has a cause.

Nor does granting the apriority of (3) "guarantee a more than contin-

gent status for the laws that fall under it." The principle does require
that causal laws obtain and that they govern all of our experience, but it
does not specify which propositions are (or express) those laws. Merely
granting that there are causal laws does not give us any special way to
deduce or to justify all (or even some) of them. That process is restricted
to inductive generalization, and with regard to it our causal judgments
are always fallible, but only because we may be mistaken in our efforts
to identify a causal law, not because sometimes such laws do not obtain.
Consequently, Kant can accept (3), "the generalizability of the causal
connection," not merely on the grounds that it is a regulative principle
at work in our attempts to empirically discover particular, causal laws,
but on the stronger grounds that it, like (1), "the universal validity of the
causal connection," is a constitutive condition of the possibility of experience.

Two premises remain for us to consider from the Argument for Causal
Determinism. Premise (4) indirectly occupied us at some length in
Chapter 2. As we there discovered, some commentators have thought
that Kant's compatibilism required him to deny premise (4), and to
embrace a thesis of noumenal or timeless agency (which is distinct from
empirical causation even at the level of tokens), in order to avoid any
lawful connection between acts of agent causality and the phenomenal
events that precede the phenomenal consequences of those acts. As I
have argued, however, all cases of causation, empirical and intelligible,
are token-token identical to phenomenal events that stand under conditions of spatial and temporal determination. But if they are temporal,
then we may empirically determine their time positions relative to one
another. But if we can so relate them in time, then there are causal laws
governing the connections between them, since the causal order makes
our temporal ordering of them possible. But this is just to assert that
there are no events that do not stand in a lawful connection to the
events that preceded them, and so Kant may maintain (4).

One will note that premise (4) implies that there is no earliest member
in the causal series, and premise (5) from the Argument for Causal
Determinism requires that, if this is the case, then for every time t, some
event in that series happens prior to t. Kant is clearly ready to accept this
premise as well. For suppose he were to deny it. Then there would be
some part of time prior to every member of our causal series. But then

there would be a temporal interval the occupants of which could not be related to the occupants of our causal series. But given that we sometimes have perceptions of objective successions, since this requires the complete determinability of all states or events (or occupants in general) in time, such a case is ruled out.

In conclusion, Kant argues for the Law of Universal Causation, and in doing so he also argues for the necessity and the generalizability of the causal connection, three presuppositions of a thoroughgoing causal determinism. Furthermore, the nature of his argument requires him to accept the other premises in our Argument for Causal Determinism, whether or not he would explicitly recognize them as also being presuppositions of a thoroughgoing causal determinism. Therefore, according to Kant, and in keeping with our definition of causal determinism, at any moment of time, the state of the world at that time and the laws of nature together determine a unique future.

Chapter 5

Kant's Theory of Free Will

Kant's exposition of his theory of the nature and freedom of the human will is not confined to any particular, easily identifiable place in the Kantian corpus. As we have seen in his early *Nova dilucidatio*, Kant broaches the topic of freedom of the will in a response to Crusius, he investigates these topics further in the Third Antinomy and its resolution from the *Critique of Pure Reason*, and he develops and expounds his mature views in his ethical writings, ranging from the *Foundations of the Metaphysics of Morals* through the *Critique of Practical Reason* to the later *Religion within the Limits of Reason Alone* and the *Metaphysics of Morals*.

Over the course of a half-century of writing and philosophical maturation, as one might expect of any thinker, Kant imposes technical terms (only to change them) and describes (only to redescribe) his views on the nature of the will and its freedom. Moreover, as one might expect of Kant, he does not adhere to the rigid boundaries he creates with his own terminology, and consequently commentators find in his texts several apparently different theories of freedom of the will with no clear way in which to relate them to one another. Any attempt to show the compatibility of his theory of free will with some other doctrine, then, should include an investigation into Kant's ambiguous use of the terms 'freedom' and 'will', so that the nature of the theory of free will in question becomes evident, and so that the resulting compatibilism is prevented from inheriting any undesirable ambiguity.

Among the more prominent phrases Kant uses when speaking of freedom, one may find "the causality of reason," "transcendental freedom," "cosmological freedom," "spontaneity," "practical freedom," "independence," "freedom in the strictest sense," "comparative freedom," "the freedom sufficient for morality," "negative freedom," "positive freedom," "heteronomy," and "autonomy." Some of these phrases refer to the same sense of freedom; some refer to different senses of freedom; some refer to more than one of the senses of freedom; and Kant sometimes uses one phrase when the context makes it clear that he means another. Consequently, not all the texts can be easily reconciled with one another, and I occasionally argue the familiar thesis that Kant is incautious when applying his own terminology. None of this is surprising but, once again, if we wish to support the view that Kant believed and had good reasons for believing that freedom of the will and causal determinism are compatible, then we need to discover the meanings of and the relations between the different phrases he utilized in the course of providing his account of the nature of the will and its freedom.

I propose to attempt to shed some light on Kant's theory of free will by way of two discussions closely connected to Kant's ethical views: first, I clarify the Kantian conception of human will by way of defending Kant from an objection brought against his moral theory, an objection which, I argue, is motivated by a misunderstanding of Kant's theory of the human will; second, I provide an analysis of the Kantian conceptions of freedom of the will by way of investigating Kant's reciprocity thesis of freedom and morality, the misunderstanding of which also leads to the same objection leveled against his moral theory.

The Imputability Problem

Like many philosophers who are interested in the foundations of ethics, Kant worries about the problem of whether morality is merely illusory—whether any actions are really morally obligatory, whether there are any actual, moral laws, and whether there are in fact any moral agents. Kant believes that to answer these questions affirmatively he must argue in favor of the nonillusory character of the necessary elements in moral activity.

Without autonomy of the will, the idea of morality is chimerical and a mere phantom of the mind. A critical examination of the faculty of practical reason is therefore required to show that pure practical reason can be effective in moral activity, and thus that the idea of a pure rational morality is more than a mere illusion. So argues Kant in the transition from the second to the third section of the *Foundations of the Metaphysics of Morals*.[1] His (and our) task, then, is to conduct such an examination and to analyze the notions he employs (autonomy, practical reason, pure practical reason).

Kant's early insistence that the very concept of causality involved in the idea of a free or autonomous will entails that a will cannot be lawless leads him to identify a free will and a will under moral laws and provokes some of his critics to charge him with establishing autonomy only at the very high price of rejecting the notion of the imputability of morally evil or morally neutral actions.[2] This imputability problem gives rise to an objection against Kant which stems from noting that this identification in the *Foundations* and the confirmation of this reciprocity of freedom and the moral law in sections 5 and 6 in the *Critique of Practical Reason* would seem to make the freedom of the will both necessary and sufficient for the moral goodness of its acts.[3] Because of the sufficiency of freedom for moral goodness, then, every free act would be a morally good act and no morally evil or morally neutral act would ever be free. Since only those actions that are free are (properly) imputable to an agent, it follows that no morally evil or morally neutral act could ever be (properly) imputed to an agent.

What has just been described is simply not Kant's view of im-

---

[1]*Foundations of the Metaphysics of Morals*, p. 71; Ak. Ed. 4:445.

[2]*Foundations of the Metaphysics of Morals*, p. 72; Ak. Ed. 4:447. For a good discussion of how this charge is motivated, see Roger J. Sullivan, *Immanuel Kant's Moral Theory* (Cambridge: Cambridge University Press, 1989), pp. 279–286. Sullivan is eloquent in his statement of the charge but is indecisive in his adjudication of the issue. For versions of the argument, also see Lewis White Beck, "Five Concepts of Freedom in Kant," p. 38; and Gerold Prauss, *Kant über Freiheit als Autonomie* (Frankfurt am Main: Vittorio Klostermann, 1983), pp. 62–115.

[3]*Critique of Practical Reason*, pp. 28–30; Ak. Ed. 5:28–30.

putability, and no one has seriously charged that Kant explicitly held such a view; the charge is that, given his premises, he is committed to such a view, however unpalatable it may be. Nevertheless, Kant accepts (and even calls attention to) the imputability of evil actions in many passages throughout his critical writings, thus clearly demonstrating that he does not accept the conclusion of the objection arising from the imputability problem.[4] If it could be shown, then, as those who advance the imputability problem argue, that the rejection of the notion of the imputability of morally evil or morally neutral actions is a consequence of Kant's ethical position, then to the detriment of his ethical theory Kant would be exposed as inconsistent.

Kant is not without an answer to this objection. By focusing on some recent work done on the *Wille/Willkür* distinction, I argue that he can escape the imputability problem. One alleged disadvantage of a defense of Kant which utilizes this distinction is that, since he draws it explicitly only much later in the *Metaphysics of Morals* and in the *Religion within the Limits of Reason Alone*,[5] one might argue that it is little more than historical speculation to claim that Kant recognized this distinction as early as the second *Critique* or even the *Foundations*. Consequently, one might argue that, whereas the Kant of the 1790s had no imputability problem, the Kant of the 1780s was subject to the objection with no solution at hand. I believe that this line of argument is motivated by a misreading of both the reciprocity thesis in the second *Critique* and the Third Antinomy in the first *Critique*, and I argue that not only can Kant give an account of moral imputability consistent with the whole of his practical philosophy but also that the imputability problem cannot even be generated from the reciprocity thesis as it stands in the second *Critique*.

Wille, Willkür, and the Nature of the Human Will

The distinction between reflective and determinate judgment Kant draws in the *Critique of Judgment* has proved a valuable interpretive device when read back into various discussions in the *Critique of Pure*

---

[4]For examples, see the first *Critique* [A551/B579n; A554–555/B582–583], and the second *Critique*, pp. 39–40, 101–103; Ak. Ed. 5:37–39, 97–100.

[5]*Metaphysics of Morals*, Ak. Ed. 6:213; *Religion within the Limits of Reason Alone*, pp. 16–39; Ak. Ed. 6: 2–44.

Reason, and it is a precedent for the fruitfulness of this type of method which looks to Kant's later writings for insight into the more obscure sections of his earlier ones.[6] Commentators on Kant's ethics such as Lewis White Beck and John Silber have focused on another distinction that Kant draws in his *Religion within the Limits of Reason Alone* and in the *Metaphysics of Morals* between two senses of 'will', which Kant terms *Wille* and *Willkür*.[7] After these commentators provide an account of the two senses of 'will', they then read back the distinction into the *Foundations* and the second *Critique* in the hopes of rescuing Kant from the imputability problem.

As Beck puts it, there have been distinguished two meanings of will: "*Wille* as practical reason, the legislative function, and *Willkür*, as the executive faculty of man."[8] According to Beck, each sense of the will has its own accompanying sense of freedom: the freedom of *Wille* is autonomy, displayed in the giving of the moral law to *Willkür* as an unconditional practical law; and the freedom of *Willkür* is spontaneity, both as a characterization of a rational agent's choosing to follow either the moral law as given by *Wille* or the inclinations presented to the agent by her sensuous nature and as a characterization of her action as an initiation of a causal series in nature. The general thrust of the explanation then comes in emphasizing that, since through *Willkür* a rational agent has this option of freely choosing between moral law and inclination, the imputability of morally good, morally evil, and morally neutral actions has been established and connected to the freedom belonging to will in the sense of *Willkür*, or the faculty of choice. Finally, Beck argues that the distinction does not commit one to recognizing two wills, but rather that *Wille* and *Willkür* are merely two different employments of the same faculty, so that in a strict sense the will gives a law to itself, preserving thereby both its freedom and its lawfulness in its actions.[9]

[6]*Critique of Judgment*, pp. 18–20; Ak. Ed. 5:179–181.

[7]Lewis White Beck, *A Commentary on Kant's "Critique of Practical Reason,"* pp. 176–208; John Silber, "The Ethical Significance of Kant's *Religion*," reprinted as an introduction to *Religion within the Limits of Reason Alone*, p. lxxix–cxxxiv.

[8]Beck, *Commentary*, p. 202; see also pp. 176–177 and note.

[9]Beck, *Commentary*, p. 201. Beck has a much fuller discussion of the same argument in his "Kant's Two Conceptions of Will in Their Political Context," in *Studies in the Philosophy of Kant* (Indianapolis: Bobbs-Merrill, 1965), pp. 224–229.

H. J. Paton, in his earlier commentary, makes suggestions along the lines later developed by Beck, insisting that "Kant expressly distinguishes between a will 'under moral laws' and a will which always obeys moral laws."[10] Paton only reports, however, that Kant made such a claim; he does not argue that Kant is entitled to make it, nor does he make it clear just how the distinction between senses of the will solves the imputability problem. Similar charges have been brought against the much fuller accounts of Beck and Silber by Nelson Potter, who argues that introducing the distinction between *Wille* and *Willkür* without giving a complete account of the relation between these two employments is only renaming, not solving, the problem of how it is intelligible that an agent is free in one sense to violate her freedom in another sense.[11] The request made by Potter is a reasonable one and, if a distinction between two different capacities of one and the same object is to be invoked as the tool for solving the imputability problem, these different capacities ought to be defined clearly and an adequate description of their relation should be made available.

So, let us begin with *Willkür*. In the *Critique of Pure Reason*, Kant characterizes the freedom of *Willkür* as freedom in the practical sense and as "the will's [*der Willkür*] independence of coercion through sensuous impulses. For a will is sensuous, in so far as it is *pathologically affected, i.e.*, by sensuous motives; it is *animal* (*arbitrium brutum*), if it can be pathologically *necessitated*. The human will is certainly an *arbitrium sensitivum*, not, however, *brutum* but *liberum*. For sensibility does not necessitate its action" [A534/B562].

It might appear that Kant is drawing the distinction between animal and human will along the same lines as the distinction between complete necessitation and lack of any necessitation, but the term "pathological" needs to be stressed here. Independence from pathological necessitation is not an automatic independence from all types of determination, for the notion of determination is wider and more com-

---

[10]H. J. Paton, *The Categorical Imperative* (Philadelphia: University of Pennsylvania Press, 1948), pp. 213–214. Paton cites the *Critique of Judgment*, p. 338n.; Ak. Ed. 5:448–449.

[11]Nelson Potter, "Does Kant Have Two Concepts of Freedom?" *Akten des 4. Internationalen Kant-Kongresses* (Berlin: Walter de Gruyter, 1974), pp. 590–596.

plex than that of pathological necessitation, inasmuch as the latter omits reason and limits itself to ideas of sense and imagination.[12] Moreover, as I argued in Chapter 2, pro-attitude, propositional determination (the determination relevant to episodes of intelligible causality) is not automatically excluded merely in virtue of the fact that an agent is free from pathological necessitation. This distinction, then, bears a striking resemblance to Kant's very early distinction between internal and external determination through which he divided the rational from the animal will.[13] And that distinction, like this one, is based not on the elimination of all determination of the will but rather on the nature of the source of that determination [cf. A802/B830].

Later in the first *Critique* Kant reinforces this reading of the distinction by declaring that a *Willkür* that is determined independently of sensuous impulses is determined through motives that are represented only by reason [A802/B830]. An immediate connection is established here between human *Willkür* and reason, and this connection distinguishes human beings from animals. In human beings, the conative component of the will is complemented by a rational component, and it is never the case that the human *Willkür* is simply pathologically necessitated to act in favor of its strongest sensuous desire, although it is free to do so. Instead of always being an inevitable and brute reaction to the most powerful sensuous inclination, human *Willkür* can look to reason for the maxim of its motivation and to pure reason (which furnishes its own nonsensuous desires) when the act in question is morally good.

These brief comments from the first *Critique* on human *Willkür*, together with Kant's elaboration of his views concerning maxims and the mediation of reason in human action in his ethical writings, suggest the following theory of human agency. In the *Foundations* Kant writes, "Everything in nature works according to laws. Only a rational being has the capacity of acting according to the conception of laws, *i.e.*, according to principles."[14] Thus, an agent possessed of a rational *Willkür* acts according to the conception of laws furnished by reason; that is, *Willkür*

[12]See Ralf Meerbote, "Kant on Freedom and the Rational and Morally Good Will," in *Self and Nature in Kant's Philosophy*, ed. Allen Wood (Ithaca: Cornell University Press, 1984), pp. 52–72, esp. p. 63.

[13]*Nova dilucidatio*, Ak. Ed. 2:400.

[14]*Foundations of the Metaphysics of Morals*, pp. 47–48; Ak. Ed. 4:412.

is *always* mediated by a maxim. In the opening of the second *Critique*, Kant defines those practical principles as "propositions which contain a general determination of the will. . . . they are subjective, or [mere] maxims, when the condition is regarded by the subject as valid only for his own will. They are objective, or practical laws, when the condition is recognized as objective, *i.e.*, as valid for the will of every rational being."[15] Reason, therefore, gives rise to maxims that are either valid for an individual or group and are based on the presumption of a sensuous desire specific to that individual or group or are valid for every rational agent and are binding independently of any nonrational desires or lack of such desires had by an individual agent.

Thus, human will (as *arbitrium liberum*), a rational *Willkür*, is distinguished from animal will (as *arbitrium brutum*) not by being independent of all types of determination but rather by being mediated by the subjective maxims or practical laws furnished by reason. As just noted, maxims and laws are propositions expressing means-end relations, the belief in which occasions a rational choice executed through *Willkür* on the basis of rationally based respect for or sensuous inclination toward the end in question. This suggests that an ascription to Kant of a theory of human agency dependent on propositional representations of moral, nonmoral, and sensuous feelings and their respective ends can be adequately defended from the standpoint of the first and second *Critiques* alone. The third *Critique* offers further evidence for this view, however. Ralf Meerbote has ascribed to Kant a Davidsonian, pro-attitude belief model of human agency (primarily on the strength of section 10 of the *Critique of Judgment*) which is in agreement with the present discussion: according to that model, "a requirement R is said to be a reason for some person P to perform action H, represented in some manner m, only if R consists of a pro-attitude of P's toward actions possessing some particular property and of a representation of P's that H, represented in manner m, has that property."[16]

This model of human agency, then, capturing Kant's general theory of acting on maxims, gives us a way of analyzing *Willkür*. The adoption of a maxim by an agent involves the conceptualizing of an end, the practi-

[15]*Critique of Practical Reason*, p. 17; Ak. Ed. 5:19.
[16]Ralf Meerbote, "Kant on the Nondeterminate Character of Human Actions," esp. pp. 140–141. See Donald Davidson, "Actions, Reasons, and Causes."

cal reasoning involved in providing practical rules that indicate alternative means to that end, and the selection of one such alternative. *Willkür*
is the capacity responsible for this selection, and hence it has often been
interpreted as the faculty of choice from among alternatives presented
by practical reason: (i) when an agent possessed of a rational *Willkür*
adopts a maxim with a view to the material of the maxim, that is, some
particular object of sensuous desire, the maxim remains a mere maxim
and the corresponding imperative is always hypothetical; (ii) when an
agent possessed of a rational *Willkür* adopts a maxim solely because of
its form of universality, however, the corresponding imperative is categorical and the maxim has the same content as an objective or practical
law of pure reason. In case (i), the rational agent may adopt a mere
maxim that happens to be in accordance with the moral law but is not
adopted for that reason and therefore has no genuine moral worth; or
the agent may adopt a mere maxim that is contrary to the moral law and
is therefore blameworthy. In case (ii), the rational agent may adopt a
maxim corresponding to an unconditional practical law *because* it is a
practical law of pure reason, and the actions resulting from the adoption
of this maxim have full moral worth.

The source of these objective or practical laws of reason is yet to be
identified, though. One of the crucial theses in the second *Critique* is
that pure reason can be practical, which is tantamount to the assertion
that there are unconditional practical laws (Ak. Ed. 5:19). But to retain a
sense of freedom for *Willkür* while simultaneously affirming its lawfulness, Kant believes that he needs to show that the will is the source of
its own laws, so that in being subject to them it also has the freedom of
autonomous legislation. Hence, Kant must find a way of creating a
connection between pure practical reason (as the only possible source of
the moral law) and *Willkür* as the human faculty of free will. This task is
accomplished by clarifying the concept of human will and by showing
that *Willkür* is only one employment of this faculty; there is another
function of human will, the lawgiving function of *Wille*, which if identified with pure practical reason could thereby bridge the gap between
the source of the moral law that is binding on the rational, human will
and the very will that it so binds. As Kant later writes, "we find *Wille* by
regression upon the conditions of *Willkür*."[17]

[17]*Metaphysics of Morals*, Ak. Ed. 6:221.

In his version of the distinction between *Wille* and *Willkür*, Paton takes this reading when he says of *Wille* that "will in this technical sense is concerned only with the law and seems to be equivalent to pure practical reason."[18] But if *Wille* must ultimately be identified with just *pure* practical reason, then Kant is rescued from the imputability problem only to be thrown into inconsistency concerning his views of law and lawlessness. As we have seen in Chapter 4, it is a consequence of the arguments in the *Critique of Pure Reason* that all the appearances in nature are necessarily interconnected, and that to admit the possibility of lawlessness in the phenomenal realm is to forfeit the unity of experience. Similarly, in the *Foundations* Kant argues that the concept of intelligible causality involved in freedom of the will also requires a type of lawfulness in the actions attributed to the spontaneous activity of the free will. This move on Kant's part is described as "curiously inadequate" even by one of his more forgiving commentators, Paton, and it is attacked even more severely by others.[19] The complaint is that Kant has obviously equivocated on the term 'causality', and if this were his only argument he would have simply left unsupported his claim regarding the lawfulness of the will. Paton gives a more plausible argument on Kant's behalf, though, by pointing out that "a lawless free will would be governed merely by chance and so could not properly be described as free."[20]

Let us suppose, then, that it is a requirement of all actions, including those that are the products of a free *Willkür*, that they conform to law. What sort of law remains, then, to stand as the law under which free actions are executed, but which is different from (although not automatically incompatible with) the natural laws under which causally determined actions are necessitated? According to our present hypothesis, in which we identified the lawgiving faculty of the human will with pure practical reason, we should turn to *Wille* for a law of pure practical reason. Now, Kant has repeatedly maintained that a law of pure practical reason is an unconditional practical law, and Henry Allison has argued that the only conceivable candidate for being a practical law is the moral law, since, as he rightly points out, Kant holds an implicit

---

[18]Paton, *The Categorical Imperative*, p. 213.

[19]Paton, *The Categorical Imperative*, p. 211; Henry E. Allison, "Morality and Freedom: Kant's Reciprocity Thesis," *Philosophical Review* 95 (1986): 393–425, esp. sec. 1.

[20]Paton, *The Categorical Imperative*, p. 211.

definition of a practical law as "an objectively and unconditionally valid practical principle."[21] Indeed, in the earlier passage quoted from the opening of the second *Critique* it appeared as if we have only two alternatives: either a practical principle is subjective and is a mere maxim or it is objective and is both a maxim and an objective or practical law.

The problem now arises in attempting to implement the *Wille/Willkür* distinction in the hopes of solving the imputability problem while simultaneously adhering to the conditions of the present hypothesis. By exercising *Willkür*, we have been told, a rational agent can either follow the law laid down by *Wille* or choose to follow the maxims of his desires. If in the exercise of *Willkür* the rational agent obeys the law of *Wille*, only morally good actions result. If, however, in the exercise of *Willkür* the rational agent chooses to follow the maxim of his desires, (i) this fact cannot simply be due to pathological necessitation connecting the agent's "choice" with antecedent natural conditions, for, if we are restricted to descriptions of a causal connection of this sort between the object of desire and the action undertaken to attain it, the *Willkür* is animal-like, or, worse yet, there is no *Willkür* at all but only mere behavior consequent on a stimulus; (ii) nor can the agent follow the maxim of his desires under the practical laws of *Wille*, since (under the present hypothesis) *Wille* has been identified strictly with pure practical reason, which only gives maxims that cannot be based on (nonrational) desires. The only explanation, then, would be that to follow his desires the agent would have to act without acting under any law at all—by mere chance—and this is impossible. Therefore, if one interprets *Wille* along with Paton as pure practical reason, and if one agrees with Allison that only moral laws are practical laws, then Kant is exempted from the imputability problem at the expense of the inconsistency of appealing to lawless acts of free will, an appeal Kant describes as an absurdity.[22]

What generates this second difficulty, which poses the dilemma of yielding either to the imputability problem or to the inconsistency of lawless activity, is the characterization of *Wille* exclusively as pure practical reason. On rather different grounds, Ralf Meerbote has proposed a

---

[21]Allison, "Morality and Freedom," p. 399. This implicit definition that Allison attributes to Kant is justified repeatedly in sections 1–8 of the second *Critique*. See also the "First Introduction" to the *Critique of Judgment*, p. 390n; Ak. Ed. 20:200–201.

[22]*Foundations of the Metaphysics of Morals*, p. 71; Ak. Ed. 4:446.

version of the *Wille/Willkür* distinction in which *Wille* is further subdi-
vided into pure practical reason and empirical practical reason, and in
which *Willkür* retains its status as a capacity to select from among alternatives offered by practical reason.[23] On the strength of the dilemma
just presented, then, we should be motivated to accept some such proposal in order to rescue Kant both from the imputability problem and
from the absurdity of lawlessness. As we discover, this division within
Wille itself is vital to a proper resolution to many of the objections raised
against Kant's ethical views. Unfortunately, however, in some of the
more important commentaries on these topics the dual nature of *Wille*
has been left unspecified or ambiguous.[24]

One possible reason for the failure to explore this suggestion is that
Kant's theory of human agency is not made explicit, and hence the dual
function of *Wille* is obscured by the sorts of phrases (which I indulged in
above) frequently used to describe the options available to an agent
possessed of a rational *Willkür* (e.g., that he is either free to follow the
directives of reason or free to follow those of the senses). To characterize
the choice in this manner, however, is to misrepresent the status of the
inclinations. The human *Willkür* is not pathologically determined, and
being *arbitrium liberum* it is *always* mediated by a maxim, that is, by a
propositional representation of a means-end relation that makes possible the activity of choosing, an activity essential to an agent possessed of
a rational *Willkür*. But the senses do not furnish the agent with maxims;
only reason has that power. Sensuous inclinations (which by definition
are nonpropositional) have no directives to give the *Willkür*, though a
human agent is subject to being affected (but not determined) by the
inclinations. If the human agent decides to act on the desires presented
to him through his sensuous nature, then *Wille* as empirical practical
reason is called on to discover various means to that end which has been
formulated by a being who, possessed of specific desires, is able to act in
the hopes of attaining the object of those desires according to a conception of causal laws relating means to ends.

---

[23]Ralf Meerbote, "*Wille* and *Willkür* in Kant's Theory of Action," in *Interpreting Kant*,
ed. Moltke S. Gram (Iowa City: University of Iowa Press, 1982), pp. 69–84.

[24]Beck, for example, in his *Commentary* says that *Wille* has been distinguished as
meaning practical reason (p. 202), but he also describes *Wille* strictly as pure practical
reason (p. 198).

With the present analysis of the human will, which distinguishes between *Wille* and *Willkür* as the legislative and executive functions of one and the same will, and with the separation of the former into pure practical reason and empirical practical reason, we are finally in a position to give an answer to the imputability problem which does not land Kant in the absurdity of lawless activity.

Allison convincingly demonstrates the equivalence of a practical law and a moral law, and since pure practical reason is the only faculty that can be responsible for the latter it is therefore the only faculty that can be responsible for the former. But to say that pure practical reason can be the source of practical laws is not to say that practical laws exhaust the sorts of laws practical reason can produce. Both pure practical reason and empirical practical reason can constrain an agent possessed of a rational *Willkür*, in the first case unconditionally and in the second case on the presupposition of some specific, antecedent desire. Thus, practical reason can issue commands to the rational agent, which Kant divides into categorical imperatives and problematical, assertorical, and technical imperatives.[25] This corresponds to his division between objective principles of morality and objective principles of skill and prudence. What is common to all imperatives, though, is that they involve an 'ought' that has the force of necessity with respect to an agent; if the 'ought' is categorical, it expresses a necessity regarding a rational being as such, and if the 'ought' is hypothetical, it expresses a necessity regarding a rational being who is also possessed of a particular, sensuous desire that she has conceptualized as an end [see A547/B575].

What is of interest here is the constraint empirical practical reason places on a rational agent with such a desire in the form, if one desires x, then one ought to do y.[26] Such a necessity could never be elevated into an unconditional practical law precisely because it is conditioned by the presence of a contingently possessed desire, and Kant never tires of reminding his reader that this will never do as the foundation of a moral law.[27] Nevertheless, necessary and universal connections are established through empirical practical reason between a type of rational

[25]*Foundations of the Metaphysics of Morals*, pp. 48–50; Ak. Ed. 4:413–415; "First Introduction" to the *Critique of Judgment*, p. 390; Ak. Ed. 20:191–201 and n. 9.

[26]*Foundations of the Metaphysics of Morals*, p. 33; Ak. Ed. 4:416.

[27]*Critique of Practical Reason*, pp. 17–28; Ak. Ed. 5:19–28.

agent (qualified by the possession of such a desire) and the means to
obtaining the object of that desire; that is, even though Kant terms this
product of empirical practical reason and desire a mere maxim, a coun-
sel of prudence, or a pragmatic law when distinguishing it from the
moral laws and rational desires of pure practical reason [A800/B828], it
is nevertheless a *law* of empirical practical reason, which is binding with
the force of necessity on any rational agent who attempts to attain the
object of her desire and which is universally valid for any rational agent
under the same conditions. So, when a *Willkür* is determined by the
content of the maxim and not by its form, the agent satisfies the relevant
condition; namely, she may then be regarded as a particular type of
rational agent (qualified by the possession of a specific desire), and the
resulting action is governed under a law of *empirical* practical reason that
prescribes the necessary means to that end.

It would have been convenient to characterize a law of pure practical
reason as an unconditional practical law and a law of empirical practical
reason as a conditional practical law. Kant is, however, adamant
throughout the opening sections of the Analytic of the second *Critique* in
his position that only laws that can determine the will irrespective on
any nonrational desires can be practical laws. Kant here clearly wants to
reserve the term 'practical law' for a law given by pure practical reason,
from which issues a categorical imperative giving the information for
the construction of a maxim, which can then be adopted by the rational
agent through *Willkür* and which can have the same content as a moral
law. His frequent protestations against thinking that what I have here
characterized as a law of empirical practical reason could ever be a
practical law might even seem to threaten or to refute outright the suggestion that the prescriptions of empirical practical reason can be considered to be any sort of laws at all. But all these protestations serve to
show is that Allison is right in believing Kant to hold an implicit definition of a practical law as "an objectively and unconditionally valid practical principle." In other words, Kant takes 'practical law', 'unconditional
practical law', and 'moral law' all to be synonymous. There is still the
question of the status of the products of empirical practical reason,
which cannot be established by appealing to the status of the products
of pure practical reason.

Either we admit, then, that empirical practical reason furnishes laws that are formulated with an 'ought' and express necessary means to achieving some end a rational agent takes as an object of desire (and thus attempts to attain in accordance with a conception of natural laws), or we are faced with the dilemma that maintains Kant is stuck with either the imputability problem or the absurdity of lawless activity. Clearly, then, empirical practical reason furnishes laws, on the strength of which the free, heteronomous action of a rational agent is termed lawful.[28]

So, when a rational agent follows the law given by pure practical reason, her actions have moral worth. On the other hand, when the rational agent follows a law that has been formulated by empirical practical reason with a view to attaining some object of desire conflicting with the moral law, her actions fail to have moral worth. In either case, the agent chooses good or evil freely and, since *Wille* and *Willkür* are the functions of one and the same will, the agent is both author and executor of her own laws.

Four Conceptions of Freedom

The imputability problem originally arises out of a confused understanding of the propositions "a free will and a will under moral laws are identical," and "freedom and unconditional practical law reciprocally imply each other."[29] To generate the imputability problem, a critic must show that these versions of the reciprocity thesis license an inference from the freedom of an action to its moral goodness. To claim, however, that such an inference is justified on the basis of the reciprocity thesis is to jumble together some very distinct conceptions of freedom. Equivocation of the term 'freedom' is an ever-present danger for both Kant and his commentators due to the great number of descriptions Kant lavishes on his own positions. In the remainder of this chapter, I attempt to

---

[28]Although several commentators make a passing but somewhat undeveloped reference to the products of empirical practical reason as laws, one person who makes explicit the dual lawgiving function of *Wille* is Bernard Carnois in *The Coherence of Kant's Theory of Freedom*, trans. David Booth (Chicago: University of Chicago Press, 1987), pp. 25–27.

[29]*Foundations of the Metaphysics of Morals*, p. 72; Ak. Ed. 4:447. *Critique of Practical Reason*, p. 29; Ak. Ed. 5:29.

clarify Kant's position by reading his theory of the freedom of the will in light of the thesis that appears in the *Foundations* and the second *Critique* concerning the reciprocity of freedom and morality. Although his comments on freedom of the will are scattered here and there, the fifth and sixth sections of the *Critique of Practical Reason* contain a crucial discussion in which Kant draws on all the relevant conceptions of freedom, including those put forth in the Dialectic of the first *Critique* as well as those he elaborates in the later ethical writings. This discussion, then, provides a testing ground for my reading of Kant's theory of freedom.

Beck has written that the second *Critique* is a bridge where two different conceptions of freedom of the will must meet. The first *Critique* contains the conception of freedom of the will as spontaneity, and the *Foundations* introduces the conception of freedom of the will as autonomy. "Some of the difficulties in interpreting the *Critique* become more manageable," Beck writes, "when we realize that its central doctrine of freedom of the will involves two different concepts of freedom and two different concepts of the will."[30] Whereas Beck is right to note that there are two different conceptions (or employments) of one and the same will, as was shown in the preceding section, one can find at least four different conceptions of freedom attaching to these different employments of the will.

Freedom as Spontaneity (Transcendental Freedom) and Freedom as Independence (Practical Freedom)

The first two conceptions of freedom are contained in the Dialectic of the first *Critique*. In his attack on rational cosmology in the Antinomies of Pure Reason Kant claims that, unless we distinguish between things in themselves and appearances, reason falls into contradiction with itself by producing incompatible theses. One such pair of theses, their proofs, and their commentary compose the Third Antinomy, in which Kant contrasts what he calls the causality of transcendental freedom with causality in accordance with the laws of nature. As we have seen in Chapter 2, in his resolution to that antinomy Kant argues that, whereas only one thesis is knowable (inasmuch as it is a presupposition of empir-

---

[30]Beck, *Commentary*, pp. 176–177.

ical knowledge in general), both may be true; in other words, the result of the Second Analogy does not entail the rejection of transcendental freedom. Kant makes the modest claim of the simultaneous thinkability or compatibility of these two types of causality and does not attempt to argue for the actuality of transcendental freedom. That latter task is left to the second *Critique*, where "with the pure practical faculty of reason, the reality of transcendental freedom is also confirmed."[31]

This transcendental freedom or causality of reason, Kant explains, is "an *absolute spontaneity* of the cause, whereby a series of appearances, which proceeds in accordance with laws of nature, begins *of itself*" [A446/B474]. And again, he describes it as "a special kind of causality in accordance with which the events in the world could have come about, namely, a power of absolutely beginning a state, and therefore also of absolutely beginning a series of consequences of that state" [A445/B473].

Such talk should no longer alarm us. As we saw in the discussion of Kant's compatibilism in Chapter 2, Kant does adhere to a theory of absolute beginnings due to intelligible causality, but it is a theory which, when properly interpreted, does not threaten or compete with his theory of the universality of subordinate or relative beginnings due to empirical causality. This twofold theory of causality is not a last-minute rescue attempt, launched in the later ethical works, in order to save Kant's moral theory; rather, it is clearly at work in the first *Critique*, and not merely in its Dialectic but also in its Analytic. For instance, Kant has already warned us in the Second Analogy itself that, if he should later speak of regarding appearances as the effect of some merely thinkable "foreign cause," his "terms would then carry with them quite other meanings, and would not apply to appearances as possible objects of experience" [A206/B252]. Thus, even if this "special kind of causality" is somehow connected to effects that are appearances in the world, whatever meanings or descriptions are appropriate to the "special causes" grouped under this kind are quite different from the meanings or descriptions appropriate to the causes that fall under the type of causality Kant explicates in the Second Analogy. And since those differences are such as to prevent the former from being regarded as possible objects of

---

[31]*Critique of Practical Reason*, p. 3; Ak. Ed. 5:3.

experience (insofar as they are considered under one of the descriptions in question), we can anticipate that the content of those descriptions will be nontemporal and nonspatial, thus rendering the objects as considered under those descriptions unfit for possible experience in virtue of violating the conditions of possibility presented in the Postulates of Empirical Thought [A218/B265].

Kant gives us a hint about what he means by this special kind of causality when he writes, "that our reason has causality, or that we at least represent it to ourselves as having causality, is evident from the *imperatives* which in matters of conduct we impose as rules upon our active power" [A547/B575]. As was noted before in the discussion of Kant's theory of human agency, what is significant about these imperatives is that they always contain an 'ought' (a term that has no meaning in nature and no place in empirical descriptions) and that they are furnished through the activity of practical reason. Thus, this special kind of causality which is equated with absolute spontaneity and with our first conception of freedom is a causality of reason through which we choose and act (or at least represent ourselves as choosing and acting) on some maxim or law that has been constructed through empirical or pure practical reason. And once again this freedom as spontaneity bears a striking resemblance to Kant's account of spontaneity in his precritical writings, as actions proceeding from internal determination or as actions elicited "through motives of the intellect applied to the will."

Such choosing and execution of that choice is the privilege of will in its employment as *Willkür*. A rational agent employing *Willkür* is free in the transcendental sense; he employs a special kind of causality of reason which requires the propositional representation of means-end connections, formulated with an 'ought', furnished by practical reason, on the basis of which he can adopt a maxim and execute the action that falls under that maxim.

This account is not yet complete, however, since in his distinction between animal and human *Willkür* Kant says something quite different about the freedom of *Willkür*: "Freedom in the practical sense is the will's independence of coercion through sensuous impulses" [A534/B562], that is, independence from pathological necessitation, not independence from determination through practical reason. Moreover, freedom in the practical sense is different from freedom in the transcendental sense, but it is closely connected with it. Kant writes that "the practical concept of freedom is based on this transcendental idea [of freedom]" [A533/B561], and again, that "the denial of transcendental freedom must, therefore, involve the elimination of all practical freedom" [A534/B562]. Although he does not, he might well have added that the denial of practical freedom also involves the elimination of transcendental freedom. In other words, the two senses of freedom belonging to *Willkür* mutually imply each other:

(i) Assume an agent possesses transcendental freedom. Then, that agent can select from among maxims presented by practical reason, and consequently his *Willkür* can be determined by practical reason. But this is to deny that the agent is pathologically necessitated, always determined merely by ideas of sense and imagination. And thus it is to affirm practical freedom. Alternatively, "as will is a kind of causality of living beings so far as they are rational [i.e., as the will is free in a transcendental sense], freedom would be that property of this causality by which it can be effective independent of foreign causes determining it" [i.e., the will is also free in a practical sense.][32]

(ii) Assume an agent possesses practical freedom. Then, since "practical freedom presupposes that although something has not happened, it *ought* to have happened" (i.e., since it presupposes the determinability of an agent by practical reason) [A534/B562], it also requires transcendental freedom, the activity of which prompts the agent to construct propositions containing an 'ought' in order to provide the maxims and laws necessary for human agency. Or, more simply, without transcendental freedom an agent with practical freedom would be lawless in his actions, which is absurd.

As is well known, Kant believes that one can claim to possess practical freedom.[33] And if practical freedom requires transcendental freedom, as I have just argued, it would seem that one could also be justified in claiming to possess transcendental freedom. This would, however, apparently conflict with Kant's reluctance to suggest that a demonstration that we possess transcendental freedom is available. As Karl Ameriks

[32]*Foundations of the Metaphysics of Morals*, p. 63; Ak. Ed. 4:446.
[33]*Vorlesungen über Metaphysik*, Ak. Ed. 28:255.

has argued, though, Kant's remarks against proofs of transcendental freedom need not be taken in the sense that we cannot have grounds for claiming to possess such freedom. Rather, Kant means that we cannot have a theoretical or speculative proof of transcendental freedom which would reveal *how* such freedom is possible. Such a proof would be clothed in the language of natural causality, and that language is not applicable in this context.[34] Furthermore, recognizing that practical freedom requires transcendental freedom gives us a way to make sense of Kant's often repeated but puzzling remark that practical freedom is sufficient for the needs of morality;[35] practical freedom is sufficient for transcendental freedom, which *combination* is sufficient for the needs of morality. Moreover, the fact that the exercise of transcendental and practical freedom still remains token-token identical to a phenomenal event should not cast doubt on the claim that these senses of freedom are sufficient for the needs of morality either, as we saw in the last section of Chapter 3.

The independence of practical freedom is a negative characterization of freedom of the will, and this "freedom from" nature can be identified with the negative conception of the freedom of *Willkür*. By contrast, Kant writes, "this freedom ought not, therefore, to be conceived only negatively as independence of empirical conditions. The faculty of reason, so regarded, would cease to be a cause of appearances. It must also be described in positive terms, as the power of originating a series of events" [A553–554/B581–582]. Hence, this "freedom to" spontaneously act can be identified with the positive conception of the freedom of *Willkür*.

We now have our first two conceptions of freedom. The first conception admits of the following descriptions: a causality of reason; the transcendental idea of freedom; spontaneity; "freedom to"; the positive conception of the freedom of *Willkür*; and since Kant's discussion takes place in his critique of rational cosmology, he also calls this the cosmological idea of freedom. Hereafter, let this conception of freedom be abbreviated WK+. Our second conception admits of the following de-

---

[34]Karl Ameriks, "Kant's Deduction of Freedom and Morality," *Journal of the History of Philosophy* 19 (1981): 53–79.

[35]For example, in *Vorlesungen über Metaphysik*, Ak. Ed. 28:267, 269.

scriptions: the practical idea of freedom; independence; the comparative idea of freedom; "freedom from"; and the negative conception of the freedom of *Willkür*. Hereafter, let this conception of freedom be abbreviated WK−. As was just demonstrated, then, an agent possesses WK+ if an only if he possesses WK−; I refer to this demonstration of mutual interdependence as Lemma I.

Freedom as Autonomy and Freedom as Heteronomy

Before I investigate the freedom attaching to the will in its employment as *Wille*, an initial objection to discussing the freedom of *Wille* at all can be set aside: in the *Metaphysics of Morals* Kant claims that only *Willkür* can be called free; *Wille* is neither free nor not free, because it does not act.[36] One should not conclude from this passage that *Wille* has no proper sense of freedom but rather that, whatever sense of freedom does belong to *Wille*, it does not involve action in the sense of WK+ or WK−. Even this is a little misleading, since *Wille* is the lawgiving faculty, which even if not an action of executing those laws is, in a sense, an action of presenting the laws to *Willkür*.

Freedom of the will in the moral sense of *autonomy* is the freedom of pure practical reason, and hence of will in one aspect of its employment as *Wille*. Kant's theory of autonomy in his ethics has been heralded as his Rousseauean Revolution and compared favorably with the Copernican Revolution which characterizes his epistemology.[37] Following the political insight he borrowed from Rousseau, namely, that actions that are lawful are genuinely free only when the laws under which they are executed are of one's own making, Kant writes, "Autonomy of the will is that property of it by which it is a law to itself independent of any property of the objects of its volition."[38] So, autonomy of the will is *Wille* as pure practical reason giving a law to an agent in which no object of sensuous desire is presupposed in the maxim delivered to *Willkür*. Kant

---

[36]*Metaphysics of Morals*, Ak. Ed. 6:226.

[37]The Rousseauean Revolution is Kant's developing of the concept of a free will to which he attached the political metaphor of autonomy based on his readings of Rousseau; see Beck, *Commentary*, pp. 197, 200. Kant also has a notion of epistemic autonomy, which I return to later in the discussion.

[38]*Foundations of the Metaphysics of Morals*, p. 57; Ak. Ed. 4:440; see also 4:447.

declares the autonomy of the will "the sole principle of all moral laws" and maintains that "this intrinsic legislation of pure and thus practical reason is freedom in the positive sense."[39] This freedom to give the moral law, which is here called by Kant the positive conception of freedom of the will, is certainly not identical with our other positive conception of freedom, WK+, since the freedom of *Wille* in its pure employment is the freedom of moral lawgiving, not the freedom of acting on maxims. Hereafter, let this positive conception of the freedom of *Wille* be referred to as the autonomy of *Wille*, abbreviated W_a.

Freedom of the will in the sense of *heteronomy* is the freedom of empirical practical reason, and hence, once again, of will in another aspect of its employment as *Wille*. Whereas Kant's theory of freedom as autonomy has been spotlighted, his theory of freedom as heteronomy has been ignored and even argued against by those who are attempting to explain Kant's views on freedom, both of which strategies lead to the imputability problem. Some commentators have suggested that acting heteronomously is to be understood as self-abnegation or as a failure to act on laws provided by *Wille*.[40] As I argued in the preceding section, however, *Wille* furnishes propositions that may determine the *Willkür* not only with moral laws in its role as pure practical reason but also with maxims in its role as empirical practical reason. Heteronomy of the will obtains when the will "seeks the law in the property of any of its objects," that is, when "the will does not give itself the law, but the object through its relation to the will gives the law to it."[41] So, heteronomy of the will is a rational agent's use of *Wille* as empirical practical reason to give directions for *Willkür* concerning means-end relations, but always under the presupposition of a contingently held or sensuously based desire for the end in question. Consequently, along with autonomous spontaneity of action we have a conception of heteronomous spontaneity of action, which is the proper characterization of the rational agen-

---

[39]*Critique of Practical Reason*, p. 33; Ak. Ed. 5:33.

[40]For examples and discussion of this issue, see Silber, "The Ethical Significance of Kant's *Religion*," p. xc; Allison, "Morality and Freedom," pp. 418–423; Wood, "Kant's Compatibilism," pp. 76–83; and Meerbote, "Kant on the Nondeterminate Character of Human Actions," pp. 143–146.

[41]*Foundations of the Metaphysics of Morals*, p. 58; Ak. Ed. 4:441; see also 4:444 for the same point.

cy of a being who acts on the maxims of empirical practical reason. As Kant says, "it is heteronomy because the will does not give itself the law but only directions for a reasonable obedience to pathological laws."[42]

This guidance of empirical practical reason, given in the form of an imperative stating means-end relations, is exactly what was called a law of empirical practical reason in the preceding section. This lawgiving activity of *Wille* is clearly not autonomy, for here a rational agent is working with desires for specific ends which are pathological; and since *Wille* as a general cognitive faculty discovers and does not create the means to the object of desire and does not dictate what the objects of (nonrational) desire shall be, *Wille* is not, properly speaking, the sole source of its empirical practical laws. Nevertheless, this activity of furnishing an agent possessed of a rational *Willkür* with the necessary information about the empirical laws in accordance with which the object of desire can be attained is a function of *Wille* that is not identical to the giving of the moral law. Accordingly, it deserves its own sense of freedom of the will. So, hereafter let this freedom of *Wille* to give empirical practical law be referred to as the heteronomy of *Wille*, abbreviated W_h.

Unfortunately, there is not a lemma that would state that an agent possesses freedom in the sense of W_a if and only if she possesses freedom in the sense of W_h. Indeed, what the second *Critique* is designed to show is that pure reason can be practical, and that *Wille* as pure practical reason does have W_a freedom as well as having W_h freedom in its role as empirical practical reason. What is worth proving, though, is that the freedom of WK+ and WK− presupposes the freedom of *Wille* in at least one of its two senses.[43] This is obvious since, as we have seen, all actions of an agent possessed of a rational *Willkür* must be executed under the laws of freedom, and since it is only through *Wille* (which provides the necessity carried in the 'ought' in the maxims it gives to *Willkür*) that the actions of WK+ can be lawful. On the strength of Lemma I, then, since WK+ presupposes the freedom of *Wille* in at least one of its two senses, so does WK−. In the other direction, either sense of freedom belonging to *Wille* presupposes WK+ and WK−. This is so,

---

[42]*Critique of Practical Reason*, p. 34; Ak. Ed. 5:33.

[43]The problem of imputability arises when it is erroneously supposed that WK+ entails and is entailed by W_a.

because if one ought to do something, one can, and both W_a and W_h give a command to an agent possessed of a rational *Willkür* in the form of an 'ought'. This is a command that could be acted on only if WK+ obtained, and the agent could be determined by reason in this way only if WK- obtained. Let it stand as Lemma II, then, that an agent possesses (W_a or W_h) if and only if she possesses (WK+ and WK−).

To summarize, four conceptions of freedom have been formulated and two lemmata proved:

WK+   the absolute *spontaneity* of an agent possessed of a rational *Willkür* in adopting a maxim and in executing the action that falls under that maxim. Also called transcendental freedom.

WK−   the *independence* of an agent possessed of a rational *Willkür* from pathological necessitation in his choices of actions and in his actions based on those choices. Also called practical freedom.

W_a the ability of a rational agent to give the moral law through *Wille*. Also called *autonomy* of the will.

W_h the ability of a rational agent to give empirical practical law through *Wille*. Also called *heteronomy* of the will

Lemma I   WK+ if and only if WK−.

Lemma II   (W_a or W_h) if and only if (WK+ and WK−).

Given the analysis of freedom presented above, to wring the imputability problem out of the reciprocity of freedom and morality one must show that every instance of WK+ is a case of acting on a product of W_a, and this is just what cannot be demonstrated; rather, it is a case of acting on a product of either W_a or W_h.

With this analysis of Kant's four conceptions of freedom of the will, we may now turn to the crucial reciprocity thesis itself as a testing ground for my reading of Kant's theory of freedom. Moreover, if successful, we will finally eliminate the imputability problem and simultaneously illuminate an important feature of Kantian ethics.

Kant's Reciprocity Thesis and Theory of Free Will

Kant's doctrine of the reciprocity of freedom and morality is at the very heart of his ethics. The very first footnote in the second *Critique* is a reminder to the reader of what Kant intends by claiming that these two concepts are reciprocal: "Though freedom is certainly the *ratio essendi* of the moral law, the latter is the *ratio cognoscendi* of freedom."[44] This frequently quoted note serves to reiterate a familiar point: what is first in the order of being is not always first in the order of knowledge. Kant first exhibits this relation and then spends a good deal of the second *Critique* giving its explanation. There is a considerable controversy over Kant's strategy in justifying this relation between freedom and morality. It is unclear whether he attempts to produce a deduction of morality in the second *Critique*, or if he did so in the *Foundations*, and thus whether he changes his mind, not simply about the necessity but about the very possibility of providing such a deduction within his critical period.[45] However, after positing the very obscure "fact of reason" that somehow breaks into the potentially vicious circle of reciprocal concepts by providing an independent warrant for the moral law, he deduces from it the concept of freedom. The preeminence of this step is announced in the Preface, where Kant writes, "The concept of freedom, in so far as its reality is proved by an apodictic law of practical reason, is the keystone of the whole architecture of the system of pure reason and even of speculative reason."[46] So, Kant boldly professes to rest the architecture of his system of reason on the reciprocity of freedom and morality, and therefore an investigation of exactly what is being reciprocally related is certainly in order.

WK+, WK−, W_a, and W_h are four different conceptions of freedom, belonging to two different employments of one and the same will, and therefore these are four different kinds (or aspects) of freedom had by a single human faculty of will. To deny this would be to forfeit the results of the Rousseauean Revolution in the discovery of autonomy; if they were not two employments of the same will, then an agent possessed of a rational *Willkür* would not be self-governed when he followed the moral law, and thus in an important sense the human agent would not be genuinely free in his moral actions. Clearly, Kant recognizes this even

---

[44]*Critique of Practical Reason*, p. 4; Ak. Ed. 5:4.

[45]For a discussion that also provides an overview of the different positions on this issue, see Ameriks, "Kant's Deduction of Freedom and Morality," esp. sec. 6; also see Henry Allison's *Kant's Theory of Freedom*, pt. 3.

[46]*Critique of Practical Reason*, p. 3; Ak. Ed. 5:3.

if he does not make it explicit, for he moves from one conception of freedom belonging to this will to another in his arguments in sections 5 and 6 of the second *Critique*, and if he is not to be accused of a gross equivocation on 'freedom' one must note his strategy in the two problems he poses.[47]

Section 5, Problem I

"Granted that the mere legislative form of maxims is the sole sufficient determining ground of a will, find the character of the will which is determinable by it alone."[48] Kant begins by granting a condition that at first appears contrary to fact: cannot an agent, utilizing WK+, adopt maxims from the products of *Wille* not only as W_a but also as W_h? The answer is that she can, but then the legislative form of the maxim would not be the sole sufficient determining ground of *Willkür*; *Wille* as W_h can give an empirical practical law that can determine *Willkür*, but it is not sufficient to do so itself; rather, a sensuously based desire is required as an additional necessary condition for this determination. Kant asks the reader to consider what follows if one grants a case in which *Willkür* is determinable by the legislative form of maxims alone, that is, by the product of *Wille* as W_a alone.

Now the question is posed, what is the character of a will in which *Willkür* as WK+ is determinable by the product of *Wille* as W_a alone? Merely to answer that it is free would be doubly trivial. Simply by repeating the conditions in the statement of the problem we know that it is free twice over, namely, in the senses of WK+ and W_a. Rather, Kant argues to another sense of freedom in his solution of Problem I: "Now,

[47]Throughout sections 5 and 6, Kant uses *Wille* as his only reference to the will, whereas the context clearly demands *Willkür* repeatedly, as is shown below. Unfortunately, Kant regularly practices a dismaying sort of consistency: he is consistent in misusing his own terminology. There are many instances of that here. He sometimes writes *Wille* when he is referring to the spontaneous actions of a free will (*Willkür*), and he sometimes writes *Willkür* when he is referring to the will which is lawgiving (*Wille*). But this does not show that he did not have a distinction between types of freedom of the will when writing the second *Critique*, any more than his occasional switch of the terms 'law' and 'imperative' or 'concept' and 'intuition' shows that he did not distinguish between those conceptions.

[48]*Critique of Practical Reason*, p. 28; Ak. Ed. 5:28.

as no determining ground of the will except the universal legislative form can serve as a law for it, such a will must be conceived as wholly independent of the natural law of appearances in their mutual relations, *i.e.*, the law of causality. Such independence is called *freedom* in the strictest, *i.e.*, transcendental sense."[49] With his emphasis on independence, what Kant means is clear, but he misspeaks here. He says in the first *Critique* that "the transcendental idea [of freedom] stands *only* for the absolute spontaneity of an action, as the proper ground of its imputability" [A448/B476, emphasis added]. Since he distinguishes sharply between spontaneity and independence, he should not say, as he does here, that independence (or freedom in the strictest sense) is transcendental freedom. On the strength of our Lemma I, however, he could correctly say that it *requires* transcendental freedom. So, Kant's conclusion that, "therefore, a will to which only the legislative form of the maxim can serve as a law is a free will," can be read in the following way: if *Willkür* as WK+ is determinable by the product of *Wille* as W_a alone, then *Willkür* must also have freedom in the sense of WK−.

Section 6, Problem II

"Granted that a will is free, find the law which alone is competent to determine it necessarily."[50] It is not apparent what is being granted here, and one must begin reading the solution to the problem before it becomes clear just which sense of freedom of the will has been presupposed. When calling on what has been granted in the statement of the problem, Kant clarifies which sense of freedom is at issue by writing, "a free will must be independent of all empirical conditions (*i.e.*, those belonging to the world of sense) and yet be determinable."[51] This is first a reference to WK− freedom and then to WK+ freedom, since it is through the former that an agent possessed of a rational *Willkür* is free from pathological necessitation and through the latter that the agent is determinable. So, granted that a will is free in the sense of WK− and WK+, the question arises, what is the character of the law that alone is competent to determine it necessarily?

[49]*Critique of Practical Reason*, p. 28; Ak. Ed. 5:29.
[50]*Critique of Practical Reason*, p. 28; Ak. Ed. 5:29.
[51]*Critique of Practical Reason*, p. 28; Ak. Ed. 5:29.

From Lemma II we know that the alternatives from which to answer are provided by the products of *Wille* either as W_a or as W_h. If Problem II had read, "Granted that a will is free, find the law which is competent to determine it," one would be unable to provide anything but a disjunction; both the laws of pure practical reason and the laws of empirical practical reason are competent to determine *Willkür*. As in the statement of Problem I, however, the statement of Problem II gives conditions through which we may eliminate one of the disjuncts, since the problem specifies that the law *alone* must be competent to determine it *necessarily*. The laws of empirical practical reason will fail on two counts: they do not determine *Willkür* completely by themselves, but rather only on the presupposition of a certain type of antecedent desire, and they do not determine an agent's *Willkür* necessarily, since the individual agent can relinquish the relevant desire and thus release himself from the force of the 'ought' in the imperative given through the law. Kant's argument in the solution to Problem II can be reconstructed as follows. Either the form or the material of a law is the determining ground of the will. But a free will is WK− and WK+ and thus cannot be (necessarily) determined by the material of the law, that is, cannot be pathologically necessitated. So, if it is determined necessarily, the only remaining alternative is that it be determined by the form of the law. Hence, Kant's conclusion that, "therefore, the legislative form, in so far as it is contained in the maxim, is the only thing which can [necessarily][52] constitute a determining ground of the [free] will," can be read as follows: if *Willkür* is free in the sense of WK+ and WK−, only the legislative form of a law can necessarily constitute a determining ground of *Willkür*. Theorem III in the second *Critique* shows the equivalence of unconditional practical laws and laws that contain the determining grounds of the will merely because of their form.[53] Since we also know that only *Wille* as W_a gives unconditional practical laws, that is, moral laws, the conclusion to Problem II is equivalent to the claim that only *Wille* as the source of moral

[52]I insert "necessarily" here because the statement of the problem includes it, and thus it is demanded in the solution to the problem.

[53]*Critique of Practical Reason*, p. 26; Ak. Ed. 5:27. "If a rational being can think of its maxims as practical universal laws, he can do so only by considering them as principles which contain the determining grounds of the will because of their form and not because of their matter."

laws (as W_a), can necessarily determine *Willkür* that has freedom in the senses of WK+ and WK−.

Consequently, the full reading of the reciprocity thesis has the following structure:

Problem I   If a will has freedom in the sense of WK+, and if it is sufficiently determinable by W_a alone, then the will also has freedom in the sense of WK−.

Problem II If a will has freedom in the sense of WK+ and WK−, and if it is determined necessarily, then the will is determined by W_a alone.

One will note that all four conceptions of freedom I have attributed to Kant have essential roles in the argument that justifies his reciprocity thesis: three conceptions play a direct role (W_a, WK+, and WK−) and one conception plays an indirect role (W_h). The qualification "determined necessarily" has the obvious purpose of ruling out of consideration W_h in order to concentrate on the complex relation of W_a to WK+ and WK−. Without separating and making clear each of these conceptions of freedom of the will, the reciprocity thesis would be either trivial or nonsensical, and thus we may conclude that the present reading of Kant's theory of the freedom of the will has passed this test of its accuracy.

It is crucial to note that "sufficiently determinable by W_a" and "necessarily determined by W_a" mean only that through *Wille* as pure practical reason a rational agent can give a universal law that is binding necessarily and unconditionally on *Willkür*. It does not mean that an agent possessed of a rational *Willkür* is restricted in her choice to adopt, among all the maxims given through *Wille*, this one corresponding to the moral law.

Whereas the principles of deontic logic resemble those of modal logic, with "it is obligatory that" replacing "it is necessary that" and "it is permissible that" replacing "it is possible that," some analogous theorems certainly do not hold in both systems. Common modal inferences are from the necessity of x to the actuality of x, from the actuality of x to the possibility of x, and thus from the necessity of x to the possibility of x. In deontic logic, however, the inferences from the obligatoriness of x

to the actuality of x and from the actuality of x to the permissibility of x are both fallacious, although the one from the obligatoriness of x to the permissibility of x is acceptable. Now, for Kant, physics is the science of the laws of nature and their objects, and ethics is the science of the laws of freedom and their objects; the first is a study of what does happen and the second of what ought to happen.[54] Just as there is a disanalogy in the types of necessity attaching to the laws at work in each science, so too there is an important difference in the consequences generated by each type of law. Whereas the application of a law of nature generates a declarative statement, a law of freedom generates a normative statement; since there is no entailment between the two, what ought to happen often does not happen, and often what does happen ought not happen.

Hence, when a rational agent is bound by the moral law, this means that he ought to perform the relevant action, but it does not follow that he will perform that action, "for though we can suppose that men as rational beings have a pure will, since they are affected by wants and sensuous motives we cannot suppose them to have a holy will, a will incapable of any maxims which conflict with the moral law."[55] Kant here draws attention to the fact that an agent who is possessed of a rational *Willkür* is capable of acting on maxims that conflict with the moral law, and therefore that the agent can look to *Wille* in both its lawgiving functions for a maxim of action. Even though the moral law is binding on the rational agent such that no desire (or lack of desire) could ever alter the necessity with which the imperative is given to him, nevertheless what is objectively necessary is subjectively contingent for *Willkür*,[56] and even in the face of the moral law an agent possessed of a rational *Willkür* can turn to his desires and empirical practical reason for a maxim suited to their attainment.

Not until the *Religion within the Limits of Reason Alone* does Kant give a fuller account of the possibility of moral failure. Moral evil, according to Kant, consists not merely in the performance of actions contrary to law but in the presence of evil maxims through which one performs those

---

[54]*Foundations of the Metaphysics of Morals*, pp. 3–4; Ak. Ed. 4:387–388.

[55]*Critique of Practical Reason*, p. 32; Ak. Ed. 5:32.

[56]*Critique of Practical Reason*; Ak. Ed. 5:25. See also *Foundations of the Metaphysics of Morals*, p. 48; Ak. Ed. 4:412–413.

actions. So, whereas unlawful conduct may be the evidence leading us to believe that an agent has an evil will, it is rather the formal ground of such actions, the supreme maxim adopted by the agent, that is responsible for her will's being evil.[57] Moral failure occurs when *Willkür* is determined in such a way as to conflict with the moral law, and Kant distinguishes three types of such failure: (i) human frailty: one incorporates the law into her maxim, but the sensuous incentives prove too strong on a given occasion, and the agent is determined by empirical practical reason in her attempt to obtain the object of those desires, even against her moral ends and her rational desires; (ii) human impurity: one incorporates the law into her maxim, but the rational desires are insufficient to motivate her, and even though she follows the letter of the law she requires sensuous inclinations to perform the correct actions (e.g., the person who tells the truth, not because lying is wrong but to enhance her reputation); (iii) human wickedness or perversity: one reverses the priority of the incentives available to her. In other words, she makes it her supreme maxim to let nonmoral incentives override moral incentives when they are in conflict, and in such perversity Kant locates human evil.[58] One should note that in each type of case the agent acts freely, since the agent is determined by empirical practical reason and thus acts with heteronomous spontaneity. It is interesting to note that Kant denies that moral failure ever occurs because an agent repudiates the law or renounces obedience to it. No matter what she does, moral incentives are present in her ever as much as sensuous inclinations, such that if either type of incentive were missing the remaining one would be wholly sufficient to determine her will. But humans are neither gods with a holy will (always determined by the law) nor animals with an *arbitrium brutum* (always determined by the senses). In us, that type of moral failure which is also moral evil is due to the preplanned subordination of one type of incentive to the other, such that the condition of one's acting morally is that such action not conflict with one's incentive of self-love and one's corresponding sensuous inclinations.[59]

Earlier I cited Paton as noting that Kant drew this distinction between being under moral laws and being obedient to moral laws, and I men-

[57]*Religion within the Limits of Reason Alone*, pp. 16, 26; Ak. Ed. 6:20, 31.
[58]*Religion within the Limits of Reason Alone*, pp. 24–25; Ak. Ed. 6:29–30.
[59]*Religion within the Limits of Reason Alone*, pp. 31–32; Ak. Ed. 6:36.

tioned that Paton did not argue that Kant was entitled to make this distinction. This analysis can serve as a justification for drawing that distinction. In section 5 we are told that if a will is under moral laws (if an agent with transcendental freedom is determinable by pure practical reason), then that will is free also in the practical sense; and in section 6 we are told that, if a will is free in both the transcendental and the practical sense (and if it is determined necessarily), then it is under moral laws. It will be determined necessarily if pure reason can be practical, a condition Kant guarantees in the corollary to section 7 in the second *Critique* [Ak. Ed. 5:31–32].

Hence, Kant concludes in the first sentence of his Remark on section 6, "thus freedom [of the will in the transcendental and the practical sense] and [being a will under] unconditional practical law reciprocally imply each other."[60] It is worth noting that this looks remarkably similar to its counterpart from the *Foundations*: "A free will and a will under moral laws are identical."

Another problem related to the reciprocity thesis remains to be addressed. In his discussion of freedom as autonomy, Kant rather one-sidedly concentrates on pure practical reason in the legislation of moral principles. The problem is in how we are to fit in the freedom to legislate the categorial principles of cognition; what is the status of pure theoretical reason in the legislation of categorial principles? For Kant's answer we may turn to his general division in philosophy between formal and material philosophy, and with regard to the latter between its sub-species, as distinguished by their use of either theoretical reason or practical reason.[61] One and the same faculty of reason is at issue, and the distinction between theoretical and practical reason is found in the distinction between the objects and the laws governing those objects in the fields of physics and ethics. According to Kant, each science has its pure and its empirical part. In the case of physics, an agent utilizing pure theoretical reason autonomously legislates the categorial principles to nature, that is, provides an a priori plan for his investigation of nature to which all synthetic, a posteriori discoveries in nature are subject; utilizing empirical theoretical reason, then, one engages in science in

---

[60]*Critique of Practical Reason*, p. 29; Ak. Ed. 5:29.
[61]*Foundations of the Metaphysics of Morals*, pp. 3–4; Ak. Ed. 4:387–388.

general and attempts to discover the particular, empirical laws of nature. In the case of ethics, an agent utilizing pure practical reason autonomously legislates the moral principles and utilizing empirical practical reason engages in nonmoral but rational activity. Although the dual nature of such legislation receives extended treatment primarily in the *Critique of Judgment*, it is clearly already a commitment of Kant's in the first *Critique* [Bxiii–Bxvii] and in the second *Critique*.[62]

The pure part of each science, which may be termed the Metaphysics of Nature and the Metaphysics of Morals, each manifests a type of autonomy in the cognitive or rational agent. In support of this observation, one should note that Kant also adopts a dual account of spontaneity, the practical spontaneity attached to moral autonomy and the epistemic spontaneity (so prominent in the Transcendental Deduction) attached to theoretical or epistemic autonomy. Thus, each seems to involve a species of volition. Although we might have thought that any species of volition is always subject to practical reason, it may be wise to revise this presupposition. Although he tends to ignore this sense of freedom in an agent, Kant *could* adopt a theory of the freedom of pure theoretical reason. Such a theory would have its place in cognitive contexts and would commit Kant to a sense of volition not directly bound up with the activity of *Willkür*. Before this is read as an objection to ascribing to him such a theory, however, note that Kant is already happy to distinguish between types of volition in his ethical system. Although there is a clear sense of volition involved in the activity of each, *Wille* is distinguished from *Willkür* by not *acting* in the same sense; in other words, Kant does not regard autonomous legislation as on a par with adopting and executing actions in accordance with maxims.[63] Whatever sense of volition belongs to practical autonomy, then, might well do for theoretical autonomy as well. Furthermore, there seem to be some appropriate contexts for mixing the language of one science with the other. For instance, although Kant is clear in his claim that there is no room for 'ought' within nature, this does not rule out the normative or prescriptive elements in the categorial principles that condition nature.

[62]*Critique of Judgment*, pp. 13, 35; Ak. Ed. 5:174, 195. *Critique of Practical Reason*, p. 29; Ak. Ed. 5:30.
[63]*Metaphysics of Morals*, Ak. Ed. 6:226.

Finally, it is instructive to note how this reading of the reciprocity thesis justifies Kant's claims that freedom is the ratio essendi of the moral law, and that the moral law is the ratio cognoscendi of freedom. It is not surprising to note that he returns to the question of whether freedom is known through morality or morality is known through freedom immediately after announcing the reciprocity of freedom and moral laws in section 6. It is not immediately obvious, however, how such a claim could be defended with the reading of the reciprocity thesis just given. In one direction, the reading is unproblematic: being a will under unconditional practical law is the reason for the knowledge of freedom of the will in the transcendental and the practical sense, of WK+ and WK−. Kant thinks that simply constructing maxims for *Willkür* (i.e., merely "being under" moral laws, whether obedient to them or not) is sufficient to make one immediately conscious of the moral law (Ak. Ed. 5:29–30). Once this is accomplished, though, the antecedent for Problem I is satisfied: *Willkür* as WK+ is determinable under the laws of *Wille* as W_a, and the proof is there given that the freedom of *Willkür* as WK− must follow. Hence, given the immediate consciousness of the moral law, one can deduce the freedom of *Willkür* in the sense of WK−. This, then, is what Kant means by the moral law's being the ratio cognoscendi of freedom.

In the other direction, the situation is not as clear. *Wille* as pure practical reason (W_a) is the source of and the reason for the existence of the moral law, but if my reading of the reciprocity thesis is correct then there must be a way in which the freedom of *Willkür* in the transcendental sense (WK+ and WK−) can be considered sufficient for the existence of the moral law. We know from Lemma II that the freedom of *Willkür* as WK+ and WK− implies the freedom of *Wille* in at least one of its two senses, W_a or W_h. Kant's aim in the second *Critique* is to show that both senses are available to *Willkür*, that reason can be purely practical as well as empirically practical, and so from Kant's point of view the faculty of *Willkür* never exists in isolation but always in conjunction with the faculty of *Wille*. Two options arise: either these are two independent wills related to one another, or they are two employments of the same will, each serving a different function. If the former were true, then Kant would equivocate on 'freedom' in the reciprocity thesis, since in that case *Willkür* and *Wille* would be two different faculties of will with no clear way to relate the types of freedom pertaining to each. But if the latter were true, then freedom of the will in the transcendental and the practical sense would not be the source of a simple equivocation on 'freedom', for according to Kant this sort of freedom requires the existence of *Wille*, and if *Wille* is the reason for the existence of the moral law then the move from *Willkür* to *Wille* is permissible; the freedom of *Willkür* in the transcendental and the practical sense involves the freedom of *Wille* as pure practical reason, and pure practical reason is the source of the existence of the moral law. This, then, is what Kant means by freedom's being the ratio essendi of the moral law.

In this chapter we have found in Kant a unified theory of the human will and its freedom. As we have now seen, this complex conception of freedom of the will is not only wholly adequate to the needs of ethics but also compatible with Kant's thesis of causal determinism. In Kantian terminology, then, we have found that the will has employment as pure and empirical practical reason and as the power of choice in rational, human agency; we have also found that, according to Kant, the human will is capable of both autonomous and heteronomous spontaneity of action, and that whereas it is pathologically affected it is not pathologically necessitated. In other words, we have found that, according to Kant, the human will is free.

Bibliography

Allison, Henry E. "The Concept of Freedom in Kant's Semi-Critical Ethics." *Archiv für Geschichte der Philosophie* 7 (1968): 96–115.

———. "Kant's *Non-Sequitur*: An Examination of the Lovejoy- Strawson Critique of the Second Analogy." *Kant-Studien* 62 (1971): 367–377.

———. "Kant's Refutation of Materialism." *Monist* 72 (1989): 190–208.

———. *Kant's Theory of Freedom.* Cambridge: Cambridge University Press, 1990.

———. *Kant's Transcendental Idealism.* New Haven: Yale University Press, 1983.

———. "Morality and Freedom: Kant's Reciprocity Thesis." *Philosophical Review* 95 (1986): 393–425.

———. "Practical and Transcendental Freedom in *The Critique of Pure Reason*." *Kant-Studien* 73 (1982): 271–290.

———. "Transcendental Affinity—Kant's Answer to Hume." In *Kant's Theory of Knowledge*, ed. L. W. Beck. Dordrecht: D. Reidel, 1974. Pp. 119–127.

———. "Transcendental Idealism: The 'Two Aspect' View." In *New Essays on Kant*, ed. Bernard den Ouden. New York: Peter Lang, 1987. Pp. 155–178.

Ameriks, Karl. "Kant's Deduction of Freedom and Morality." *Journal of the History of Philosophy* 19 (1981): 53–79.

———. *Kant's Theory of Mind.* Oxford: Clarendon Press, 1982.

Aquila, Richard E. "Kant's Phenomenalism." *Idealistic Studies* 5 (1975): 108–126.

——. "Necessity and Irreversibility in the Second Analogy." *History of Philosophy Quarterly* 2 (1985): 203–216.

——. *Representational Mind: A Study of Kant's Theory of Knowledge*. Bloomington: Indiana University Press, 1983.

Atwell, John. "The Intelligible Character in Kant's First *Critique*." *Akten des 5. Internationalen Kant-Kongresses* (1981): 493–500.

Baldner, K. "Causality and Things in Themselves." *Synthese* 77 (1988): 353–373.

Beattie, James. *Essay on the Nature and Immutability of Truth* [1772]. New York: Garland, 1983.

Beck, Lewis White. *The Actor and the Spectator*. New Haven: Yale University Press, 1975.

——. *A Commentary on Kant's "Critique of Practical Reason."* Chicago: University of Chicago Press, 1960.

——. *Early German Philosophy*. Cambridge: Harvard University Press, 1969.

——. *Essays on Kant and Hume*. New Haven: Yale University Press, 1978.

——. "Five Concepts of Freedom in Kant." In *Stephan Körner—Philosophical Analysis and Reconstruction*, ed. J. T. J. Srzednicki. Hingham: Kluwer, 1987. Pp. 35–51.

——. "Kant on the Uniformity of Nature." *Synthese* 47 (1981): 449–464.

——. "Kant's Two Conceptions of Will in Their Political Context." In *Studies in the Philosophy of Kant*. Indianapolis: Bobbs-Merrill, 1965. Pp. 224–229.

——. "A *Non-Sequitur* of Numbing Grossness?" In *Essays on Kant and Hume*. New Haven: Yale University Press, 1978. Pp. 147–153.

——. "Once More unto the Breach: Kant's Answer to Hume, Again." In *Essays on Kant and Hume*. New Haven: Yale University Press, 1978. Pp. 130–135.

——. "A Prussian Hume and a Scottish Kant." In *Essays on Kant and Hume*. New Haven: Yale University Press, 1978. Pp. 111–129.

——. "A Reading of the Third Paragraph in B." In *Essays on Kant and Hume*. New Haven: Yale University Press, 1978. Pp. 141–146.

——. *Studies in the Philosophy of Kant*. Indianapolis: Bobbs-Merrill, 1965.

——, ed. *Kant Studies Today*. La Salle, Ill.: Open Court, 1969.

Beiser, Frederick C. "Kant's Intellectual Development: 1746–1781." In *The Cambridge Companion to Kant*, ed. Paul Guyer. Cambridge: Cambridge University Press, 1992. Pp. 26–61.

Bennett, Jonathan F. "Commentary: Kant's Theory of Freedom." In *Self and Nature in Kant's Philosophy*, ed. A. W. Wood. Ithaca: Cornell University Press, 1984. Pp. 102–112.

——. *Kant's Analytic*. Cambridge: Cambridge University Press, 1966.

——. *Kant's Dialectic*. Cambridge: Cambridge University Press, 1974.

Berofsky, Bernard. *Determinism*. Princeton: Princeton University Press, 1971.

——, ed. *Free Will and Determinism*. New York: Harper and Row, 1966.

Bird, G. *Kant's Theory of Knowledge*. London: Routledge and Kegan Paul, 1962.

Bossart, William H. "Kant's Doctrine of the Reciprocity of Freedom and Reason." *International Philosophical Quarterly* 8 (1968): 334–355.

Brittan, Gordon G., Jr. "Kant, Closure, and Causality." In *Kant on Causality, Freedom, and Objectivity*, ed. W. L. Harper and Ralf Meerbote. Minneapolis: University of Minnesota Press, 1984. Pp. 66–82.

——. *Kant's Theory of Science*. Princeton: Princeton University Press, 1978.

Broad, C. D. "Kant's First and Second Analogies of Experience." *Proceedings of the Aristotelian Society* 25 (1925–1926): 189–210.

Brunton, J. H. "The Second Analogy and Levels of Argument." *Kant-Studien* 62 (1971): 378–391.

Buchdahl, Gerd. "Causality, Causal Laws, and Scientific Theory in the Philosophy of Kant." *British Journal for the Philosophy of Science* 16 (1965): 187–208.

——. "The Conception of Lawlikeness in Kant's Philosophy of Science." In *Kant's Theory of Knowledge*, ed. L. W. Beck. Dordrecht: D. Reidel, 1974. Pp. 128–150.

——. "The Kantian 'Dynamic of Reason' with Special Reference to the Place of Causality in Kant's System." In *Kant Studies Today*, ed. L. W. Beck. La Salle, Ill.: Open Court, 1969. Pp. 341–374.

Burkholder, L. "The Determinist Principle as Synthetic and *a Priori*." *Kinesis* 4 (1971): 43–57.

Butts, Robert E. *Kant and the Double Government Methodology*. Dordrecht: D. Reidel, 1984.

Carnois, Bernard. *The Coherence of Kant's Doctrine of Freedom*. Trans. David Booth. Chicago: University of Chicago Press, 1987.

Cassirer, Ernst. *Kant's Life and Thought*. Trans. J. Haden. New Haven: Yale University Press, 1981.

Cassirer, H. W. *Kant's First Critique*. London: George Allen and Unwin, 1954.

Chisholm, Roderick M. "Freedom and Action." In *Freedom and Determinism*, ed. Keith Lehrer. Atlantic Highlands, N.J.: Humanities Press, 1966. Pp. 11–44.

——. *Person and Object*. La Salle, Ill.: Open Court, 1976.

Cooke, Vincent M. "Kantian Reflections on Freedom." *Review of Metaphysics* 41 (1988): 739–756.

Crusius, Christian August. *Entwurf der nothwendigen Vernunft-Wahrheiten* [1745]. Darmstadt: Wissenschaftliche Buchgesellschaft, 1963.

Davidson, Donald. "Actions, Reasons, and Causes." In *Essays on Actions and Events*. Oxford: Clarendon Press, 1980. Pp. 3–19.

——. "Causal Relations." In *Essays on Actions and Events*. Oxford: Clarendon Press, 1980. Pp. 149–162.

——. "Freedom to Act." In *Essays on Actions and Events*. Oxford: Clarendon Press, 1980. Pp. 63–81.

——. "The Material Mind." In *Essays on Actions and Events*. Oxford: Clarendon Press, 1980. Pp. 245–259.

——. "Mental Events." In *Essays on Actions and Events*. Oxford: Clarendon Press, 1980. Pp. 207–225.

——. "Psychology as Philosophy." In *Essays on Actions and Events*. Oxford: Clarendon Press, 1980. Pp. 229–244.

Davies, Martin. "Boethius and Others on Divine Foreknowledge." *Pacific Philosophical Quarterly* 64 (1983): 313–329.

Dennett, Daniel C. *Elbow Room: The Varieties of Free Will Worth Wanting*. Cambridge: MIT Press, 1984.

den Ouden, Bernard, ed. *New Essays on Kant*. New York: Peter Lang, 1987.

Dodge, Jeffrey R. "Uniformity of Empirical Cause-Effect Relations in the Second Analogy." *Kant-Studien* 73 (1982): 47–54.

Dryer, D. P. "Bennett's Account of the Transcendental Dialectic." *Dialogue* 15 (1976): 118–132.

——. "Kant's Second Analogy." In *Kant on Causality, Freedom, and Objectivity*, ed. W. L. Harper and Ralf Meerbote. Minneapolis: University of Minnesota Press, 1984. Pp. 58–65.

——. *Kant's Solution for Verification in Metaphysics*. London: Allen and Unwin, 1966.

Dworkin, Gerald, ed. *Determinism, Free Will, and Moral Responsibility*. Englewood Cliffs, N.J.: Prentice-Hall, 1970.

Ewing, A. C. *Kant's Treatment of Causality*. London: Kegan and Paul, 1924.

——. *A Short Commentary on Kant's "Critique of Pure Reason."* Chicago: University of Chicago Press, 1950.

Fischer, John M. "Incompatibilism." *Philosophical Studies* 43 (1983): 127–137.

——. "Introduction: God and Freedom." In *God, Freedom, and Foreknowledge*, ed. J. M. Fischer. Stanford: Stanford University Press, 1989. Pp. 1–56.

——. "Introduction: Responsibility and Freedom." In *Moral Responsibility*, ed. J. M. Fischer. Ithaca: Cornell University Press, 1986. Pp. 9–61.

Flint, Thomas P. "Compatibilism and the Argument from Unavoidability." *Journal of Philosophy* 84 (1987): 423–440.

Flynn, James R. "The Logic of Kant's Derivation of Freedom from Reason." *Kant-Studien* 77 (1986): 441–446.

Fogelin, R. J. "Kant and Hume on Simultaneity of Causes and Effects." *Kant-Studien* 67 (1976): 51–59.

Foley, Richard. "Compatibilism and Control over the Past." *Analysis* 39 (1979): 70–74.

Frankfurt, Harry G. "Alternative Possibilities and Moral Responsibility." *Journal of Philosophy* 66 (1969): 828–839.

——. *The Importance of What We Care About*. Cambridge: Cambridge University Press, 1988.

Friedman, Michael. "Causal Laws and the Foundations of Natural Science." In *The Cambridge Companion to Kant*, ed. Paul Guyer. Cambridge: Cambridge University Press, 1992. Pp. 161–199.

Ginet, Carl. "The Conditional Analysis of Freedom." In *Time and Cause: Essays Presented to Richard Taylor*, ed. Peter van Inwagen. Dordrecht: D. Reidel, 1980. Pp. 171–186.

——. "Might We Have No Choice?" In *Freedom and Determinism*, ed. Keith Lehrer. New York: Random House, 1966. Pp. 87–104.

Goodman, Nelson. *Fact, Fiction, and Forecast.* 4th ed. Cambridge: Harvard University Press, 1983.

Gram, Moltke S., ed. *Interpreting Kant.* Iowa City: University of Iowa Press, 1982.

Greenwood, T. "A *Non-Sequitur* of Numbing Grossness," *Kant-Studien* 72 (1981): 11–30.

Gregor, Mary. *The Laws of Freedom.* Oxford: Basil Blackwell, 1963.

Grünbaum, Adolf. *Philosophical Problems of Space and Time.* 2d ed. Dordrecht: D. Reidel, 1973.

Guyer, Paul, ed. *The Cambridge Companion to Kant.* Cambridge: Cambridge University Press, 1992.

——. *Kant and the Claims of Knowledge.* New York: Cambridge University Press, 1987.

Harper, William L. "Kant's Empirical Realism and the Distinction between Subjective and Objective Succession." In *Kant on Causality, Freedom, and Objectivity*, ed. W. L. Harper and Ralf Meerbote. Minneapolis: University of Minnesota Press, 1984. Pp. 108–137.

——. "Kant's Empirical Realism and the Second Analogy of Experience." *Synthese* 47 (1981): 465–480.

Harper, William L., and Ralf Meerbote. "Kant's Principle of Causal Explanations." In *Kant on Causality, Freedom, and Objectivity*, ed. W. L. Harper and Ralf Meerbote. Minneapolis: University of Minnesota Press, 1984. Pp. 3–19.

——. "The Second Analogy in Recent Literature." In *Kant on Causality, Freedom, and Objectivity*, ed. W. L. Harper and Ralf Meerbote. Minneapolis: University of Minnesota Press, 1984. Pp. 167–172.

Hasker, William. "The Transcendental Refutation of Determinism." *Southern Journal of Philosophy* 11 (1973): 175–183.

Hoffman, W. Michael. "An Interpretation of Kant's Causal Determinism." *Idealistic Studies* 5 (1975): 139–163.

——. "An Interpretation of Kant's Solution to the Third Antinomy." *Southern Journal of Philosophy* 13 (1975): 173–185.

Hook, Sidney, ed. *Determinism and Freedom in the Age of Modern Science.* New York: Collier Press, 1958.

Horgan, Terence. "Compatibilism and the Consequence Argument." *Philosophical Studies* 47 (1985): 339–356.

Hudson, Hud. Review of Henry E. Allison's *Kant's Theory of Freedom* (Cambridge: Cambridge University Press, 1990). *Kant-Studien* 82 (1991): 219–222.

———. "The Significance of an Analytic of the Ugly in Kant's Deduction of Pure Judgments of Taste." In *Kant's Aesthetics*, ed. Ralf Meerbote and Hud Hudson. Atascadero, Calif.: Ridgeview, 1991. Pp. 87–103.

———. "*Wille, Willkür*, and the Imputability of Immoral Actions." *Kant-Studien* 82 (1991): 179–196.

Hume, David. *Enquiry concerning Human Understanding*. Ed. L. A. Selby-Bigge. 3d ed. Oxford: Clarendon Press, 1975.

———. *A Treatise of Human Nature*. Ed. L. A. Selby-Bigge. Oxford: Clarendon Press, 1964.

Irwin, Terence. "Morality and Personality: Kant and Green." In *Self and Nature in Kant's Philosophy*, ed. A. W. Wood. Ithaca: Cornell University Press, 1984. Pp. 31–56.

Jackson, Frank. "What Mary Didn't Know." *Journal of Philosophy* 83 (1986): 291–295.

Jones, William T. *Morality and Freedom in Kant*. London: Oxford University Press, 1940.

Jordon, James M. "Determinism's Dilemma." *Review of Metaphysics* 23 (1969): 48–66.

Kalin, Martin G. "Idealism against Realism in Kant's Third Antinomy." *Kant-Studien* 69 (1978): 160–169.

Kant, Immanuel. *Kants Gesammelte Schriften*. Berlin: Königlich Preussische Akademie der Wissenschaften, 1902; later volumes published by Georg Reimer and Walter de Gruyter.

———. *Critique of Judgment*. Trans. Werner S. Pluhar. Indianapolis: Hackett, 1987.

———. *Critique of Practical Reason*. Trans. Lewis White Beck. New York: Macmillan, 1985.

———. *Critique of Pure Reason*. Trans. Norman Kemp Smith. New York: St. Martin's Press, 1929.

———. *Foundations of the Metaphyscis of Morals*. Trans. Lewis White Beck. 2d ed. New York: Macmillan, 1990.

———. *Lectures on Ethics*. Trans. Louis Infield. Indianapolis: Hackett, 1930.

———. *A New Exposition of the First Principles of Metaphysical Knowledge*. Trans. John A. Reuscher. In *Kant's Latin Writings*, ed. Lewis White Beck. New York: Peter Lang, 1986.

———. *Prolegomena to Any Future Metaphysics*. Trans. Lewis White Beck. Indianapolis: Bobbs-Merrill, 1950.

———. *Religion within the Limits of Reason Alone*. Trans. Theodore M. Greene and Hoyt H. Hudson. New York: Harper and Row, 1960.

Kemp Smith, Norman. *A Commentary to Kant's "Critique of Pure Reason."* 2d ed. New York: Humanities Press, 1962.

Kim, Jaegwon. "Phenomenal Properties, Psychophysical Laws, and the Identity Theory." *Monist* 56 (1972): 177–192.

———. "Psychophysical Laws." In *Actions and Events: Perspectives in the Philosophy of Donald Davidson*, ed. Ernest LePore and B. P. McLaughlin. New York: Basil Blackwell, 1985. Pp. 369–386.

Kitcher, Patricia. "Kant on Self Identity." *Philosophical Review* 91 (1982): 41–72.

———. "Kant's Paralogisms." *Philosophical Review* 91 (1982): 515–547.

———. "Kant's Real Self." In *Self and Nature in Kant's Philosophy*, ed. A. W. Wood. Ithaca: Cornell University Press, 1984. Pp. 113–147.

Kripke, Saul. *Naming and Necessity*. Cambridge: Harvard University Press, 1972.

Lamb, James. "On a Proof of Incompatibilism." *Philosophical Review* 86 (1977): 20–35.

Lehrer, Keith, ed. *Freedom and Determinism*. New York: Random House, 1966.

Leibniz, Gottfried Wilhelm. *Philosophische Schriften von G. W. Leibniz*. 7 vols. Berlin, 1875–1890.

———. *Discourse on Metaphysics*. Trans. George Montgomery. La Salle, Ill.: Open Court, 1902.

LePore, Ernest, and Brian P. McLaughlin, eds. *Actions and Events: Perspectives in the Philosophy of Donald Davidson*. New York: Basil Blackwell, 1985.

———. "Actions, Reasons, Causes, and Intentions." In *Actions and Events: Perspectives in the Philosophy of Donald Davidson*. New York: Basil Blackwell, 1985. Pp. 3–13.

Lewis, David. "Are We Free to Break the Laws?" *Theoria* 47 (1981): 113–121.

———. "Counterfactual Dependence and Time's Arrow," and "Postscripts to Counterfactual Dependence and Time's Arrow." In *Philosophical Papers*, vol. 2. Oxford: Oxford University Press, 1986. Pp. 32–52, 52–66.

———. *Counterfactuals*. Cambridge: Harvard University Press, 1973.

Lovejoy, Arthur O. "On Kant's Reply to Hume." *Archiv für Geschichte der Philosophie* 18 (1906): 380–407.

Łukasiewicz, Jan. "On Determinism." In *Polish Logic*. Oxford: Clarendon Press, 1967.

MacDonald, Cynthia. *Mind-Body Identity Theories*. New York: Routledge, 1989.

McDowell, John. "Functionalism and Anomalous Monism." In *Actions and Events: Perspectives in the Philosophy of Donald Davidson*, ed. Ernest LePore and B. P. McLaughlin. New York: Basil Blackwell, 1985. Pp. 387–398.

McLaughlin, Brian P. "Anomalous Monism and the Irreducibility of the Mental." In *Actions and Events: Perspectives in the Philosophy of Donald Davidson*, ed. Ernest LePore and B. P. McLaughlin. New York: Basil Blackwell, 1985. Pp. 331–368.

Meerbote, Ralf. "Butts' *Kant and the Double Government Methodology*: Supersensibility and Method in Kant's Philosophy of Science." *Nous* 23 (1989): 266–270.

———. "Kant on Freedom and the Rational and Morally Good Will." In *Self and Nature in Kant's Philosophy*, ed. A. W. Wood. Ithaca: Cornell University Press, 1984. Pp. 57–72.

———. "Kant on the Nondeterminate Character of Human Actions." In *Kant on Causality, Freedom, and Objectivity*, ed. W. L. Harper and Ralf Meerbote. Minnesota: University of Minnesota Press, 1984. Pp. 138–163.

———. "Kant's Functionalism." In *Historical Foundations of Cognitive Science*, ed. J. C. Smith. Dordrecht: Kluwer, 1990. Pp. 161–187.

———. "*Wille* and *Willkür* in Kant's Theory of Action." In *Interpreting Kant*, ed. M. S. Gram. Iowa City: University of Iowa Press, 1982. Pp. 69–84.

Melden, A. I. *Free Action*. London: Routledge and Kegan Paul, 1961.

Melnick, Arthur. *Kant's Analogies of Experience*. Chicago: University of Chicago Press, 1973.

Murphy, J. G. "Kant's Second Analogy as an Answer to Hume." *Ratio* 11 (1969): 75–78.

Nagel, Gordon. "Substance and Causality." In *Kant on Causality, Freedom, and Objectivity*, ed. W. L. Harper and Ralf Meerbote. Minneapolis: University of Minnesota Press, 1984. Pp. 97–107.

Narveson, Jan. "Compatibilism Defended." *Philosophical Studies* 32 (1977): 83–86.

Paton, Herbert J. *The Categorical Imperative*. Chicago: University of Chicago Press, 1948.

———. *Kant's Metaphysic of Experience*. 2 vols. London: George Allen and Unwin, 1936.

Pears, David F., ed. *Freedom and the Will*. New York: St. Martin's Press, 1963.

Pippin, Robert. *Kant's Theory of Form*. New Haven: Yale University Press, 1982.

Pluhar, Werner S. "Introduction." In Kant, *Critique of Judgment*, trans. W. S. Pluhar. Indianapolis: Hackett, 1987. Pp. xxiii–cix.

Posy, Carl. "Transcendental Idealism and Causality: An Interpretation of Kant's Argument in the Second Analogy." In *Kant on Causality, Freedom, and Objectivity*, ed. W. L. Harper and Ralf Meerbote. Minneapolis: University of Minnesota Press, 1984. Pp. 20–41.

Potter, Nelson. "Does Kant Have Two Conceptions of Freedom?" *Akten des 4. Internationalen Kant-Kongresses* (1974): 590–596.

Prauss, Gerold. *Erscheinung bei Kant*. Berlin: Walter de Gruyter, 1971.

———. *Kant über Freiheit als Autonomie*. Frankfurt am Main: Vittorio Klostermann, 1983.

———. *Kant und das Problem der Dinge an Sich*. Bonn: Bouvier Verlag H. Grundmann, 1974.

Reichenbach, Hans. *The Philosophy of Space and Time*. Trans. Maria Reichenbach and John Freund. New York: Dover, 1958.

Rescher, Nicholas. "Noumenal Causality." In *Kant's Theory of Knowledge*, ed. L. W. Beck. Dordrecht: D. Reidel, 1974. Pp. 175–183.

Rotenstreich, Nathan. "Will and Reason: A Critical Analysis of Kant's Concepts." *Philosophy and Phenomenological Research* 46 (1985): 37–58.

Saunders, John Turk. "The Temptations of Powerlessness." *American Philosophical Quarterly* 5 (1968): 100–108.

Schipper, E. W. "Kant's Answer to Hume's Problem." *Kant-Studien* 53 (1961–1962): 68–74.

Schopenhauer, Arthur. *The World as Will and Representation*. 2 vols. Trans. E. F. J. Payne. New York: Dover, 1969.

Scott-Taggart, M. J. "Recent Work on the Philosophy of Kant." In *Kant Studies Today*, ed. L. W. Beck. La Salle, Ill.: Open Court, 1969. Pp. 1–71.

Sellars, Wilfred. *Essays in Philosophy and Its History*. Dordrecht: D. Reidel, 1974.

Silber, John R. "The Ethical Significance of Kant's *Religion*." Reprinted as an introduction to Kant, *Religion within the Limits of Reason Alone*. New York: Harper and Row, 1960.

Singer, Brent A. "Kant's Conception of a Causality through Freedom." *Auslegung* 13 (1986): 63–70.

Slote, Michael. "Selective Necessity and Free Will." *Journal of Philosophy* 79 (1982): 136–151.

———. "Understanding Free Will." *Journal of Philosophy* 77 (1980): 136–151.

Smart, J. J. C. "Sensations and Brain Processes." In *Modern Materialism: Readings on Mind-Body Identity*, ed. John O'Connor. New York: Harcourt, Brace and World, 1969. Pp. 32–47.

Strawson, Peter F. *The Bounds of Sense*. London: Methuen Press, 1966.

Suchting, W. A. "Kant's Second Analogy of Experience." In *Kant Studies Today*, ed. L. W. Beck. La Salle, Ill.: Open Court, 1969. Pp. 322–340.

Sullivan, Roger J. *Immanuel Kant's Moral Theory*. New York: Cambridge University Press, 1989.

Taylor, Richard. *Action and Purpose*. Englewood Cliffs, N.J.: Prentice-Hall, 1966.

———. "Determinism and the Theory of Agency." In *Determinism and Freedom*, ed. Sidney Hook. New York: Collier Press, 1958. Pp. 224–230.

———. *Metaphysics*, 4th ed. Englewood Cliffs, N.J.: Prentice-Hall, 1991.

Van Cleve, James. "Another Volley at Kant's Reply to Hume." In *Kant on Causality, Freedom, and Objectivity*, ed. W. L. Harper and Ralf Meerbote. Minneapolis: University of Minnesota Press, 1984. Pp. 42–57.

———. "Four Recent Interpretations of Kant's Second Analogy." *Kant-Studien* 64 (1973): 71–87.

van Inwagen, Peter. "Ability and Responsibility." *Philosophical Review* 87 (1978): 201–224.

———. *An Essay on Free Will*. Oxford: Clarendon Press, 1983.

———. "The Incompatibility of Free Will and Determinism." *Philosophical Studies* 27 (1975): 185–199.

———. "The Incompatibility of Responsibility and Determinism." In *Moral Responsibility*, ed. J. M. Fischer. Ithaca: Cornell University Press, 1986. Pp. 241–249.

———. ed. *Time and Cause: Essays Presented to Richard Taylor*. Dordrecht: D. Reidel, 1980.

Vermazen, Bruce, and Merrill B. Hintikka, eds. *Essays on Davidson*. Oxford: Clarendon Press, 1985.

Walsh, W. H. "Kant on the Perception of Time." In *Kant Studies Today*, ed. L. W. Beck. La Salle, Ill.: Open Court, 1969. Pp. 160–180.

———. *Kant's Criticism of Metaphysics*. Edinburgh: Edinburgh University Press, 1975.

———. "Kant's Transcendental Idealism." In *Kant on Causality, Freedom, and Objectivity*, ed. W. L. Harper and Ralf Meerbote. Minneapolis: University of Minnesota Press, 1984. Pp. 83–96.

Ward, A. "On Kant's Second Analogy and His Reply to Hume." *Kant-Studien* 77 (1986): 409–422.

Watson, Gary, ed. *Freewill*. Oxford: Oxford University Press, 1982.

Weldon, T. D. *Kant's "Critique of Pure Reason."* Oxford: Clarendon Press, 1958.

Wiggins, David. "Towards a Reasonable Libertarianism." In *Essays on Freedom of Action*, ed. Ted Honderich. London: Routledge and Kegan Paul, 1973. Pp. 31–61.

Wilkerson, T. E. "Time, Cause, and Object: Kant's Second Analogy of Experience." *Kant-Studien* 62 (1971): 351–366.

Williams, M. E. "Kant's Reply to Hume." *Kant-Studien* 55 (1965): 71–78.

Wolff, Christian. *Philosophia prima sive ontologica*. Frankfurt, 1730.

———. *Vernünftige Gedanken von Gott, der Welt, und der Seele der Menschen, auch allen Dingen überhaupt*. 4th ed. Frankfurt and Leipzig, 1729.

Wolff, Robert Paul. *Kant's Theory of Mental Activity*. Cambridge: Harvard University Press, 1963.

Wood, Allen W. "Kant's Compatibilism." In *Self and Nature in Kant's Philosophy*, ed. A. W. Wood. Ithaca: Cornell University Press, 1984. Pp. 73–101.

———, ed. *Self and Nature in Kant's Philosophy*. Ithaca: Cornell University Press, 1984.

Young, Michael J. "Functions of Thought and the Synthesis of Intuitions." In *The Cambridge Companion to Kant*, ed. Paul Guyer. Cambridge: Cambridge University Press, 1992. Pp. 101–122.

Zweig, Arnulf, ed. and trans. *The Essential Kant*. New York: New American Library, 1970.

———. "Reflections on Noumenal Freedom." *Akten des 5. Internationalen Kant-Kongresses* (1981): 614–619.

Index